JEFFREY DAHMER's
DIRTY SECRET

Dennis,

Thanks for all your forensic support and friendship over the past years. Enjoy this book and we hope to solve this case soon. Best Regards,

Ian

Dahmer's Slip of the Tongue?

IN THE SUMMER OF 2002, in the true crime section of a used bookstore, I found a 1997 book by former FBI serial-killer profiler Robert Ressler titled *I Have Lived in the Monster* that included a transcript of an interview he'd conducted with Jeffrey Dahmer in January 1992. Browsing it, Dahmer was talking about finding his last Milwaukee murder victim and had made light of a coincidence, that Konerak Sinthasomphone was the younger brother of Somsack Sinthasomphone, who he'd been arrested for sexually assaulting three years earlier:

> *"He was the brother of the one that [I'd photographed]. I was just walking in the mall, ran into him, didn't know him from Adam—how many are the chances of that happening? Astronomical."*

When I read this, I stared at it. Was this a slip of the tongue by a serial killer who severed heads, who'd admitted being in Miami when the Walsh child was reported lost—and who trolled for children to abduct in a shopping mall?

Didn't know him from Adam?

In 1991, Hollywood police seemed to have decided that Dahmer's movements here would be too difficult to trace 10 years after the fact. Despite the handicap of another 11 years since then, I decided on the spot in the bookstore to do the legwork Hollywood hadn't done and learn everything I could about Jeffrey Dahmer—and especially his time in Miami.

Other true crime books by
Arthur Jay Harris

SPEED KILLS
FLOWERS FOR MRS. LUSKIN
UNTIL PROVEN INNOCENT

JEFFREY DAHMER's DIRTY SECRET

The Unsolved Murder of Adam Walsh

~

Arthur Jay Harris

BOOKSURGE

JEFFREY DAHMER'S DIRTY SECRET is a journalistic account of the actual investigation of the abduction murder of Adam Walsh in Hollywood, Florida in 1981. The events recounted in this book are true. Names that have been changed are noted in the text as such. Research has been done using author interviews, law enforcement and other public records, published and broadcast news stories, and books. Quoted sworn testimony has been taken verbatim from transcripts.

Copyright © 2009 by Arthur Jay Harris
Published by arrangement with the author.

ISBN: 1-4392-3627-5

Cover and author photos: Sandy Levy, Miami, Fla.
Cover and typographical design: Bruce Kluger, New York

Photographic usage of *Hollywood Sun-Tattler* newspapers courtesy Hollywood Historical Society, Hollywood, Fla.

Mug shot of Jeffrey Dahmer, courtesy Milwaukee Police Department.

Photographs, updates, links and additional materials available at www.arthurjayharris.com.

First printing: August 2009

In 1996, at the request of news organizations but over the bitterest objections of Hollywood Police and the Walsh family, a judge ruled that Florida law required that the long-unsolved murder case file of Adam Walsh, killed in 1981, must be made public.

In advance of the exposure of the files, charges flew:

"The city of Hollywood and its police department lacked the experience to conduct an investigation of this magnitude."

—Richard Witt, in 1996 the chief of police, Hollywood, Florida

"Now, details previously known only to the police and the killer will be known to all—making it almost impossible to find out who the real murderer is."

—John Walsh

Introduction

DAHMER, JEFFREY—SERIAL KILLER WHO LIVED IN THE MIAMI AREA at the time Adam Walsh was abducted.

In 1994, a Hollywood, Florida cold case detective reviewing the never-solved Adam Walsh murder case of 1981 wrote that in a seven-page master summary of 70-plus people who over the years had been briefly suspected of the crime or who had given information regarding it. His purpose was to organize the huge, rambling case file and see if in the passage of time some neglected lead might leap off the page, requiring a fresh look.

The case was the largest in the history of the low-rise seaside city of Hollywood, and a festering sore besides because police, despite monumental work, had never made an arrest. It was all the more notorious because the child's severed head had horrifically been found, and the boy's father, John Walsh, afterwards had crusaded to change American laws and awareness regarding missing children and then had become the long-running host of a hyper-aggressive crime-fighting television show, *America's Most Wanted.*

Unfortunately, the Dahmer line the detective wrote got no

rise out of him.

As Hollywood Police had quickly learned after Dahmer's capture in Milwaukee in 1991, he'd lived and worked about 15 minutes by car from where six-year-old Adam was last seen alive, the toy department of Sears in the Hollywood Mall, where his mother had left him alone on a summer Monday around noon for no more than 5-10 minutes, she said. Although Hollywood Police never found anyone who remembered Dahmer in South Florida, Dahmer himself had admitted being here then. He even said later he remembered seeing the story on the news. But he denied killing Adam—so convincingly that the cold case detective hardly bothered to retrace the previous investigation. To the original lead detective, Dahmer said that summer he didn't have a vehicle—essential for a kidnapping. He wasn't attracted to children that young. He didn't know where the Hollywood Mall was. He was busy working 12-hour days every weekday and most weekends. Besides, he'd already admitted to more murders than Milwaukee police had evidence of, so why would he lie about this one? Dahmer looked him straight in the eye when he denied it, the detective said—and he believed him.

Yet two separate witnesses had come forward to Hollywood Police within days of when Dahmer was arrested and his photo was all over the news. They both reported encountering Dahmer at Hollywood Mall that day 10 years earlier when Adam disappeared.

That's not all. Within days of the original event, both witnesses initially had told Hollywood police what they'd seen—without knowing Dahmer's name. Through the media, the police had asked for anyone with information to come forward. A flood of tips ensued. But in that flood their statements—and as it much later turned out, potentially crucial statements of others too—had been lost, ignored, or filtered out before they reached detectives.

One witness said that Dahmer, drunk, disheveled, menacing

and hovering, tried to pick him up. When the witness refused, Dahmer shot him an evil stare, then stormed away. Scared but expecting Dahmer would approach someone else, who'd need help, he followed Dahmer at a safe distance through the mall, into Sears, then into its toy department.

The other witness saw Dahmer in the parking lot outside Sears grab a struggling, protesting child he thought was Adam and hurriedly throw him "like a sack of potatoes" into a blue van that then screeched away. That witness stood shocked, he'd never seen anything like that before. How could anyone do that to a small child?

Another witness, who was initially believed, had also described Adam's kidnapper stealing him into a blue van that sped away. For a month, the blue van was Hollywood's best lead.

But Hollywood Police were never bowled over by the Dahmer witnesses. Although Dahmer had volunteered the names of the places where he'd worked and lived in nearby North Miami Beach, both establishments were gone by 1991. He left no police records—that is, that the Hollywood detectives found. Without supporting witnesses or records, and a suspect's denial, how could a murder case be made?

On the other hand, Jeffrey Dahmer was a noted convincing liar, especially to law enforcement. He severed his victims' heads—and Adam's head was found severed. He'd already killed his first victim (by his count) and severed his head three years before Adam. Plus, all the murders he admitted to were in states that didn't have the death penalty. Florida famously did and still does. He also had a conviction for masturbating in a public place in front of two 12-year-olds and another for indecent exposure, and he admitted to such behavior often.

Hollywood Police didn't interview Dahmer until a year after his Milwaukee arrest and then only after John Walsh insisted. In a Wisconsin prison, the lead detective spent just an hour with Dahmer. When he returned to Florida, he convinced

Walsh that Dahmer was innocent.

Dahmer was murdered in prison two years later. Had Hollywood done as much as I did, considering my handicap of arriving 11 years after them, they would have had a chance to try Dahmer for Adam's murder. Now it is too late. We can only speculate whether a jury would have sent Dahmer to Florida's electric chair, his richly deserved fate. Then we would have had a legal conclusion instead of a prison inmate vigilante lynching.

One item Hollywood police never found was Dahmer's name on a Miami police report 20 days before Adam disappeared. He reported a dead homeless man, who'd already turned blue, lying next to a dumpster—a dumpster Dahmer was seen eating out of about a week before. A few feet away was an electric meter room where the dead man apparently had slept—and afterward maybe also Dahmer, then homeless himself. He said he'd stepped over the dead man for days—although it was more likely he'd just dragged him out of the meter room, because the dumpster was in a well-trafficked alley, behind a pizza shop.

In the next 20 days, with the help of his new employer—whom police also never bothered to find—Dahmer apparently rented his motel-apartment room. The last time he'd lived alone in his own place, three years earlier at home in Ohio after both his parents had briefly abandoned him, he'd picked up a hitchhiker, then killed and dismembered him.

They also never found a number of supporting witnesses who had seen Dahmer's evil eye stare exactly as the mall witness reported describing it.

One was the man who probably knew Dahmer best, his roommate on a U.S. Army base in Germany, who immediately recognized his banal pickup line to the witness. He also thought Dahmer possibly had killed a few times in Germany—German *polizei* had later suspected him of serial murders of women, although Dahmer admitted killing only men. The roommate had found blood- and mucus-covered buck knives in his room, and once Dahmer returned wearing blood-encrusted clothes after a night out.

He also knew that Army M.P.s had arrested Dahmer a few times for masturbating in front of German children in a local park, although they never entered charges and had merely brought him back to his room, with a brief explanation.

An Army nurse who had taught him anatomy also had seen Dahmer's evil eyes. She thought he might have been a serial rapist. When both she and Dahmer were on the base in Germany, on three occasions badly sodomized men were rushed to her hospital, one close to death.

For his alcoholism, the Army kicked out Dahmer early—dumped him back home on an unsuspecting America, really—but without a dishonorable discharge to blot his record. From Germany he came to Miami. His Miami employer, who also saw his evil eye, said Dahmer would occasionally come to work, weekdays in the mid-morning, drunk and disheveled and he'd send him home. He also disputed Dahmer's statement about his hours; they were only part-time, weekdays only. As well he contradicted Dahmer regarding his hair length. One of the mall witnesses insisted to the detective it was long, Dahmer said it wasn't, and the detective believed Dahmer, reasoning that he'd recently left the military, therefore it couldn't have been long. But the employer said it *was* long. So did the bunkmate, who saw Dahmer on his last day in the Army.

The police didn't know that at Dahmer's place of work, or its nearby sister store, was an unmarked blue pizza delivery van, easily accessible to employees, that often disappeared for hours and even days without documentation or consequences.

Even when I told the cold case detective most of this information in 2002, he still wasn't much interested. After I broke the story in a newspaper and on television in 2007 and then the national media picked it up, Hollywood police claimed they'd since re-interviewed the two mall witnesses—but it wasn't true; they hadn't done even that. John Walsh's reaction was inconsistent. Initially he said on camera that the local state attorney needed to examine the new evidence. But days later his show issued a statement that he trusted the police's word that they had done a full investigation of my work and correctly dismissed it.

This although Walsh had once said the Hollywood Police in this case was guilty of "incredible incompetence," and his lawyer suggested they were "the biggest bunch of bungling idiots since the Keystone Kops."

This was the same Hollywood police force that at a dramatic late Friday-night press conference, two years after the murder, had announced they'd solved the crime: a Jacksonville drifter named Ottis Toole had confessed. The police chief claimed that he knew things that only the slayer could have known. Everything he'd told them had checked out, said an interviewing detective from Jacksonville.

Actually, Toole was a serial false-confessor who Hollywood and Jacksonville detectives needed to guide with the facts during repeated grillings over a period of days. On his own he got the simplest of facts ridiculously wrong—beginning with the statement that the child was wearing mittens—in South Florida—explained only by his thinking that the kidnapping took place in January, not July. After luring the child into his car on the premise of candy and toys inside, he hit the power door lock button to ensure that the child couldn't easily escape—except that his car was discovered *not* to have power door locks. He also initially blamed the murder on his drifter-partner—until the partner was proven to be in jail in another state that day.

As shown in the transcripts, released 13 years later, when it became clear Toole needed help, the detectives dropped him obvious hints, showed him photos of the case, and gave him heavily weighted multiple-choices—which he *still* didn't always answer correctly. Step by step they unfolded the entire case.

But as the process went on, he repeatedly tried to recant. That's when the detectives double-teamed him into continuing, hoping he'd eventually produce at least a single relevant true fact on his own. He never did.

To Hollywood's further embarrassment, before the press conference they hadn't conferred with the state attorney, who the next Monday refused to accept the case without corroboration. Detectives wasted months trying to establish that on the day Adam disappeared, Toole had been at least in the same county. In fact, they could never prove where he was that day, or even establish he'd *ever* been in the county. Meanwhile, largely depending on whether the Jacksonville detective was in the room, Toole recanted—and re-confessed—and re-recanted over and over.

All of this could have been avoided because it was obvious at the start. Toole and his partner Henry Lee Lucas were already in a crazy competition to admit to the most killings—hundreds, between them, suggesting, had their statements been true, they were the most sociopathic killing machines in the history of police work. Meanwhile, less-than-skeptical detectives from all around the country embraced them to clear out their unsolved cases. They similarly told the pair their facts and accepted their confessions. The game finally ended when a law enforcement officer timelined their claimed murders and realized they couldn't have been in distant states at nearly the same times.

Even before Toole's confession, Hollywood police already had wasted more months' effort trying to bully the Walsh family live-in nanny into confessing. Although his circumstances were irregular he didn't come close to the criminal profile of someone who would have murdered a child and severed his head. In truth he was anything but a criminal.

Years later, John Walsh blamed Hollywood police for trying too hard to solve the crime by forcing the facts. He called the investigation into the live-in nanny an "easy out" for the cops, a "dead-end lead" and "their first big mistake." Reve added,

"It's almost like they're trying to frame him. The detectives are getting pressure from the top to solve this case."

John also said for publication that Toole's confession was beyond contempt. But four years later in 1996, just before Adam's police case file up to that point was made public, Walsh decided, after all, that Toole most likely *was* Adam's killer. By then even the Hollywood Police had long given up thinking he had committed the murder.

Since then, Walsh has continued to say that Toole killed his son, even after, in summer 2007, the ABC News show *Primetime* revealed that inside the electric meter room behind the sub shop where Dahmer worked a crime scene investigator had discovered a pattern of blood spatter she thought indicated a homicide, and a rusty axe and sledgehammer next to it. Dahmer had admitted using a sledgehammer on a victim before 1981, and the axe was no less grotesquely suggestive. Before broadcast, ABC had offered to present Walsh its facts, but Walsh declined and as well refused their invitation of an interview. Instead he sent an ex-cop who insisted, still, that Toole killed Adam, and promised a presentation of new evidence he'd found which *America's Most Wanted* would air within a month. It didn't.

As the chief of Hollywood police had done in October 1983, a new chief announced at another surprise press conference in December 2008 that the case was solved, Toole killed Adam Walsh. Live on cable news, Chief Chadwick E. Wagner offered no new evidence. But this time the Walshes were present, teary, and grateful for this day of closure, and national media followed in agreement.

Case now officially closed, the police offered reporters CD-ROM copies of the complete case file. (After the 1996 court-ordered opening of the file, the police had denied all public record requests to see material in the file generated since then, and no one had again challenged them in court.) In it was a document written by Chief Wagner that he personally had

16

reviewed a summary of the case prepared by Walsh's ex-cop investigator and agreed with it.

At the press conference, in discouraging reporters that police had finally found the smoking gun evidence in the case, Wagner said, "If you're looking for that magic wand or that hidden document that just appeared, it's not there."

Wagner was wrong. In the newly released part of the case file, police did have the smoking gun evidence that solved the case.

Only he didn't realize it.

The police had had it since 1996. Worse, it had been offered to them in the first week or weeks of the case, in 1981. They hadn't taken it. Had they, the case would have been solved in 1991, correctly, not in 2008, wrongly.

That evidence proved the case against Jeffrey Dahmer.

1
The Fledgling Serial Killer

THERE'S A FUCKING HEAD IN THE REFRIGERATOR!
Whether or not that was shrieked by a Milwaukee police officer first on the scene in Jeffrey Dahmer's apartment—a *Milwaukee Journal* reporter wrote it, though not in the newspaper—there *was* a fucking head in Dahmer's refrigerator. It was not alone, either. Inside the rooms, as best as such things can be hidden, the police as they searched through the overnight found ten more: three in the freestanding freezer, two on a shelf in the hall closet, two in a computer box, and three more in a filing cabinet. Four still had flesh remaining on the skulls. Some were painted gray. Police also found a collection of formaldehyde-filled glass jars holding detached male—yes, private parts.

Being discovered by law enforcement with 11 severed heads on your premises—especially considering you live alone—places you in one of the more compromising positions imaginable. So Jeffrey Dahmer, hardly a dummy and likely a

18

genius, on the spot changed life strategies: the lonely serial killer became a serial talker to a rapt audience of detectives.

Although the cops searched Dahmer's apartment without his consent or with a search warrant, Dahmer's nightmarish confessions eliminated the similarly nightmarish possibility that everything the cops found in his apartment could have been tossed out in court as illegally obtained. So maybe he wasn't so smart after all.

He admitted seventeen murders, total, including some for which there was no evidence in his apartment. Of the remainder, the one that stood out was the one he claimed was his first, in the Ohio township rancher house on a country road where he'd grown up. Why did he volunteer it? Maybe he wanted to come completely clean, as he claimed. Or maybe he figured that the cops in his hometown would search missing-persons records and discover it themselves.

Dahmer was captured in 1991. The Ohio murder was thirteen years earlier, in 1978.

He told Milwaukee detectives he couldn't remember the victim's name. It didn't really matter to him, so he hadn't committed it to memory. They were the same age. He'd met him in an Akron bar, brought him home, and they'd had sex. Days later, when the Summit County, Ohio, Sheriff's Department did search its records and showed Dahmer a photo, he said he recognized him. He even recalled his name as Steve.

Steven Mark Hicks, the Ohio detective told him.

Although they hadn't known each other, both boys had just graduated rival high schools—Revere for Dahmer, Coventry for Hicks—in the same county, which includes Akron. It was a Sunday—June 18, 1978.

Dahmer then changed his story. No, he didn't find Steve in a bar. Instead, it was late that afternoon, around five, he was driving his father's Oldsmobile back from a bar where he'd been drinking, and he saw Steve hitchhiking in front of the Bath Township Police Department, at the intersection of

Cleveland-Massillon Road and West Bath Road, about a mile from the Dahmers' house. It was a warm day and the hitchhiker was shirtless.

For the previous two years, Dahmer had been fantasizing about meeting a good-looking hitchhiker and "sexually enjoying him," he said. This was his chance.

Jeff passed him in the car then stopped. Should he do it? Nobody was home, his father had separated from the family and was living in a motel, and his mother had taken his little brother and left for Wisconsin about a week before, he said. Steve said he'd been to a rock concert. When Jeff asked if he could buy some pot from him, Hicks agreed to go to Dahmer's house, where they'd smoke, drink some beer, and listen to music.

He realized Steve wasn't gay, and no, they didn't have sex.

After a few friendly intoxicants in his bedroom while music played, Steve wanted to get back on his way, but Jeff wanted him to stay longer. Desperately. They fought, with their fists— until Jeff lifted a barbell rod and smacked Steve in the back of the head. Then he used it to strangle him to death.

You never forget your first kill, he said.

That's assuming, of course, it was his first kill, for which we only have the word of Jeffrey Dahmer. At first he'd claimed he'd met his victim in an Akron bar. Should law enforcement have taken Dahmer's word on anything that couldn't be proved by physical evidence or what someone else said?

Whether or not it was his first, Dahmer still had to dispose of the body. Later that night, with Steve already late for both his family and his friends, Dahmer dragged him into the gravel crawl space under his house. At 5'11, 160, Steve was only slightly smaller than himself. Dahmer masturbated over him. Upstairs, unable to sleep, he decided to get rid of the evidence.

The next day he bought a hunting knife, and waited until that night to slit open Steve's belly. Seeing its viscera, he masturbated again. He cut off one arm then created other pieces. He severed his head. "Bagged each piece. Triple-bagged it in large plastic trash bags," he said. He loaded the bags in the back of the Olds then at three A.M. drove back roads with the idea of going to a ravine ten miles away, where he was going to toss them.

Halfway, he said, a police car pulled him over, suspecting him of DUI because he'd crossed the median. The cop called for backup and administered a drunk test—which he passed. One cop shined his flashlight into his car and saw the bags.

"What's this stuff?"

"Just garbage," Dahmer answered. He said he'd meant to take it to the dump earlier. "And they believe it, even though there's a smell," Dahmer told the homicide cops in 1991. They gave him a ticket.

He returned home, abandoning his plan. He put the bags back in the crawl space, except for the head, which he took to the bathroom, washed on the floor, and then masturbated over. Then he put it back with the rest of the body. The next morning he placed the bags outside in a ten-foot long buried drainage pipe, smashed down the front of the pipe, and left them there.

In another version he said he buried the bags in his wooded backyard.

Six days after the murder, Steve's mother, Martha, filed a missing-persons report with the Summit County Sheriff. He had long brown hair, and she'd last seen him wearing blue jeans and blue tennis shoes. The Sunday before, his brother had dropped him off near their home so he could hitchhike about 20 miles to Chippewa Lake, which had a wooden roller coaster, where he spent the day with friends. A logical route to there went through Bath. Although Martha bugged detectives for years, and the family offered a reward for information, until 1991 nobody had reported anything.

Nature or nurture? Was Jeffrey Dahmer born a killer, or did his environment shape him toward who he became? The few known details of his home life paint a bleak picture. In his initial confession to Milwaukee police, he said his parents were "constantly at each other's throats." His Army roommate, who knew him as a 21-year-old, said he couldn't stand to talk about his mother, and could barely manage to talk about his father. "I don't have a mother and my father is a bastard," he once said to him. Much of his family story comes from his father, Lionel Dahmer, a Ph.D. chemist who wrote a book. Unsurprisingly, considering their divorce, Lionel speaks unkindly of Jeff's mother, Joyce Flint Dahmer. Lionel's own sins, he wrote, were largely of omission, failing to connect with his son and his wife or recognize the evil his eldest became capable of.

Lionel described arguments with Joyce that turned physical: "On some occasions, when I would fight back vigorously, [she] would seize a kitchen knife and make jabbing motions." Several times the police had to break up arguments, said a neighbor, mother of four, child playmates of the eventual killer. "At the time I knew him, there was something devastating going on in his life, and there wasn't anybody there to help him. I feel bad about that." Another neighbor said, "He always seemed to be alone." A third neighbor described Joyce as "a very hyper person."

Days after Lionel appeared on *Dateline NBC* to promote his book—and Stone Phillips had blindsided her on camera with Lionel's published quotes about what he said was her postpartum depression after having Jeffrey—Joyce attempted suicide, by pills and gas from her kitchen oven. On a handwritten will dated two years earlier, wrote the *Fresno Bee*, she added a note that descended into illegibility: "It's been a lonely life—especially today." Also, she wrote, since the beginning of her marriage, Lionel "has physically and mentally abused me. Now he [is] reaping financing [sic] rewards for continuing to do so. He is evil inconade [sic] and is the real monster."

Jeff and his mom largely lost contact with each other

between 1978 and March 1991, when she called him. In the next four months—was it coincidental?—he killed at least eight people. In prison, Jeff seemed to ask for forgiveness. "Mom, you must hate me," he told her during a visit. She didn't, though she was horrified by his crimes. "When I think of what [Jeff] did, I stop breathing," she told a Milwaukee newspaper writer she trusted. Another time, to the same reporter, in what must have been at least an attempt at a joke, she said she was considering writing her own book: *What To Do If You Ever Become A Serial Killer's Mother.*

In Lionel's family biography, when Jeff was small, "almost every week seemed to bring another round of illness. He often contracted ear and throat infections that would keep him crying through the night. Over and over, he was taken to the university clinic for injections, and after a time, his little buttocks were covered with injection lumps, and he began to lash out at the nurses and doctors who labored to treat him." At four, he needed surgery for a double hernia. When he awoke from sedation, in pain, he asked his mother if the doctors had removed his penis.

That same year Jeff first became fascinated with dead animals. To know where this is going, you don't need a degree in child psychiatry. There had been a terrible smell under the house. Lionel found the source—rodents killed and picked clean by other wild animals. After he collected them into a bucket for disposal, Jeff stuck his hand into it, to play with the bones.

At age six, Jeff broke several windows of an abandoned building. When Lionel took him fishing, he seemed captivated by fish entrails. Games Jeff played with other children involved stalking and concealment. His first grade teacher noticed he was shy, reclusive, unable to communicate with other children, and profoundly unhappy.

In third grade, Jeff killed his first animals. He caught tadpoles and brought them as a gift for a favorite teacher. The teacher gave them to another classmate, and after he showed them to Jeff, in disappointment Jeff later snuck into his classmate's garage and dumped motor oil in their water.

According to Lionel, Jeff was molested at age eight by an older boy in the Bath neighborhood where they'd just moved. In 1991, Jeff vehemently denied it to police.

After age ten Jeff's posture grew rigid, especially when others approached him. He preferred to be alone in his room or to blankly watch television. By early high school, undetected by his parents, he began drinking heavily and smoking pot. A neighbor perceived his budding homosexuality and told her child to stop associating with him.

On his bicycle, carrying a supply of plastic garbage bags, Jeff collected road kill—mainly dogs and foxes. After cutting into them to reveal their internal organs, he burned their flesh with acid and bleached their bones—his father anxiously had wanted him to learn chemistry, and although Jeff didn't let on to him, he did in fact have an interest. Since the animals were already dead, it didn't matter, he reasoned. Then he buried them in an animal cemetery he created on a neighbor's property. Or, as neighbors asserted, he kept their skeletons in a backyard shed. Once, on a tree branch in the woods, enshrined by a cross of sticks, he nailed a skinned and gutted dog's head. Neighbors added that they also found impaled cats and frogs. He also brought home a pig's head from science class and kept its skull. When neighboring children found ashes from a series of small fires he set, they thought it was evidence of cult worship.

Asked later if he enjoyed dissecting animals, he said he did not. Nor did he get pleasure from killing animals, although he claimed he had a friend who did. As the passenger in his friend's car, he'd watch along the road for dogs to hit. One day they killed six. Once he watched a beagle puppy fly over top of the car. "I've never seen such a look of terror in an animal's eyes. It was sickening," he recalled under questioning.

He managed only a C and D average in high school,

although many recognized his very high intelligence. Often he was drunk in class on scotch or gin, and he kept a bottle in his locker. A classmate who first knew Jeff at age 12, later a sociology professor who wrote her Ph.D. thesis about him, said, "If a 16-year-old drinking in an 8 A.M. class isn't calling out for help, I don't know what is." She added, "Anyone who met him would say, he was the most bizarre person they'd ever met."

He encouraged a reputation for taking dares to do stupid stunts. Once, for 20 bucks, 10 classmates took him to Summit Mall in Akron for a spastic tour de force—witnessed by the future sociologist. For courage, he drained a six-pack of beer. At the Woolworth's lunch counter, he used an umbrella to knock over water glasses, as two patrons barely avoided a soaking. Leaving, he bleated like a lamb—a signature effect, according to his buddies. In a health food store, he sampled wheat germ then spit it out and screamed, "I'm allergic! I'm allergic!"

"We always saw him as the type to commit suicide, not harm somebody else," said a woman who had been his prom date. For the record, at the conclusion of that evening she remained unkissed. Nor had they danced together. In fact, he left her alone for an hour; when he returned, he said he'd gone to McDonald's. They parted with a handshake.

As he later admitted, Jeff first fantasized about killing a man in his senior year. He'd seen a jogger taking the same route, and his plan was to lie in wait, club him with a baseball bat, then drag him into the woods and have sex with him. One day he actually did stalk the man's path, he said. But the man never passed. In March of that year, drinking alcohol and smoking pot at home with a classmate, he pointed at six stuffed animals he said came from a taxidermist. "I always wanted to do that to a human," he said.

When his parents' marriage was at its nadir, Lionel slept in another room in the house and rigged a string tripwire with keys attached, to awaken him should Joyce enter. According to Lionel, Joyce filed for divorce; the *Milwaukee Journal* wrote that Lionel filed for it, in November 1977, although Joyce had first suggested the thought to him. They both alleged "extreme cruelty"—a detail unsaid in Lionel's book, although he did say Joyce had had an affair. Lionel left the house for a motel. By July 24, 1978, the date the marriage was dissolved, Jeff was already 18 and therefore not the object of any custodial dispute—unlike his 13-year-old brother David. Lionel argued that Joyce shouldn't have custody of him because of her "extensive mental illness". She won anyway. He had to pay $625 a month in alimony and child support.

That summer, Lionel stayed in touch by telephone with his sons, but by mid-August his calls to the house were no longer answered. After seven days of calling, then three of driving past the house without stopping, he knocked on the door.

Opening it, Jeff looked embarrassed. Where's your mother? Lionel asked. Where's your little brother?

"Gone. They moved out." He wouldn't say where or when they'd left.

Jeff wasn't alone. Friends, whom Lionel described as stoned, were in the midst of a séance trying to contact the dead. A chalk pentagram had been drawn on a round table. Lionel chased them away. He also discovered that the refrigerator was broken.

During that summer, Jeff said in his police confession, he'd had his first feelings of abandonment.

Immediately, Lionel moved back into the house, but with his girlfriend Shari, who would become his second wife—step mom to a child who, unknown to her, had already killed. During the next month Lionel confirmed that Joyce had taken David to her family's home in Wisconsin.

Meanwhile, Jeff was scheduled in about a week to leave for college, Ohio State in Columbus. One afternoon Shari caught Jeff drunk one afternoon, and Lionel followed by reading him the riot act. Until then Jeff had successfully hidden his drinking from his father.

At Ohio State, Jeff's alcoholism continued. Living in the 23-floor student residence hall Morrill Tower, in his first semester he earned a grade point average of 0.45. Jeff's best grade was a B-minus in riflery. When Lionel came to bring him home for winter break, he found a trophy row of beer and wine bottles at the top of his closet. His roommates told him Jeff drank daily, usually until he passed out, and he wouldn't get up until the middle of the afternoon. To get drinking money, he regularly sold his blood to a blood bank. His roommate from Cleveland later told the Ohio State student newspaper, the *Lantern*, that he "used to take bottles to class with him and came back drunk." He had no friends and got no mail. The high school classmate, later the sociology professor, saw him her last time "passed out on the street in Columbus. I remember thinking he was gone then."

At home, Lionel gave his son an ultimatum: get a job or join the military. For a few mornings he dropped him off at the mall to look for work. One afternoon he picked him up "dead drunk," Lionel wrote. Instead of taking him home, he told him to sober up and then call him back.

The call never came. Late that night, Lionel returned to the mall, couldn't find him, then called police. They'd picked him up hours earlier for drunk and disorderly.

Lionel married Shari on Christmas Eve, 1978. Five days later, he escorted Jeff to an Army recruitment station, where he enlisted for three years, to be followed by three additional years in the Army Reserves.

Jeff began service in January 1979. He spent four months at Fort McClellan, Alabama, in basic training and specialty instruction to be a military policeman. During a furlough home Lionel thought the Army was straightening him out.

They were not. His M.P. career ended when two privates beat him bloody while he was drunk, and his entire unit got in trouble. The Army then transferred him to Fort Sam Houston, Texas, to train as a medical specialist.

In June 1979 the Army sent him to Baumholder, Germany. His room commander, twelve years later, called him an obnoxious drunk and a passionate racist. Another soldier said Jeff would spend weekends on his bunk, headphones on, listening to heavy-metal music like Black Sabbath, drinking martinis he mixed in a nifty bar-in-a-briefcase kit, until he passed out.

Beginning in May 1980, Jeff was written up about a dozen times for disobeying orders and reporting for work late, drunk or in improper uniform. In February 1981 the Army put him in alcoholic rehab but within weeks a counselor recommended he be declared a "failure." Dahmer's commander then initiated a Chapter 9 discharge.

Returned stateside to Fort Jackson, S.C., Dahmer was discharged on March 26, 1981, ten months short of his three-year commitment. He was discharged honorably, but with mention on his record of "alcohol or other drug abuse". Lionel didn't even know Jeff was out of the Army until his trunk arrived on his doorstep. Inside were his fatigues, but nothing to suggest where he'd gone.

As a parting gesture, the Army had offered him a one-way commercial air ticket anywhere in the country. Not wishing to face the music from his father, Jeffrey Dahmer chose to fly to Miami, Florida.

2
The Disappearance

MONDAY, JULY 27, 1981

```
                    INCIDENT REPORT
         INCIDENT NUMBER: HW-81-056073
       POLICE DEPARTMENT—HOLLYWOOD, FLORIDA

::::::::::::::::::::::::::::::::::::::::::::::::::::::::::::::::::::::

INCIDENT TYPE: MISSING PERSON JUVENILE
LOCATION: 300 HOLLYWOOD MALL
TYPE PREMISE: RETAIL STORE CHAIN STORE: Y
DISP: 7/27/81
TIME AND DATE OF INCIDENT: 1355 7/27/81
DAY: MON SUBJECTS: 2 VEHICLES: 0

------------------------ SUBJECT #1 ------------------------

STATUS SUBJECT: REPORTEE
NAME: REVE WALSH
```

RACE/SEX/DOB: W-F, 7/24/51
ADDRESS: 2801 MCKINLEY STREET

------------------------ SUBJECT #2 -----------------------

STATUS SUBJECT: MISSING PERSON—JUVENILE
NAME: ADAM WALSH
RACE/SEX/DOB: W-M, 11/14/74
ADDRESS: 2801 MCKINLEY STREET
HEIGHT: 3-06 WEIGHT: 045 HAIR: SANDY, BL
EYES: HAZEL BUILD: THIN COMPLEX: MEDIUM
FURTHER DESCRIPTION: SEE NARRATIVE

---------------------------- TEXT ----------------------------

JUVENILE WAS LAST SEEN WEARING A RED AND
WHITE STRIPED SHIRT WITH GREEN ADIDAS GYM
SHORTS, CREAM COLORED CANVAS CAPTAIN'S HAT
WITH A BLUE RIM AND YELLOW RUBBER SANDALS.
REPORTEE ADVISES THAT THE ABOVE MISSING
PERSON WAS LAST SEEN IN THE TOY DEPARTMENT
OF SEARS DEPARTMENT STORE. MISSING PERSON
WAS TO MEET REPORTEE WHEN SHE WAS DONE WITH
HER BUSINESS IN ANOTHER PART OF THE STORE,
NAMELY THE LAMP DEPARTMENT. REPORTEE
RETURNED TO TOY DEPT APPROXIMATELY TEN (10)
TO FIFTEEN (15) MINUTES AFTER SHE LEFT THE
MISSING PERSON AND THE MISSING PERSON WAS
NOT TO BE FOUND. REPORTEE LOOKED FOR
MISSING PERSON FOR APPROXIMATELY FORTY (40)
TO FORTY FIVE (45) MINUTES BEFORE CALLING
POLICE.
UPON ARRIVAL, THE UNDERSIGNED OFFICER
TOOK INFO FROM THE REPORTEE AND THEN
NOTIFIED NCIC/FCIC AND REPORT WAS TAKEN BY
BADGE #617. THE UNDERSIGNED, REPORTEE, AND
THE GRANDMOTHER THEN CONDUCTED A STORE TO
STORE SEARCH OF THE MALL WHICH PROVED
FRUITLESS. THE UNDERSIGNED OFFICER

CONTINUED SEARCH AND AT APPROXIMATELY 1700
HOURS HANDED THIS INVESTIGATION OVER TO LT.
WALSH. NO FURTHER INFORMATION AVAILABLE AT
THIS TIME. ---

REPORTING OFFICER: CSO M DONAHAY, SQD 5
BADGE: 1334 ENTRY: 0310 07/29/81

Sears, in the Hollywood Mall, was a mile and a half from
the Walshes' home. Adam's mother Reve Walsh said she
parked her gray Checker—a passenger car version of the famous
oversized cab—just outside the door of the catalog desk and
entered hand-in-hand with Adam. Although the initial police
report narrative does not mention the time, she later told the
first police officer who arrived that it was about 12:30 in the
afternoon.

Right in front of them was the toy department. To sell
what was the first generation of home video games, Sears had a
display where kids could play for free. Passing it, there was a
small crowd of kids, three deep, already playing. It was July,
summer vacation, and Adam wanted to play too. "That was our
ritual," Reve wrote in John's book (published in 1997),
entering by that door of Sears "[a]nd Adam begging me to let
him play the video game."

She relented. "Okay. I'm going to the lamp department for
a minute. Right over there. You stay here and I'll be right over
there."

"Okay, Mommy. I know where that is," he answered.

Sears had bronze lamps on sale, 20-40% off, as advertised in
Good Housekeeping. Yet the one Reve wanted she couldn't
find, and a young clerk told her it wasn't in the store. The
department manager was at lunch, she said, and Reve told her
she'd come back.

When she returned to the videogames, at most ten minutes
later, she thought, Adam wasn't there.

Nor were any of the kids she'd just seen.

She looked through some aisles, including in the lamp department, then found another clerk. "Have you seen my son? He was just here a minute ago." The woman hadn't. Nor had anyone else she asked.

"I kept saying, 'you don't understand. My son is a little boy who does not wander off.' And all the while, a horrible, cold fear was building. I knew something was wrong. Really wrong. I was absolutely convinced of it."

Outside the garden shop entrance she spotted Jean Walsh, her husband John's mother, who also lived in Hollywood. Seeing her was a relief. "Do you have Adam?" "No, what's the matter? Why are you crying? Oh, my God, let's find him."

Both of them started searching the rest of the store and the mall. Reve showed around a wallet photo of Adam. It was his first-grade school picture in which he wore the same shirt he was wearing that day—an Izod Lacoste with thick red and white stripes, thin green stripes and a sewn alligator emblem.

Still, nobody recognized him.

Reve asked a woman at the catalog desk what she should do, thinking she should call the police. The catalog clerk told her not to get excited, children commonly got lost in the store. She gave Reve the house phone, which connected to the switchboard operator. Reve asked that Adam be paged to the toy department, but store policy, the operator apologized, was to only allow pages to the customer service desk.

"Adam Walsh, please come to customer service."

"Customer service?" she wrote. "How was he supposed to know where that was, or how to get there? That was how much they were prepared for what was happening." A little later, at Reve's insistence, a second announcement: "Adam Walsh, please meet your mother in the toy department."

No boy appeared.

The catalog clerk suggested maybe the child had gone into the mall. Reve answered that Adam wouldn't do that, but she checked anyway, running up and down the mall.

"I was crying. I couldn't help it. I was so scared. We had looked everywhere, in the store and the mall. I had run out to the parking lot and checked the car, twice. I had asked everyone in sight if they had seen my little boy."

The Hollywood police arrived. Besides issuing a Be On the Lookout radio call to their officers, they didn't know what to do. They suggested maybe he'd left the store, become disoriented, and started walking home. Impossible, Reve insisted. It wasn't a pedestrian-friendly walk, and he was only six years old.

Nevertheless, she called the home of Adam's best friend, Clifford Hofman, certain he wasn't there. Clifford's parents immediately came to Sears to help look. She walked back outside, looked in dumpsters, looked inside every car in the parking lot. "I spotted a man who was loading things into a camper, bags of groceries, camping supplies. I started screaming that he must have taken my son. But it turned out that he was just some guy going on a camping trip.

"By that point I was grasping at straws. I would try any suggestion at all. Anything. Because by now everything was already so far from reality that nothing made sense. It was like a bad dream, one where you can't get there from here... I was trying to reach my child, but he couldn't hear me... It was like the life was being sucked right out of me."

At some point, she wrote, a teenage female plainclothes store security guard approached her. She was upset because, she said, she had kicked some children out of the store. She wasn't sure whether Adam was one of them.

A policeman suggested that Jean Walsh drive to her grandson's McKinley Street home and see if he was there. She did that. First she knocked on neighbors' doors to check with them. None had seen him. Nor had anyone at the playground nearby. Then she entered the house and went through it room by room. The phone rang, and her son John was calling. In his book, she wrote, "I told him we had been up at the mall and had lost track of Adam." John followed that with his recollection that he first learned about it when Reve called him from a pay phone. He quoted Reve: "John, something is wrong here. Really wrong. Adam is missing and I need you to get here."

John immediately left his office, in Bal Harbour, 20 minutes south of Hollywood. In his car he took his younger brother Joe, who worked with him, and they stopped on the way in Sunny Isles to tell their friend Jimmy Campbell. In his own car came his business associate and mentor, John Monahan.

Arriving at Sears, John wrote: "I walked in and saw the back of Reve and called her name. She turned around. Her face was white, absolutely ashen, and it was obvious that she had been crying. A terrible, desperate look was in her eyes... But the only words she spoke were, 'It's Adam, John... I can't find Adam.'"

Initially, officers spread out from the store to cover a radius they thought a little boy in rubber sandals was able to wander. But as afternoon became early evening, they realized they needed help. Every available Hollywood police officer was asked to search for Adam Walsh. The entire detective bureau turned out, plus 22 patrol officers requested overtime after their shifts ended so they could keep looking. Police boats combed canals. With searchlights aimed at the ground, the Broward County Sheriff's helicopter search team hovered over fields and golf courses.

At 7:30, police asked for help from Jack Simons, head of the Hollywood Citizens' Crime Watch. Prepared for such occasions, Simons spread the word through phone chains. They'd already carved a city map into 97 neighborhoods, and everyone in advance had assigned sections in which to look. Volunteers walked streets and alleys near their homes, calling out Adam's name. They searched dark places, dumpsters and under garbage can lids, and asked others on the street if they'd seen him.

No one found any clues at all.

When the Walshes and their own search party finally left the mall, they decamped at the Hollywood Police station, directly across the street from Sears. They left Reve's Checker where she'd parked it, in the second spot from the store's corner, unlocked the door, and Reve made Adam an impromptu bed, with his blue blanket and toys and books. They wrote a note and propped it inside the windshield: "Adam, stay in the car. Mommy and Daddy are looking for you."

By 10 o'clock, police asked Simons to set in motion his group operation's second phase: again, he started his phone chains, and by 11, about 60 volunteers arrived at the Hollywood Police station, ready to comb everywhere Adam might have reached on foot. Meanwhile, other members called radio and television stations, asking them to publicize the search.

At three in the morning, without any success, they quit for the night, pledging to return to the police station the next morning.

Tuesday July 28

By nine o'clock Tuesday morning, more than a hundred Crime Watchers had gathered at the police station. Simons asked them to cover the same areas, then return every three hours. By now people were searching all over the city, the airport, bus station, on the beach, and in other shopping areas. Riders on horseback surveyed fields. Three people monitored citizens' band radio frequencies. Meanwhile, police cadets and off-duty officers searched wooded areas and swamps.

At 10, Reve Walsh and her husband John appeared before television news cameras at the police station, teary-eyed and exhausted from lack of sleep. Their appeal would be broadcast on the noon news. They hoped either Adam would be watching or someone who had seen him.

"Adam, we're looking for you, and we miss you. We love you," said his father. "Look for landmarks, Adam. Look for landmarks and you'll be able to find your way home."

Police printed a missing flyer with a photo of Adam in a white V-neck T-ball team shirt and red cap, a Louisville Slugger gripped in his baby fingers with chewed-down nails. Smiling for the camera, he showed off his mother's big hazel eyes. His two front teeth were missing, and his brown hair was sweaty and tousled. His nickname was Cooter. Police distributed the flyer to Florida Power and Light workers, Southern Bell telephone crews, letter carriers, and taxi drivers.

> MASSIVE SEARCH LAUNCHED FOR BOY,
> ADAM WALSH DISAPPEARED FROM SEARS MONDAY
> AFTERNOON
> —*Hollywood Sun-Tattler*

That was the headline in the *Hollywood Sun-Tattler* in its home-delivered afternoon edition. By the time its reporter, 26-year-old Charlie Brennan, arrived, the Walshes had already consulted a psychic named Dr. Fisher—Brennan didn't get her first name or credentials. She thought Adam might have left the mall heading south. Brennan didn't mention that if he had, he would have walked smack into the police station.

The evening *Miami News* mentioned the search in a brief on their local news page, quoting a police spokesman. While raising the possibility of a kidnapping, he said it wasn't suspected. "The kid is probably trying to get home and is probably lost somewhere, and we're searching the city for him."

With the publicity came a shower of phone tips. Since the department was already stretched thin—on the case were 54 officers and detectives, many of whom had volunteered their off-duty time—the police allowed John, Reve, and their family members and friends to sit in the third-floor detective bureau and answer and log those incoming tips. The arrangement was highly irregular, and it reflected the trust the police had in the Walshes' innocence.

An employee of a convenience store near Hollywood Mall told John's brother Joe Walsh he'd seen Adam get into a white car that went west on Hollywood Boulevard. A mall bakery worker said she'd seen him wandering the mall. Someone else said he'd seen him at St. Matthew's Catholic Church in nearby Hallandale. Other reports had him spotted as far away as Miami Beach and West Palm Beach.

Finally at 8:30, Jack Simons called off the Crime Watch search. Everyone was exhausted, and since all areas of the city had been searched at least twice, further efforts would be futile, they felt. Simons went home but couldn't fall asleep.

Wednesday July 29

SIX-YEAR-OLD WAS KIDNAPED, POLICE BELIEVE
—*The Miami Herald*

Haggard and bleary-eyed from the all-night search for his six-year-old son, John Walsh burst into tears.

"He was an immensely loved little boy and we will go to any lengths to get him back," said Walsh, announcing a "substantial" reward for the freckle-faced Hollywood boy with a missing tooth.

Later in the day, in the *Sun-Tattler*'s home edition, Walsh expanded on that theme: "He's either dead, or someone has him. He's probably in a dead panic to reach me. Somebody's hopefully got him. If he's outside the county, there's not much we can do about it."

Police spokesman Fred Barbetta suggested they begin searching the area's many waterways, a system of canals that drained the Everglades. "If he's in the water, this is when he'd come up." Jack Simons shared a similar pessimism. "We're not looking for someone walking around right now. We're looking for whatever is left."

Also irregular was the fact that John Walsh had emerged as the story's primary spokesman, speaking from the police department. The press found him far more compelling than the usual police public information officer or press release.

"The worst thing that could happen is that he's in a canal somewhere," the *Sun-Tattler* quoted Walsh, his voice reported as shaking. "Nobody at the police department believes that's what happened. Nobody wants to believe it."

Later in the day, Walsh offered to pay a reward of $5,000, which he put on a new "missing" flyer. Apparently as a guide to how much they could afford, he described himself as vice president for marketing for the $26 million Paradise Grand Hotel resort in Nassau, Bahamas, then under construction.

Referring to the fight between the four kids, the *Herald* reported it happened about the same time Reve left Adam at the video game. But a store security guard broke it up and ordered the combatants out of the store. Later interviewed by police, the boys "remembered seeing Adam heading towards the lamp department where his mother was."

Thursday, July 30

NO CLUES
BOY, 6, STILL MISSING
—*Hollywood Sun-Tattler*

The *Sun-Tattler* reported that Adam was Broward County's biggest missing-child mystery since the 1976 disappearance of eight-year-old Lisa Lynn Berry. She'd last been seen at a Hollywood bowling alley, and the community had gathered to search for her. Within a day volunteers found her pink pants and green sweater. Days later her body was found. It turned out Lisa Berry's kidnapping and murder hadn't been random. Her mother's friend was convicted for the crimes.

Police were asking people who'd seen anything unusual at Sears on Monday to come forward. They also wanted to question the four boys—two white, two black, all between 10 and 12—who'd fought over the Atari games and had been thrown out of the store by security guard Kathy Shaffer, "on the chance it happened at the same time Adam disappeared," said Sgt. Dennis Naylon.

"He respects authority. Maybe he thought he was responsible for something. Maybe he followed them out of the store for some reason."

At nine in the morning at the Hollywood police station, Willis Morgan arrived to report what he'd seen. By then police had already listened to hundreds of tips. Trying to help, citizens called in names of people down the block who they thought were child molesters, wives suggested their ex-husbands, and others had just thought they'd seen Adam. The lobby receptionist pointed Morgan to an officer at a special desk the department had set up to receive walk-in tips.

Morgan said he'd been in the Hollywood Mall around noon on Monday. He was browsing at Radio Shack when a man approached him, wanting to talk. The man was large, drunk and disheveled, and had shaggy hair and a crappy grin.

"Hi there, nice day, isn't it?"

Morgan, 34, looked like a powerful man but because a motorcycle accident had left him with a prosthetic leg, he couldn't walk away quickly. He was scared. He tried to look away, but then the man's eyes turned angry, demonic, and piercing.

He stared for a number of seconds, then finally he got the message and left. At first Morgan was relieved. Then he thought, maybe the guy would approach someone else who'd need help. From a safe distance, Morgan followed him. The man walked through the mall and entered Sears. Staying behind him, Morgan saw him go into the toy department. But that led nowhere else, and since Morgan didn't want the man to double back and see him, he abruptly left. He did, not feeling safe until he got into his car, locked the door, and drove away.

That night he saw on the late local news that a child was missing from Hollywood Mall. When he arrived at work, Wednesday evening as a pressman at the *Miami Herald*, he told his buddies, who insisted he go to the police. His workday ended at 5:30 A.M., and he'd stayed up so he could get to the police station by nine.

The officer asked if he had a receipt from a purchase at the mall that Monday to prove he'd been there. He hadn't. Had he seen a tag number of a getaway car? He said he'd only seen the man inside the mall. The officer took his name and phone number and said they'd call him if they needed him. Morgan felt like a jerk for coming.

While some were criticizing Hollywood police for not doing enough, police responded that they'd never had a week like this one. Besides Adam, in the past five days they'd also had a rape of a five-year-old girl and the discovery of a dead woman in a canal.

Meanwhile, the *Sun-Tattler* reported, a secretary at an asphalt company had organized at least three hundred truck drivers to search fields, walking together ten feet apart, in undeveloped southwest Broward.

John Walsh said he'd been having trouble eating the past two days. "I tried to have some soup, but I can't hold anything down. I just gag it back up." Nor had he or Reve been able to sleep, he said.

"Everybody—psychics, police, friends, family—they all say they're sure he's still alive," he said. But at other moments Walsh conceded anything was possible. "I don't need to tell you how many people are walking around out there who just don't think straight."

Just peeking into Adam's room and seeing his toys and clothes was crushing to Reve, he said. However, he was comforted by the support of those around him, especially his younger brother Joe and a friend, James Campbell, who since Monday had devoted all their time to following every lead from the psychics, or just staying close to him.

The article wrote glowingly of John and Reve's strength and endurance, how they were always ready to give another newspaper interview, go on TV, or answer tipsters' calls:

> Wiping tears from his eyes for what seems like the hundredth time this week, running his hands through jet-black hair flecked with silver, Walsh sums up what Hollywood Police have discovered—"It's like he disappeared from the face of the earth."
>
> "I can't tell you how much I love that boy," he adds. "He's such a joy."

Meanwhile, state Marine Patrol officers were searching canals, which, since drug smuggling had become such big business locally in the past five years, were now common places to dump bodies. Sometimes fishermen would find them. 1981 would be the historical peak year for homicides in South Florida. If Adam had been murdered and dumped in water Monday, the day he disappeared, then Wednesday was the day to look because bodies underwater start decomposing after 36 to 48 hours. Then they surface.

PSYCHIC AIDS SEARCH FOR LOST BOY
—*Fort Lauderdale News*

Her hands touching the controls of Sears's Atari game to sense its "vibrations," Micki Dahne, a psychic with a local radio show, told Reve that Adam was scared, but okay.

Dahne also met Kathy Shaffer, the Sears security guard, in tears. The *Fort Lauderdale News* reported Shaffer had since told the police she ordered Adam as well as the four other boys to stop fighting over the video game and leave the store.

Friday, July 31

YOUTH MIGHT HAVE SEEN BOY BEFORE HE DISAPPEARED
—*The Miami Herald*

POLICE BELIEVE BOY ALIVE; REWARD NOW $25,000
—*Hollywood Sun-Tattler*

Had Adam been fighting, and was he one of five boys ejected from the store? Or was he a passive spectator of a fight, confused as to whether he as well had been ordered to leave the store?

The police and the Walshes were expounding the spectator theory. "It's possible Adam was standing there watching and was shooed from the store with the other kids," Lt. Richard Hynds told the *Miami Herald.* Lost in all this was Shaffer's change of story, to where she now she thought she *had* thrown Adam out of the store. A new detail apparently from Shaffer was added: she sent the white boys out the store's north door, and the black boys out the south.

But how many white boys had she expelled, two or three? Police were still saying two.

The 12-year-old Hollywood boy who said he'd played video games with the boy he thought was Adam told police he'd last seen Adam between 1:30-2:00. Because that changed the timeframe, the *Sun-Tattler* reported, police were now speculating that Adam was still alive. However, to believe that Adam had been seen in the toy department even at 1:30 contradicted Reve's timeline of events. She said she'd left Adam at 12:30, returned for him no more than fifteen minutes later, then searched 45 minutes before calling police.

The *Miami Herald* interviewed the child, but at his parents' request didn't publish his name. They quoted Lt. Hynds saying the child had offered the best information so far in the case. "This boy is a really credible source and the son of a prominent citizen. His family is very religious. I know he's telling the truth."

The boy told the *Herald* that a little boy matching Adam's description watched him playing the video spaceship game with a girl. Then he asked the smaller boy to play. They played two rounds, the older boy winning both. Then two 12- to 13-year-old boys demanded a turn, grabbing the game's controls from the smaller boy, who held on and told them, "It doesn't belong to you."

To the boy speaking to the *Herald*, one of the bullying kids looked as if he was going to punch the smaller kid in the face, so he told the smaller boy to leave so he wouldn't get hurt. Relinquishing the joystick, the smaller boy watched nearby for a few moments, then left.

The boy thought Adam's missing photo looked like the child he saw, but it wasn't an exact match. "This kid was a different size. He wasn't exactly skinny but he wasn't a blob either."

During their game, the boy also remembered, while the on-screen rockets and missiles were flying, the little boy had said, "Oh, wow," and "Oops! You missed one." Reve had told police that Adam said things like that. But the Hollywood boy didn't say anything to the *Herald* about a security guard breaking up a fight, or kids kicked out of the store. Adam had simply walked away, he said, the fight averted.

In the *Herald*, Lt. Hynds nonetheless connected the fight and Shaffer's ejections, which might incidentally or unintentionally have included Adam. But in the *Sun-Tattler*, the detectives held to Shaffer's original story that she'd removed only four children. Adam wasn't in the fight, he was merely watching, they said.

Left unsaid in the already conflicting stories was that if the Hollywood boy was accurate, there may have been no connection between Adam and the fight—and if his recollection of the time was right, he might have seen Adam at least a full hour after Reve first left him.

The *Herald* also reported the Walshes were now convinced Adam had been kidnapped, and that they'd raised their reward to $10,000. By that evening the *Sun-Tattler* reported it was $25,000.

Saturday, August 1

MISSING BOY WAS SEEN BY 3
—*The Miami Herald*

Police also thought 10-year-olds Timothy Pottenburgh and his cousin, and their grandmother, were credible when they reported seeing Adam apparently enter a blue van outside Sears on the day he disappeared.

Without naming them, police told the *Miami Herald* they'd seen Adam walking near the toy department Monday about 1:30—after they'd heard the store intercom page him. The grandmother said the boy they saw fit Adam's description: slight build, striped shirt, green sandals.

They next saw Adam outside the store's north exit—the same one Reve said they'd entered. He turned left toward the parking lot. From the same exit they saw a man run, enter a blue van, and drive toward the boy, nearly hitting the Pottenburgh clan. Adam fled around the side of the building, chased by the van. Curious, Timothy looked around the corner. From 25 yards away, he spotted the van, parked, its door open, then watched it speed away. He didn't see Adam.

The family described the man as white, about six feet tall,

muscular, with dark bushy hair, wearing jeans and a T-shirt. The van, they said, was shiny dark blue, late model, with mag wheels, dark-tinted windows, and a chrome ladder in the back.

On Friday, through the local news media and radio, police had started asking the public to be on the lookout for blue vans. They also called Hollywood Crime Watch, and its members began driving their assigned areas, calling police with their sightings.

"We're more sure now that he's probably been kidnapped," Lt. Hynds said.

In its news pages, the *Sun-Tattler* reprinted Adam Walsh's Missing handbill, offering the $25,000 reward. As well, a local direct advertiser stuffed copies in its regular mailing to 50,000 homes. The handbill had Adam's T-ball photo, Hollywood police phone numbers, a "non-police" number in Miami (likely Walsh's office), the Walsh family home address, and toll-free numbers so anyone in Florida or the rest of the U.S. could call. It also read:

> We are willing to negotiate ransom on ANY terms. Strict confidentiality. DO NOT FEAR REVENGE! We will not prosecute. We only want our son. If desired, contact any radio or T.V. station, newspaper or any other media as a neutral party for negotiations or information. Do not fear revenge. We want Adam home.

At Sears's parking lot, a few hundred people met to distribute another hundred thousand copies.

A Hollywood city commissioner suggested the city contribute $5,000 to the reward. John Walsh said people across the country had been sending money—five to several hundred dollars. He also wanted to spread the word via TV.

He promised Ralph Renick, Miami's Walter Cronkite, "If

you put me on, I won't break down. I won't." The *Herald* wrote that WTVJ's Renick didn't think Walsh could handle live TV, so he'd instead suggested a taped interview. But Walsh convinced him, so he and Reve went on the Friday 4:30 newscast for three minutes. With Adam's stuffed animal in Reve's lap, holding hands, the Walshes did fine. The *Herald* reporter followed them to the Hollywood police detective bureau, where a Tarot card reader insisted she do their reading. John Walsh told the reporter they'd already met with 15 clairvoyants, 13 of whom said Adam was alive.

Now that searches of canals, swamps, and undeveloped areas hadn't produced his body, the Walshes thought Adam was probably in the hands of an abductor. And since that person hadn't responded to offers to pay ransom, he or she likely was someone who wanted a child.

John also talked about finding Reve in Adam's bed, crying. Since then he'd locked the door to the child's room.

Sunday, August 2

BOY'S REWARD FUND RISES, BUT LEAD VANISHES
—*Fort Lauderdale News*

The Walshes increased their reward to $50,000, but the Pottenburghs, who hadn't wanted to get involved in the first place, were refusing to let police hypnotize Timothy to help him recall what he saw.

By herself, police said, the grandmother wasn't a good witness because she was partially blind. All she could say for certain about the incident was that a van had almost run them over.

Days later, Walsh was quoted in the *Fort Lauderdale News*: "If it wasn't going to hurt the child, well, maybe the woman can put herself in my position. What if it were her little boy who was missing?"

Monday, August 3

POLICE CHECKING VANS FOR MISSING 6-YEAR-OLD
—The Miami Herald

As a result of their request to the public for help spotting late-model shiny blue vans, police had received "tons" of calls. They'd checked 50 of them but without success.

"One lady called in this morning who said she had a dream that Adam was in a wheelchair being pushed down a long white corridor by a black male," said a police spokesman. "Now, you tell me how we're going to start looking for black males going down long white corridors."

Tuesday, August 4

THE ORDEAL OF ADAM'S PARENTS
—Hollywood Sun-Tattler

The entire week, *Sun-Tattler* reporter Charlie Brennan had stuck to the Walshes. He wrote that John and Reve had become almost as familiar to South Floridians as their missing son. In a media blitz, they'd appeared on local TV "morning, noon, and night," as well as on the front pages of all the area's newspapers. They'd refused no media request. Often they were crying, and always they pleaded for someone to bring them back their boy.

"Most couples are fortunate enough never to have to open up their hearts—their lives, even—before millions of people at a time when the core of their family is ripped out without warning. And most couples would not be doing it so well."

The late edition reported that after stopping "hundreds" of blue vans, police were now downplaying the lead. "Some of them have been stopped twice. It's hardly safe to drive a blue van in South Florida these days," said Lt. Hynds.

3
The Billy Goats Gruff

IN THE DAYS AFTER JEFFREY DAHMER'S CAPTURE, the press discovered that Billy Joe Capshaw had been his bunkmate in the Army, the 2d Battalion, 68th Armored Regiment, 8th Infantry Division, stationed in Baumholder, Germany, through 1981—before the Army discharged Dahmer early for alcohol abuse and he came to Miami. They were both trained as medics—nurse's assistants.

In 1991, Capshaw was serving six months for negligent homicide in the Garland County Jail, in his native Hot Springs, Arkansas. He explained that while he went into a bar, he'd left the keys in his car so a friend's 15-year-old stepdaughter could listen to the radio. Without his permission she drove away, wrecked his car, and accidentally killed someone. The state had held him liable.

Capshaw told *The New York Times* that he and Dahmer drank together. But drunk, Dahmer would become "stony-faced" and violent with him.

"You could tell in his face that he wasn't joking. It was for real. That's why it bothered me. It was a whole different side.

His face was blank. It was kind of like he was cross-eyed-like. An expression like he just wasn't there. I've never seen it on anyone else's face."

I read this quote to Willis Morgan, the Hollywood Mall witness who'd told police Dahmer had tried to pick him up. "I could say those words verbatim," he replied.

I'd anticipated difficulty finding Capshaw, but he'd posted a website:

"I was roommates with Jeffrey Dahmer for 18 months during my time in the military. I was age 17 when the abuse started and 19 when it finally stopped. I was raped, molested, tortured, drugged, daily beat with an iron pipe, stabbed. Jeffrey also tried to remove my prostate. I've been in therapy for many years now."

That sounded crazy. Was it credible that a U.S. soldier could become, in effect, someone's sex slave? When I reached him, Capshaw explained that at the time, the Army didn't want to deal with homosexual rape. He'd just entered the service days after his 17th birthday—"I didn't know what to do." All the other soldiers were older, including Dahmer, by at least two years. And Capshaw had never before traveled more than a few miles from home.

He'd been in psychotherapy since he came home, in November 1981, and a doctor named Eugene Watermann had helped him tremendously. For the first five years, he said, "I couldn't get out of bed." Even for the first 20 years, he described himself as Rip Van Winkle, asleep or not participating much in the rest of the world. Dr. Watermann had helped him reawaken. Meanwhile, for post-traumatic stress disorder, citing in a document that "he was tortured by a roommate," the Army had given him a disability pension, eventually in 1998 granting him 100 percent disability, and a substantial lump sum.

As I spoke with Capshaw, he was calm and reasonable, not

the "country bumpkin" as another bunkmate had described him in a 1991 *Arkansas Gazette* story. He agreed his story sounded difficult to believe. He hadn't mentioned his rapes in the 1991 stories because until very recently he wasn't ready to admit them. He did tell the *Hot Springs Sentinel-Record* that Dahmer "was violent" and "drunk all the time." Of his decision to talk about the rapes now, he said, "It's not much of a life keeping that stuff inside."

On the Internet I found corroboration. Linda Sue Swisher, a retired licensed practical nurse who'd served at the same time, wrote on her own web page:

> The saddest part of my time in the army came after I was out for a few years. Jeffrey Dahmer, the cannabalist/murderer, was one of the medics that I had trained for ER work during my tour in Baumholder, West Germany, just north of Landstuhl. There were 3 young, slender, dark complected men who were so seriously assaulted that: a) They could not crawl away from where they were found (needing serious surgery); b) In spite of collecting rape kit evidence against whomever had hurt them, the MP's would not start a case of any kind (just a lover's argument); and c) The one man who had emergency surgery to save his life had to get a permanent colostomy, but still would not press charges or tell anyone what had happened. Out of approx. 18,000 men on post these were the only men who even came close to reporting being raped.

I found Swisher's phone number, in Washington state. When I told her why I was calling, I heard her gasp. It took most of a long conversation before she finally caught her breath. She was elated that someone wanted to listen.

When she saw Dahmer's photo in the newspapers in 1991, she said, "Oh shit. I taught this guy anatomy." She'd had recurring nightmares since. "Out of all the people who came through the ER as patients or went through the medic refresher program, you could show me their pictures and I wouldn't have a clue." But Dahmer's she remembered instantly.

"There was something totally wrong about him. Something anti-social." As a nurse, she pointed out, her most basic skill was observation.

The three male rapes had occurred within months of one another, she said, and during the time Dahmer was stationed on base. She'd been assigned there between September 1977 and November 1980. According to Dahmer's Army records, he served there from July '79 to March '81.

She only matched the rapes and Dahmer when she saw his newspaper photo. "I was staring at his picture in the paper," she said. She thought the Army could have stopped him.

All three men had been badly sodomized, suffering several anal tears, she said, but one, a Hispanic man, had a rupture much higher—of his sigmoid colon, above his rectum and anal pouch. He was found screaming in pain, and had lost so much blood he would have died in 30 minutes had they not stabilized him.

Because the base hospital essentially acted as an emergency room and transported the traumatized patients to the larger army hospital in Landstuhl, Swisher didn't get to learn much about the victims. But she said they were all "fairly short men, not particularly well-built." She knew that all three survived, and when she asked a JAG officer whether the incidents would be prosecuted and the rape kit evidence she'd preserved used, her answer was, "Boys will be boys, it was a lover's spat."

The Army was then prosecuting rapes against women, she said, but "I never once saw a woman who required immediate surgery. I never, ever saw the kind of damage that happened to these men."

What especially stuck in her mind was a snapshot of Dahmer during a training class she gave. The program was six weeks long and contained 20 students. Along with classes, trainees did practical work on the emergency room day shift at the base hospital—the 56th General Hospital. Dahmer didn't make it to the next level. "It didn't seem he was paying attention in class, he didn't ask questions, he wasn't doing anything more than just showing up," Swisher said. As an instructor, she was looking for enthusiasm and pathos as well as ability. Many of her trainees had only the equivalent of a sixth grade education plus a high school equivalency diploma.

The snapshot occurred on the day they worked on a human anatomy model. It was plastic but life-sized and didn't have ribs to cover its internal organs. Like in the child's game Operation, Dahmer was to use forceps to replace its liver where it belonged.

Clutching the liver, Dahmer's "eyes were like ice." But he smiled—the first and only time she'd ever seen him smile. "His eyes didn't match his smile," she said. "In that minute of time, it was so clear to me, the violent evil I was looking at in his eyes. From all those people I saw there, how come I'm so haunted by that one snapshot?"

It was also ironic, she thought, that Dahmer, who lacked anything close to normal human empathy, had been assigned by the Army as a medic.

Swisher's description of Dahmer's eyes matched Morgan's, even to use the word evil. When I read her a book quote from Shari Dahmer, Jeff's stepmother, that she'd seen the violence behind Jeff's "dull, unmoving mask," Swisher said, "That describes him in class to a T."

Swisher's mention of the word liver recalled Capshaw's similar observation. In their room, he said, Dahmer had a small refrigerator on which he kept a combination lock. When Capshaw asked what was in it, Dahmer answered, "I got some liver in there. I don't want anybody to take it." Since they were stationed in Germany, Capshaw had assumed he meant liverwurst. In his 1992 prison interview with Hollywood Police lead detective Jack Hoffman, however, Dahmer volunteered that in his Milwaukee apartment, he'd removed at least one human liver—as well as other organs and body parts—and cooked and eaten them.

The room, Capshaw described, had three beds, but except for one week, he and Dahmer were the only two in it. It had a double-decker bunk; Capshaw slept on top, Dahmer the bottom. The room's door could be locked from either side, and Dahmer took away Capshaw's key, so as a result, when he was inside, Capshaw was Dahmer's captive. When Dahmer left, he locked Capshaw in, sometimes overnight.

"I jumped out the window the first couple times," Capshaw said. But when he landed, from the second story, he hurt himself badly. He stopped doing that, he said, because it left him weaker and less able to resist.

When Capshaw did leave the room, he was nearly always within Dahmer's sight, even in the lavatory and mess hall. "He had me completely covered," he said. He wasn't assigned to work duty. He described a non-regular Army, post-Vietnam tour, where work assignments could be permanently ducked and "everyone's doing their own thing" under poor or absent supervision.

When he had the chance, "I asked, begged, pleaded, bargained for a room transfer," but his superiors—his room commander, his sergeant, and his lieutenant—refused him. "I was locked in the room with a fucking serial killer, and they did nothing."

On the one occasion he pulled guard duty, he begged the lead officer in charge to help him. His response was, "So the baby wants out of his room." Capshaw reacted by taking the superior's .45 pistol from his holster then tried to kill himself. When he pulled the trigger there was no bullet in the chamber. Capshaw was subdued and the gun was removed from him. He was taken to the guard shack for the rest of the shift, but afterwards was returned to the room with Dahmer. "I was surprised I didn't kill myself at that guard duty," Capshaw said.

One barracks mate, David Rodriguez, remembered that Capshaw "would hang out with Dahmer." He described Capshaw, then, unflatteringly, as an illiterate hillbilly, and Dahmer as a loner who only caused trouble when he was drunk. Dahmer was also a slick liar, he said, but he'd never have guessed he'd become—or was already—a serial killer. He didn't note any evil in his eyes.

Another barracks mate, Michael Masters, told the Associated Press in 1991 he did see "sinisterness" in Dahmer. "He was on a steady decline in life. He was on a losing skid and didn't know how to pick himself up." On *Larry King Live*, he said he thought Dahmer had killed someone in Germany, although he declined to elaborate. When he first saw the stories about Dahmer's murders in Milwaukee, he told King, "It put chills up my spine."

Masters told a Knight Ridder reporter that Dahmer never revealed anything homosexual. But in his Hollywood police interview, although he denied any homosexual sex before he lived in Milwaukee, Dahmer did recall an encounter in Germany when he said he was assigned to the hospital in Landstuhl, which would have been before he met Capshaw:

> One of the sergeant majors, I think he was either the type of sergeant with two bars underneath or three, he had his own apartment and one night I was drinking in the local NCO [non-commissioned officers] club, he approached me, said he had a party going on back at his place, asked me if I wanted to go back. I said sure. And we went back, turned out there was nobody in the apartment, just him. And he lights up this bowl of hash, smoked some hash, drank some beer, he goes, takes his shower, comes back and tries to get me to hop in bed with him. I said, No thanks, so I just go walking out,

staggering out after that hash, that was good hash, and uh, so that was the first time I'd been approached.

To Milwaukee police a year earlier, Dahmer had said that in the Army he hadn't time or opportunity for sex that might have led to murder because he was busy and living among a group of men. But most weekends, Rodriguez said, Dahmer would disappear from the camp, and no one would know where he went. As for him being busy, assigned to the motor pool, Dahmer would "crawl into a vehicle and go to sleep. He was like, Hey, fuck you, I don't have to do that stuff." In his Milwaukee police confession, Dahmer had said he'd liked the structure of military life.

Rodriguez was initially skeptical about Capshaw's story. But after a discussion, he conceded, "maybe he's telling the truth."

Capshaw was incensed at the report of Rodriguez's interview. He didn't remember Rodriguez's name but later thought he recalled him by a nickname. "I was a little short fat boy, young and dumb. But I'm not dumb anymore," he said. Nor was he fat. One of the few things he did in his first five years home was pump iron every single day; at his peak he could lift 385 pounds. At his most buff he had a 19-inch neck and a 34-inch waist. As for short, he said he was about two inches shorter than Dahmer, and in 1981 maybe 30 pounds lighter. There was also a two-year age difference. Capshaw was 17, and thought he looked 14 or 15 because he had hardly any hair on his body, and just stubble on his chin. "Plus he was insane. He was different than just a regular person."

As for those who knew what was happening to him but wouldn't help, "I don't know why they picked on me like that, those dirty sons of bitches."

He recalled a time he'd escaped the room during a terrible beating, but in the hallway others helped Dahmer hold him down and drag him back, even hitting him themselves. Although to the others he may have seemed drunk, Dahmer had drugged him, probably by slipping something in his drink. From the drug and his beating he'd urinated in his pants and on his mattress, which his barracks-mates laughed at. Capshaw was even written up for failure to obey an order and for being drunk and disorderly in quarters, and has an incident date for it: May 30, 1980.

"There was more than one person keeping me in that room," he said. "They're calling me pussy, and I'm getting the hell beat out of me."

Capshaw went to the hospital numerous times—documented by Army medical records he's since received—for, among other things, a broken foot, hip, and a nervous breakdown. "I always had a cast on—an arm, a leg," he said. He said he's still got scars all over his body from cuts and stabs from knives and ice picks, and from being hit by a metal pipe—part of the bed frame.

The most painful of all was being struck on the tips of his fingers. He learned after a while that the less he resisted, the less his abuse. These many years later he remains in chronic pain and often has trouble walking and getting out of bed. In 2007, his sergeant, in a public Internet forum, denied knowing about any of his trips to the hospital.

"The pain brings back the past," Capshaw said.

But the worst Dahmer did to Capshaw was a quarter-to-half-inch incision he made under Capshaw's scrotum while he was drugged and rope-tied. When he awoke, still dazed, "I remember blood and tugging" and Dahmer over him, cutting, he said. In the emergency room—three or four days later, still bleeding—the doctor asked, "Man! What happened?" He still gets treatment for that wound.

He also thought he was one of the badly sodomized men Swisher spoke of, though not the worst-off of the three. Dahmer would take him to the hospital, but after every incident, he was returned to his room, with Dahmer.

The prostate story had sounded implausible—until Swisher mentioned the anatomy model liver. Swisher said one of the basic skills she taught medics was how to suture with an ordinary scalpel. Although suturing was to repair wounds, using a scalpel was a skill Dahmer had put to use, as evidenced in his Milwaukee apartment.

In July 1991 the *Boston Herald* quoted Rodriguez saying they received six weeks of first aid training, including how to perform tracheotomies and splinting. He said Dahmer showed no particular interest. Rodriguez also mentioned that the course taught anatomy. "It didn't look like he ever took an interest in the anatomy."

In Jack Hoffman's 1992 interview, conducted alongside Milwaukee-based FBI Special Agent Dan Craft, Dahmer impressed them with his knowledge of how to autopsy the people he'd killed. Hoffman asked where he'd learned it, or if he'd had any books.

> DAHMER: No, it was trial and error, I really didn't know that much about the anatomy at that time.
> CRAFT: You were a medic.
> DAHMER: Right. But that was just general field, real general knowledge. Probably had as much knowledge as either of you would.

But Capshaw said Dahmer knew anatomy very well, and in fact taught Capshaw, who later became a paramedic. The class may have bored Dahmer because it was so elementary, he thought. He covered their room's walls with anatomy posters stolen from the hospital dispensary and kept a collection of anatomy books. "Jeffrey Dahmer was a smart guy. A lot smarter than the press gave him credit for," he said. That agreed with what Michael Masters had told *The New York Times.* "If you were to test his I.Q., I'm sure it would be 145 or above."

Capshaw said he knew Dahmer better than anyone else, even his father. He saw Dahmer's dualities, which depended on whether or not he'd been drinking, or more specifically, whether his drunkenness had reached critical mass. "The real Jeff was a stunning person. He was very likable, good to be around." In contrast, "the drunk Jeff will kill you," he said, briefly employing the present tense. "After a certain amount of alcohol, he got that look in his eyes, and you knew it was coming."

As a medic, Dahmer had access to the infirmary's drugs, he said. The routine was, Dahmer would drug him, tie him up, and assault him with a sharp object. When he assaulted him sexually, sometimes it was violent, other time it was more like molestation. But afterwards, "he'd cuddle me, pet me, like he loved me, like a wife. Jeff loved me, in his own special way."

Similarly there was a difference between Dahmer in public and Dahmer inside Capshaw's room. When Stone Phillips had interviewed him in prison on *Dateline NBC* in 1994, Capshaw said, "He sat like a little innocent kitten. Behind closed doors he was a completely different person."

But Capshaw had never imagined Dahmer was a killer until the 1991 story broke. However, he did recall seeing, as he said others did as well, about five times when Dahmer had bloodstains on his clothes, usually under his jacket, or scratch marks on his face, hands, and forearms, and blood on his legs and feet.

Once, when Dahmer returned from staying out overnight, the whole front of his shirt and pants was bloody. When he removed his shirt, encrusted blood ripped skin from his stomach. Dahmer explained only that he'd gotten into a fight. "I knew something worse than a fight had happened," Capshaw said. He knew the blood wasn't Jeff's, but Jeff was angry so Billy was afraid to ask. Billy remembered when that was— Thanksgiving Day.

Other times, when Capshaw broke into Dahmer's wall locker, he found six-inch buck knives, which he'd dispose of but Dahmer would always replace. One time he found a knife stained with blood and mucus. He also found vials of a drug called ketamine hydrochloride, an anesthetic which Swisher said was then available at the infirmary. Now only legally used on animals, in humans it produces hallucinogenic effects as well as a detachment from bodily sensations, amnesia, and coma. It's considered a "date-rape" drug, close in family to PCP, another animal tranquilizer, and in recreational or club settings has been called "Special K" or "Vitamin K".

Dahmer may have used hallucinogens himself. He once asked Capshaw if he'd ever had his eyes dabbed with LSD. Capshaw hadn't. But ketamine is significantly more powerful a mind-altering drug than LSD, writes Jay Stevens in his book *Storming Heaven*. He quotes a ketamine "user's report" published in *High Times*: "I'm moving through some kind of train tunnel. There are all sorts of lights and colors, mostly in the center, far, far away... and little people and stuff running around the walls of the tube, like little cartoon nebbishes."

At least twice that summer, Capshaw said, Dahmer called him from Florida. The calls were a form of stalking, he thought. He didn't want to take them, but did. Dahmer sounded like he'd been drinking. The first call, he said he'd been sleeping on the beach, like a beach bum, but he'd found a job and a girlfriend. "He told me he had sex with a girl. That was his main objective for calling me. He was awful happy. He wanted me to know he was getting better." At the time, however, Capshaw was scared and got off the phone as soon as he could.

When Capshaw was later able to check his Army medical records, he found two infirmary reports of a panic attack that included chest pains, heart palpitations and shakiness. He'd gone to the hospital the first time about an hour after the call, he remembered. The first report was dated nine P.M. July 26, 1981, and the second was 6:30 the next morning—July 27.

Later that Monday, Eastern time in the U.S., Adam Walsh disappeared from Hollywood Mall.

Dahmer had told Jack Hoffman that when he arrived in Miami he'd only had enough money to last a week at a hotel, and that he hadn't planned very far ahead. As a result he had to sleep in the open, on the beach, until he got a job a month or so later. Capshaw didn't believe Dahmer ever didn't think very well ahead, and disputed that Dahmer left the Army short of money. When Capshaw was discharged, the Army gave him $1400 in mustering-out pay, and he thought Dahmer would have had a similar amount, plus other money he'd saved—and likely stolen from Billy.

After two months in Germany, Capshaw said, he stopped getting paid. As well, he stopped getting mail. Billy had designated some of his pay to go to his sister in Arkansas, to help pay her medical bills. When those checks stopped, and his family stopped hearing from him, they desperately tried to reach him, by mail and telephoning Germany, only to be told he was AWOL. They couldn't afford to go there themselves. Not until he was discharged and sent home, escorted, did they know where he was.

Beyond Dahmer, Capshaw blamed his sergeant, the one who denied knowing he'd spent any time in the hospital. It was his responsibility, Billy argued, to get his soldiers paid. However, the sergeant had become friendly with Dahmer, he said. And the sergeant, at the time, had little oversight, he thought, because of a stretched-thin command.

Another dereliction of responsibility, Capshaw said, was the Army's failure to charge Dahmer after arresting him for masturbating in a public area, at least twice. Base military policemen returned Dahmer to his room after catching him in a place Capshaw thought was named Family Park. The M.P.s told Billy he'd done it in front of children. One of the times, even though it was snowing, Jeff was wearing just his boxer shorts. He'd left the room in his uniform. Another time he was returned, his pants were around his ankles.

Capshaw said the park was a 30-minute walk from the barracks. "He took me there. He got me drunk on Paul Masson wine. He made one of his first assaults on me. I was one scared dude." In general Dahmer masturbated a lot in front of Capshaw, before or after tying him up and beating him. He also masturbated in the barracks shower and got in fights when other soldiers caught him.

In his Hollywood police interview, referring to his 1982 arrest in Milwaukee for lewd and lascivious conduct in front of others, Dahmer added that he'd done similar things that whole year. "But there was no assault on any children or anything, it was just masturbation," he said.

Whether or not Dahmer was an out-and-out pedophile of small children, he did collect and read young children's books, Capshaw recalled. One of his favorites was "The Three Billy Goats Gruff," a folk tale about goats, a bridge, and a troll. The first billy goat passes over the bridge and is seized by the troll, who wants to eat him. He saves himself by persuading his captor that coming next is a fatter billy goat, which will make a better meal. The story repeats for the second goat. When the third, and fattest, billy goat crosses, he's able to butt the troll into the water, and all three goats pass freely.

"The Billy Goats Gruff, comin' to get ya," Dahmer would threaten jokingly, Capshaw said.

Did this story contain a moral for Dahmer, the cannibal? Pick an unwieldy victim in a moment of greed and stupidity and it would be he—the troll—who'd be victimized.

Yet "The Billy Goats Gruff, comin' to get ya" suggested a role-reversing sequel, The Return of the Billy Goats. Whereas in the children's story the smaller goats could only survive by practicing deception, now, grown up, gruff *in extremis*, they were no longer at a disadvantage. That would make Dahmer a billy goat and Capshaw the troll. In his mind, was Jeff replaying someone's victimization of him when he was smaller? Was

Capshaw a convenient substitute for that person, whom he felt justified in revenging through torture, deception, control—and nearly, murder? Was there even, deep in his mind, a thought of doing good by stopping or eliminating somebody bad? Was he assimilating both roles of victimizer and victim, troll and billy goat?

Linda Swisher said she didn't remember details, but there were a lot of abducted children around Baumholder when she was serving. She thought they were local Germans. The children were terrified, but not killed.

She remembered the park Capshaw mentioned, around a lake that was off-limits to American soldiers, who too often made trouble for the locals. The park had a lot of kids because it was the only place they could swim.

She better recalled a murder investigation at the time, of a black American woman whose burned body had been found stuffed into the trunk of an abandoned car—a Mercedes, she thought. There were posters on roads for hundreds of miles around. The German *polizei* had never been able to identify her, and the picture on the poster was of a unique gold cross left on her body.

Capshaw remembered a black woman nurse at the Baumholder hospital after Dahmer broke Billy's hip. He described her as a nice-looking young woman who held his hand and listened to what had happened to him. Dahmer was present as well, so he knew Capshaw had confided in her. Swisher too recalled a black woman nurse at the Baumholder hospital who worked in the pediatric clinic. She couldn't recall her name, but she was in her early 20s and "always had a listening ear." There weren't many women then at the base, and even fewer black women, she said.

He also remembered that when he first came to Germany in February 1980 he was warned to be careful when leaving the base. A month before, a man had been found mutilated nearby, his entire trunk sliced. Capshaw's bunkmates knew the man; his name was Hans, he was a hitchhiker from close by Idar-Oberstein who'd partied at their barracks and was friends with Jeff Dahmer. A night or so before he was found dead, he was seen leaving with Dahmer.

Swisher as well remembered the body of a black soldier fished out of the Family Park lake and brought to the hospital. She referred to him as "the pond man," and she thought he'd been murdered, possibly in the summer of 1980. Capshaw said he also remembered that, he'd been in the hospital at the same time, for his broken hip.

The German newspaper *Bild* had reported in 1991 that German federal police had five unsolved murders of unidentified mutilated women near the provincial capital town of Bad Kreuznach—30 miles northeast of Baumholder—that occurred between 1979 and 1981. The women were aged 14-30, they'd been stabbed and cut up, and Dahmer was considered a suspect. The Associated Press reported that only four of the five killed were women. Another report said that German prosecutors had reopened at least nine unsolved murders to check for connections to Dahmer.

Only one victim was identified by name: Erika Handtshuh, 22, described as a hitchhiker, reported the *Milwaukee Journal*. She was found in Gräfenbach, a suburb of Bad Kreuznach, stabbed, strangled, her hands bound with cord, and frozen in the snow on November 30, 1980.

That day was a Sunday. Thanksgiving Day in 1980 was November 27. It was the only Thanksgiving Day Billy and Jeff were together.

Capshaw believed Dahmer spent at least some of his weekends away from his bunk looking to pick up people. Once, he remembered, Dahmer returned and his mouth was so damaged he needed dental surgery to pull his teeth back into place. Someone had slugged him, Capshaw figured.

I told him the pickup line the man gave Morgan, "Hi there, nice day, isn't it?"

"That's Jeff. Oh, yeah. He'd always tell people things like that. Like, 'Beautiful day, isn't it?'"

Morgan had said that in an instant, Dahmer's eyes had turned demonic. "That sounds like him. His anger was something. In a millimeter of a second, he turned from good to bad—and then he'd attack. A kid (like Adam) wouldn't know how to deal with it. If you've ever seen that—I promise you, you will never forget that eye contact." When I told him that Morgan had an above-the-knee leg prosthesis that hobbled his walk, he said, "Jeff preyed on people who had that kind of problem."

I asked, the last time he saw Dahmer, how long was his hair? Morgan had told Hoffman the man's hair was long in the back but Hoffman responded that Dahmer, recently out of the military, couldn't have grown long hair that quickly.

Capshaw answered the question: "We never got haircuts. When I got out, it was over my ears. Things were not military."

Morgan had also thought Dahmer was ready to pull a knife on him. Capshaw said, "I know how he kills. He lunges—he's unpredictable. He never made any sounds. He didn't talk much." Also, Capshaw said, wherever Dahmer went, he always wore an army-issue waterproof green jacket with many large pockets, in which he would keep his six-inch lock-blade serrated knife, which opened to 12 inches; foot-long cuts of nylon rope; and sometimes an ice pick and anesthesia drugs. The same jacket was designed for jungle weather as well as cold, and Dahmer wore it year-round. Although Morgan didn't see the man inside the mall wearing it, the man Bowen said he saw, who threw a child into his already-running blue van, wore something like it—on a steaming hot July day in South Florida. Capshaw surmised that Dahmer could have left the jacket in the van, then when he returned to it, he put the jacket over his shirt to change his appearance.

Capshaw was discharged in October 1981, and sometime

either around Thanksgiving or Christmas Dahmer arrived at Capshaw's home in Hot Springs driving a two-tone brown station wagon that his mother thought was a Chevrolet. (Dahmer later told him, by phone, his father had given him a beat-up old car.) Billy wasn't home, he was staying with a friend a few blocks away where he was a shut-in, paranoid and afraid to leave the house. He now reasoned that Dahmer intended "to finish me off" because he knew too much. He'd since read that Dahmer killed his new friends when they wanted to leave—and Capshaw had never left him, because he couldn't.

Dahmer left a belated birthday card. It had a drawing of W.C. Fields holding a beer mug and was signed "To a fellow guzzler on his 19th birthday." Capshaw said Dahmer liked the famously misanthropic Fields, and once spoke what he thought was one of his lines: "The only good kid is a dead kid." Although it wasn't an actual Fields quote, Capshaw said Dahmer meant it.

4
The Discovery

TUESDAY, AUGUST 11, 1981

SEARCH FOR ADAM GOES ON TV
BOY, 6, MISSING 16 DAYS
HEAD OF BOY FOUND IN CANAL
—*Hollywood Sun-Tattler*

To appear this morning on ABC's *Good Morning America* with other parents of missing children, John and Reve Walsh had flown to New York. While there, they were also trying to get on NBC's *Today Show*, and *Phil Donahue*, which taped in Chicago. Sitting by the phone in their hotel room at the St. Moritz on Central Park, the Walshes speculated to Charlie Brennan of the *Sun-Tattler* on why someone was trying to destroy their family.

"John has never stepped on anyone as long as I've known him," said Reve.

"The business we're in, we don't step on people or make enemies," John agreed.

Since the Walshes were planning to ask *GMA* viewers to call a number if they'd seen Adam, Southern Bell installed five phone lines in the old Hollywood police building, now serving as a temporary search headquarters.

Capt. Bob Mowers was a little skeptical: "They might get some good information, but they'll also hear from every... nut in the nation." Lt. Richard Hynds speculated that the investigation could go on indefinitely. "You get strange cases like this sometimes."

Beneath the *Sun-Tattler*'s six-column banner headline on the Walshes, the remainder of the top of the page was occupied by an ominous wire story datelined Vero Beach, in central Florida: *Head of boy found in canal.*

While fishing on a bank of a canal Monday evening at 6:45, two orange grove ranch hands had seen something floating, a hundred feet away. It looked at first like a doll's head. When they put a rowboat in the water and paddled toward it, they realized the head was human.

The men, Robert Hughes and Vernon Bailey, radioed their office to have them call police. At 7:20, the Florida Highway Patrol arrived. The scene was remote, swampy, and brush-filled, just off the northbound side of Florida's Turnpike, about seventy-five yards from mile marker 130. That was 125 miles north of Hollywood, fifty miles southwest of Vero Beach.

The site was located in Indian River County, just north of its border with St. Lucie County, so FHP called police and fire rescue from both counties to help them look for the rest of the body or other clues. Long past nightfall, they searched the canal banks and dove into the water, without success.

At 11:20, Indian River County Sheriff's Det. Donald Coleman showed the head to Lt. Sid DuBose. Both agreed it appeared to be Adam Walsh. The Indian River sheriffs notified Hollywood police. Also, a Vero Beach funeral home took the remains to the Indian River Memorial Hospital morgue.

At ten past midnight, the search was called off until

daylight. But Coleman and DuBose waited at the scene for Hollywood detectives to arrive. At 12:15 A.M., the *Sun-Tattler* city desk called Brennan in his hotel room. He'd been asleep about an hour. "They've found a head of a young male floating in a canal. It might be Adam Walsh." Trying to return to sleep, he kept hearing, "They've found a head."

At 1:18 Det. James Gibbons, Sgt. Dennis Naylon, and I.D. tech Ron Young arrived at the scene. The Indian River detectives took them to the morgue where the Hollywood officers concurred, it looked like Adam. At two o'clock Naylon asked nurses to awaken Indian River County Associate Medical Examiner Franklin Cox so he could come to the hospital's autopsy room. He'd been told before nine P.M. about the head. At 2:40 A.M., Cox arrived and began his examination. He noted five cutting and chopping wounds stretching along the back of the victim's neck to almost the edge of both corners of his mouth. There was no evidence of any facial mutilation. It took him just eight minutes to conclude that the head appeared to have been intentionally severed by a blade like a meat cleaver.

Just before four o'clock, *Good Morning America* line producer Amy Hirsh took a call from a Florida police officer asking her to tell the Walshes that a head had been discovered. She was shocked, she later recalled, as well as left with the impression that the head was very likely Adam's. Hirsh told the officer, "You call him, no way I'm going to do that." She gave him the number at their hotel. When his phone rang, John Walsh answered, although later he couldn't recall specifically who it was. They wanted to know the name of Adam's dentist.

He wrote: "They were couching it. Saying everything in a way so as not to panic me. They didn't really think it was Adam's remains. Another boy [in Tampa] was missing, a boy a little older. And they thought it might be him." Walsh gave them the name of the dentist, and was told that John Monahan would be going up to Indian River County.

Hirsh said between four-thirty and five she called John herself and told him "You don't have to go through with this," meaning the show. They could arrange to fly them home immediately, and "we'll understand." Walsh wrote that he answered, "We have to go ahead with the appearance. You're our only hope. This is the only chance we have to get Adam's photo on national television." Besides, he wanted to show photos of other people's missing children to get publicity for them.

After show host David Hartman arrived at about four-thirty, Hirsh told him about the calls and that the Walshes still wanted to do the show. "Awfully gutsy of them," said Hartman.

Charlie Brennan called John while he was shaving. "Charlie," John wrote he said, "I don't know anything. They're getting the dental records." Brennan thought there wouldn't be confirmation either way for a while.

Walsh wrote that he didn't tell any of this to Reve. "I didn't tell her anything. I was scared to death, hoping against hope. I had a horrible, paralyzing feeling. But I wasn't going to let anybody know. I was the guy with the stiff upper lip."

He prepared for his show appearance:

I knew exactly what I was going to say. I had it all memorized… If they gave me thirty seconds, I was going to cram it all into thirty seconds. If they gave me five minutes, I could go on longer, about how [Adam] acted and what his favorite games were, everything about him.

I knew that Reve wasn't going to say much. It was my job to do the talking… But I had it down. I was going to do it all… 'Stay focused,' I told myself. 'You've got to stay focused.'

Brennan reported differently, that Reve knew. At breakfast

with her, John, and Jane Walsh, he wrote that Reve said, half to herself, "It's not Adam. It could be anyone."

Admitting he had the same intuition as Brennan, John said they'd already decided to do the show anyway. "What else can I do? If Adam's dead, I still have to give it a shot for all the other [missing] children."

At six o'clock the Walshes arrived on the set of *Good Morning America*. Hartman found them in the Green Room—the guests' lounge—and took them aside. "I understand you've had a call," he said. He repeated the offer that the show could put them on the first flight home. "Absolutely not," John told him.

At seven, in Indian River County, the search team resumed, now with an airplane, several helicopters and airboats, prepared to examine a full mile radius on each side of the turnpike. The Hollywood officers, having worked through the night, became part of it.

GMA went on air at seven as well. All morning executive producer George Merlis had been fighting with the network's standards and practices unit—the censors—over whether they could post on air the toll-free phone numbers the Walshes wanted people to call if they had information about Adam or the other missing children to be mentioned on the show. The censors were afraid that an avalanche of calls to those numbers would crash AT&T's phone lines, and in retaliation, AT&T might pull the plug on the entire ABC network. Merlis told the censors, nonsense.

Sometime before 7:30, in the midst of this argument, the show's unit manager Debbie Cox-Riches interrupted Merlis in the control room. She had a Florida policeman on the line asking to speak to John Walsh. Recollecting, Merlis thought the police agency was the Florida Highway Patrol, possibly a lieutenant, who asked him if Walsh could be given a discreet area to take the call.

The Walshes were still in the green room. Merlis had the

call transferred to David Hartman's dressing room, took John there, and closed the door. During the call Merlis recalled Walsh as very much in control. "He put down the phone and said, 'It still may not be Adam.'"

Merlis walked him back to the green room where Reve had waited. During a break, Merlis went to the set to brief Hartman.

Air time for the Walshes and Kristin Cole Brown, of Child Find, was set at 8:15. Moments before, John called Hollywood police. They told him Indian River County's judgment was that the head was almost certainly Adam's—99 percent certain. Brennan wrote that Merlis told the Walshes they could back out. Merlis recalled he said that only to John. The answer, again, was no.

Off-camera, Merlis recalled, Hartman said to the Walshes, "I have to ask you about this." John replied, "That's okay."

On set, designed to look like a suburban living room, complete with window blinds and modern art, Hartman sat in his wicker chair. On the couch to his right was Brown, then Reve, then John. On the show for their seven minutes, John looked and sounded fairly natural, although downbeat. Reve, on the other hand, said nothing the entire appearance. Only once did she even try. Her eyes stared straight ahead, down, or occasionally toward John when he spoke. Neither cried. John wrote, "The whole time, Reve was sitting there next to me. Not saying a word. Looking like a bomb had gone off in her head." Hartman described her as "catatonic."

The interview was clearly hard for Hartman as well. He stuttered through the opening part, while cute family pictures of Adam appeared on screen. Hartman later said it was his most dramatic moment in all the 12 years he did the show:

HARTMAN: John and Reve Walsh are from Hollywood, Florida. They have a son, Adam, he is six years old, but they haven't seen him for more than two weeks now.

Adam and his mother were shopping in a shopping center, a department store, he was playing in the toy department while Mrs. Walsh went to buy something else just a few feet away. When she came back to get him, Adam was gone. Mr. and Mrs. Walsh—John, Reve, if I can—John, this has been a long night particularly—it's been a long two weeks, God knows, but it's been an even longer night. What happened last night? Can you tell us?

JOHN: Well, amongst many sightings and reported possible clues on Adam they have found the remains of a young person in Florida that at this time they are trying to identify whether it is Adam or not. At this point they feel there is a good possibility it is not Adam. Therefore they felt we should come on and carry the word of Adam to the public because there is a good likelihood that he is still out there with his abductors.

Watching in the studio, Charlie Brennan was stunned. He knew John didn't believe that. Hours later he quoted what Walsh had just said as "We have good information the body found last night is not Adam's."

The *Fort Lauderdale News*, watching from their newsroom, quoted him more precisely: "At this time they feel there is a good possibility it is not Adam. They feel there is still a good possibility he is out there [alive]."

HARTMAN: And you were advised this morning by what, the police authorities?

JOHN: By several police authorities, Hollywood Police as well as the FBI and urged to go on and give Adam the best possible chance.

Over more pictures of Adam, John described him as 6½, with sandy blond hair, freckles, missing a front tooth, slight build, about 45 pounds and 3½ feet tall.

JOHN: He's a very introverted, sheltered, but very bright little boy. He's a little gentleman.

HARTMAN: What kind of help have you had in the last couple of weeks? Who has helped him?

JOHN: Overwhelming community support. It was the largest search in the history of South Florida for a little boy, conducted in the Hollywood area. All the official organizations joined in the search. Park rangers, fish and wildlife, game as well as many other police departments, citizens' crime watch volunteers and individuals.

Also helping, Walsh mentioned, were Burger King, Eastern and Delta airlines, big theme parks elsewhere in the state, thousands of letter writers from across the country, and contributors to Adam's reward for information fund, which he said had now topped $120,000.

JOHN: And of course the media was phenomenal. The media in South Florida kept the word of Adam on the television stations and in the newspapers for nine days. Which I think is a long time.

Kristin Cole Brown spoke about problems other parents of missing children had encountered in dealing with authorities trying to help. After photos of some of those missing children appeared on screen, John added: "I can't tell you the horror it is of losing a child. It would be hard to relay that to someone."

HARTMAN: I don't think anybody can...

JOHN: But the lack of organized efforts on the part of federal and state governments to assist parents in locating their children after they leave the immediate area is totally unbelievable in a country of our size.

The segment ended, as it did every show, at exactly 8:22:55. Merlis and Hartman differ in remembering what happened next. Merlis thought the Walshes and Hartman all stayed where they were sitting. John turned to Reve and told her: "It is Adam." She broke down on the set.

"John and Reve sat there for some time while she wept. The local news cutaway—five minutes long—was going on, preceded by two minutes of commercial and one minute of station I.D. and commercial, so there were about seven minutes from the time the segment ended until we had to clear the set and David had to open the next half hour. I don't recall how long John and Reve sat there. David is a devoted father and this must have been very hard for him. He had another half-hour of show to do after witnessing this and he did it like the professional he was, betraying none of the emotion he must have felt."

In Hartman's memory, all three stood up after the segment ended. Hartman thanked them then John guided him behind the set, as someone guided Reve away. Hirsh Rogers remembered it that way as well. Behind the set, alone, John told Hartman, "It is Adam's head they found."

"We both cried," Hartman said. They stayed behind the set for only 30 seconds, maybe a minute. "But I had to finish the show." Asked how he did that, he answered, "I don't know." It was that much harder, he said, because at the time, his oldest child, of three, was six, like Adam. It was his recollection that John was going to tell Reve back in the hotel.

Brennan called his city editor, Chuck Joyce, and told him what he'd just seen Walsh say on TV was wrong. At the 8:30 daily story conference, Joyce relayed that to managing editor Jerry Esslinger. They decided that since at any time that morning the story could change, the paper needed to be ready for all instances: that the head was verified as Adam; it was *not* Adam; or no determination by press time. They needed to compose three possible front pages, each with a completely different tone. They also kept a hotline open to Hollywood police, who were on a hotline with the Vero Beach sheriff.

The Walshes stayed in the Green Room forty minutes after their segment, Merlis said. Then John came into the control room and thanked everyone. "More than a few of us broke down," Merlis remembered. Walsh wrote that everyone wished them good luck and said they were praying for them.

By nine o'clock, ABC's limo returned the Walshes to the St. Moritz. To relieve the unbearable tension, Reve, Jane, and Brown wanted to go to the Plaza Hotel to eat. Brennan reported that he and John went back to John's hotel room to wait for John Monahan to take Adam's dental records to Vero Beach. It would be a horrible irony for Monahan to see John Walsh's dead son, fished out of the water.

As Walsh mechanically tossed clothes into his suitcase, he became enraged, Brennan wrote.

> I'm sure He's still up there. But I don't know what purpose He had for this, or what test, what reason... What logic? It's beyond the human comprehension. Maybe Adam's better off not growing up in this world. Look what happened to our little boy.
>
> I'll never be the same the rest of my life. How could Adam have met the one person who would do this, out of the thousands of people in Sears who would have helped him?

Nor did he mince words for law enforcement, or the lack of government support for families of missing children:

> There's more money spent for taking care of stray dogs at the ASPCA than there is on looking for missing children. The FBI waited and waited and waited. They waited for word. Florida Highway Patrol waited for

word. Meanwhile, the Hollywood Police, those poor guys, are busting their tails for 14 grand a year.

I hope to God they catch him, because they told me that once someone does this kind of thing, it gets easier to do it again.

Whoever did this had to have a vehicle, it had to be registered somewhere. He was functioning in society. And now he'll probably just move to another state and get another dishwasher's job and the FBI could care less.

I'm getting super-conscious of the strange people out there. All I can say to people is, don't take anything for granted.

In his own writing, Walsh says he was alone in his hotel room.

"I sat on the bed, by myself, saying, 'It can't be. Nobody could do this. Nobody. Nobody could kill this little boy. There is no creature on the planet who could do that.'"

At eleven o'clock, driven by his personal valet in his white Mercedes-Benz, John Monahan arrived at Indian River Memorial Hospital to meet with Franklin Cox. With Monahan was Lt. Hynds—they were personal friends—and Marshall Berger, Adam's dentist, carrying the child's dental records. Dr. Cox had already examined the child's teeth, noting a dental filling on his last lower left molar and a missing upper right incisor. More than once in print, Adam had been referred to as "gap-toothed."

Dr. Berger's records matched. John Monahan looked at the child's face and agreed.

It was Adam.

This is how Brennan reported it:

Just after 11:30, a phone rang at the St. Moritz. John Walsh answered it.

"Give it to me straight," he demanded.

How could Brennan, or anyone, have left John alone at that moment? Yet deadline was already an hour and a half past, and his newspaper was relying on him. Brennan had no choice. He raced to his room and rang his office.

Walsh recalled the worst moment of his life this way:

And then the phone rang.

"Is this Mr. John Walsh?"

"Yes, it is."

"Mr. Walsh, we are so very sorry to have to tell you this. But the remains that were found last night in Vero Beach have been positively identified as Adam's."

I went down.

Right onto the floor. It felt like somebody took a huge, wooden stake and shoved it into the wall of my chest.

Like somebody killed me right there on the floor.

I couldn't breathe. I thought I was having a heart attack. It felt like I was dying.

"Please let me trade places with him..."

Death would have hurt me so much less.

I thrashed and I screamed. I yelled and pushed over the mattress and smashed things. I broke glass and a picture frame and tore off the sheets and threw lamps and kicked the table over.

I was like a wounded animal. Dying the way a wounded animal dies. I could not deal with it. It was unbearable, unbearable. I thought that my heart was going to explode...

The little boy I had waited all my life to have was dead.

Security guards came to his door, asking if they could get him a doctor. "I don't think I answered them," Walsh wrote. "I was saying, 'How am I going to tell my wife? How am I ever going to tell Reve? How can I tell her? She's his mother. I can't tell her this.'"

He called the Plaza to page his sister Jane. He told her, "You must not tell Reve. Don't tell her. I will tell her. Bring her back to me at the hotel. Do it right now. Because I have to tell her."

When they got to the door of the hotel room, John opened it.

And I said, "Our baby's dead."
And Reve said, "I know."

As John watched, "the spirit that had made her who she was slowly collapsed into her. As if her whole being was caving in on itself... she went from being a girl to an old woman right before my eyes."

All John could say to her, over and over, was I love you.

Already so far past deadline, the *Sun-Tattler* desperately worked to get as much of the story as they could into the paper. Press time was delayed for an hour. Tearing up its hopeful front page, they replaced it beginning with a simple, stunning, urgent banner headline with a subhead:

ADAM WALSH FOUND DEAD
DISCOVERED IN VERO CANAL

NEW YORK—Adam has been found.

John and Reve Walsh of Hollywood received the worst possible answer to the mystery of their only child's mysterious disappearance at 11:35 this morning.

The remains of a young boy found floating in an Indian River County canal late Monday are those of Adam, 6 years old.

Adam's father received a call at the St. Moritz Hotel in Manhattan from family friend Jeff O'Regan saying the two-week search for Adam is over.

Adam's mother was away from the hotel with friends when the news came.

"Oh Christ, oh Christ, who could do this to my little boy," the 35-year-old father cried. "Who could cut his head off?"

Throughout the day, police officers searched along the turnpike from Orlando to Miami, including thirty-five miles of canals. In the afternoon someone called the Indian River Sheriff's office to say the rest of the body was within a mile of where the head was found. But searchers didn't find it.

At noon, Franklin Cox spoke to Broward County medical examiner Ronald Wright, who asked to do the autopsy. Deferring to his bigger-city counterpart, Cox agreed, packed the remains in ice, and gave the package to Hollywood Det. Ron Young, who accepted a ride back to Fort Lauderdale in Miami television station WCKT's news helicopter.

Dr. Wright signed for the remains at 2:15. He too noted five distinct blows to the back of the child's neck and lower rear portion of his skull. He thought a very sharp bladed instrument at least 5¼ inches in length had inflicted the blows.

He said Adam was dead when he was decapitated. By examining the inside of his skull, he could say he'd been dead at least ten days before he was found.

Because of the air traffic controllers' strike, the Walshes' flight home from Kennedy airport was delayed more than two and a half hours. Waiting at the New York Delta terminal, hearing that reporters from every major local news agency had gathered to await them at Fort Lauderdale airport, John and Reve reluctantly decided to speak to them.

They slept most of the flight. Jane Walsh talked to Charlie Brennan about the issue in general of missing children; Kristen Cole Brown, who'd formed Child Find to help families find their missing children, had told the Walshes that as many as 50,000 children each year aren't recovered.

"It's over for us, one way or the other. But for some of these women, they still go to sleep at night, not knowing where their children are. John's not going to forget them.

"John wants to help these people get publicity, and he'll do that. He could walk away and say 'The hell with the world.' But that's not my brother."

They finally arrived just after 11 P.M. They spoke to reporters for four minutes, refusing questions.

Reve's arm tucked under his shoulder, his eyes red, once again he broke into tears:

> I really don't know what to say. Other than I'm sure you know our hearts are broken.
>
> We were fortunate in the fact that we had a lot of friends and some resources to look for Adam, and we gave it our best effort to bring him back. I just wish it had a happier ending.
>
> I don't know who would do this to a six-year-old child. I can't conceive of it. It's beyond the realm of reality.

He thanked the Hollywood Police, the volunteers who'd searched for Adam, the community that had prayed for him, and the press too, but was bitter about the lack of state and federal help:

> I can't tell you how we feel. But maybe by me saying this will make some people aware of how hard it is, and how little cooperation people get that have missing children.
>
> We have a huge computer in Washington, D.C. that is for stolen cars. But we have no kind of a central location for missing children. Monies are spent and

funded for natural resources and to save endangered species, but yet there's no federal or state organization to help in the search for missing children.

This is a great country and we have a lot of resources but it appears to me that our priorities are in the wrong order. Maybe these words will help save some other little children from what happened to Adam.

Her face taut, Reve was briefer and less demonstrative:

I don't know what is happening in this world. I really don't. But Adam evidently is too good for this world. He's much greater than this world, and he didn't deserve to live in this world. He was too good, and you know, only the good die young.

5

Man In A Blue Van

WEDNESDAY, AUGUST 12

ADAM MAY HAVE BEEN DEAD SINCE
HE DISAPPEARED; POLICE NEED CLUES
—*Hollywood Sun-Tattler*

"The ordinary criminal, with this much heat, would have dropped the kid off by the roadside, stabbed him, smothered him or just killed him," Lt. Richard Hynds speculated to the *Miami Herald.* "But this, this mutilation is the work of a psychopath."

"This person is a nasty animal that needs to be eradicated from the earth," said Broward County medical examiner Ronald Wright. "Assuming that this is the first such killing, there will be more. These kinds of people don't quit."

The Sun-Tattler quoted Wright that Adam might have been killed July 27, the day he went missing. But the *Herald* quoted him saying the autopsy alone couldn't determine the cause or time of death because the head had been disfigured, possibly by alligators or turtles. He'd have to conduct clinical tests, which would take four days.

Tests on brain tissue might reveal a better idea of time of death, and testing the cut on the spinal column at the base of the head would help determine the decapitation instrument, Broward Medical Examiner's office chief investigator D.P. Hughes explained to the *Miami News*. The severing was uneven, Wright told the *Sun-Tattler*.

To the *Fort Lauderdale News*, Wright added that the head was in an advanced state of decomposition. It had areas of discoloration, but he couldn't tell whether they were bruises from a beating or something else.

Hughes said dismembered bodies are typically scattered, and Lt. Hynds concurred: "There had to be a massive amount of blood lost when the head was severed, and we didn't find any near the canal." Bacterial tests from water samples taken from the site would also need to be done.

Hynds added that the site where the head was found was inaccessible from the road, which meant the killer stopped his car and walked to it. However, the next day, in the *Sun-Tattler*, Hynds contradicted himself: "He could have just stuck his arms out the window and dropped it there. He may not even have left the car."

In the afternoon, the Walshes held another press conference, this time to announce funeral services, and that much of the money donated to the reward fund for Adam's safe return would now be given to Child Find and the Dee Scofield Project. To handle that money and new donations, they set up an Adam Walsh trust fund, in care of a Miami attorney.

"In our situation, the Hollywood police were fantastic, and their efforts were day and night. But once the child has left the area, the search becomes fruitless."

A Mass of the Angels, spoken at Catholic funerals of children younger than seven—who are considered to be without sin—would be held 10 A.M. Saturday. Cremation would be early the next week. Said John Walsh, "We'll scatter his ashes at sea, because that boy loved the water so much."

Walsh addressed questions that the murder might have been related to his business. "[The police] searched my background totally, from getting out of college and going to work, through the last few years, and my business associates (voluntarily) came forth. I'm in sales and marketing. I entertain people and try to get them to come to hotels, and I'm not in the type of business to alienate people. I'm a salesman.

"The people I'm involved with are wealthy on their own right. They have children. If it really is for a ransom, there was no ransom demand, so it's been eliminated. This person was a sick, sick person."

At three P.M., after more than 500 officers at the Vero Beach site had combed land, water, and ditches, finding nothing, the search was concluded.

Thursday, August 13

What Timothy Pottenburgh had reported was the police's best lead, Lt. Hynds told the *Herald*. All over the state, police had stopped hundreds of blue vans and checked registrations. "I'm afraid to drive my own blue van," Hynds told the *Fort Lauderdale News*.

In the wake of events, the Pottenburghs let Ron Hickman speak to Timothy and his grandmother at length. Timothy said he and his grandmother were in Sears's toy department when he saw a man reading comic books, loitering. He described him as white, mid-twenties, five-ten to six-foot, with dark curly hair and a mustache, wearing a multi-colored tank top. This concurred with what the family had described two weeks earlier, a man that was white, about six feet tall, muscular, with dark bushy hair, wearing jeans and a T-shirt.

Shortly after, Timothy said he saw a small boy leave the

store through the north door, and the man followed him out. The man ran to a navy blue van parked near the entrance. The little boy walked around Sears to the west side, near the garden shop. As Timothy and his grandmother stepped off the sidewalk to walk to their car, the blue van nearly hit them as it turned the corner.

Then, in front of the garden shop, the blue van stopped, and Timothy saw the van's passenger side door slide open and two hands motion to the little boy, standing in the west parking lot. The boy then walked to the van and was pulled inside. He thought the person in the van was wearing a stocking mask.

On his first recollection, Timothy had said all he'd seen at the curb was the van, door open, where the boy might have been. He hadn't seen the boy enter, nor had he mentioned the mask. Carolyn Hudson, Timothy's grandmother, repeated that she hadn't seen any of this, except for the blue van that almost ran them over. Nor was she certain exactly when it happened.

At the end of the interview, Hickman again asked Marilyn Pottenburgh, would she now allow her son to be hypnotized? Finally she relented.

In an attempt to profile Adam's killer, Hollywood police legal advisor Geoff Cohen called Dr. Mark Reisner, a psychologist employed by the Los Angeles Police Department.

Because the evidence was thin, Reisner could offer only a general profile:

Sex: Male

Age: 19-35 years of age, probably in his early to late twenties.

Race: Caucasian or Latin. Expressed the opinion that this type of conduct was not generally inter-racial.

Mental Status: Borderline psychopathic/psychotic personality with a tremendous homosexual conflict expressed in violence and rage. Probably a loner and not liked by many people. Individual unlikely to brag or talk about this act.

Unlikely that he will exhibit any remorse or guilt over act or confess to the abduction or murder.

Educational Background: Little formal education. Lower socio-economic background.

Occupational Skills: Probably has held many unskilled or minimally skilled laboring jobs.

Social Relations: Identifies with and is attracted to children. May sometimes work with children. Poor relationships with both females and males.

Criminal History: Almost certainly has abducted or attempted to abduct a child in the past. Almost certainly has sexually assaulted a child in the past. Very likely that he has been arrested and imprisoned for such acts.

Reisner also said the decapitation indicated there had been sexual contact with the boy. Further, after the abduction, the individual would seek an isolated environment, and that he would maintain control over the boy by using both deception and physical force.

Friday, August 14

In the morning, a Fort Lauderdale man named Eugene Menacho called Hollywood police to say that a blue van had nearly collided with him as he was driving to Sears on July 27, between 12:30 and 1:00 P.M. He was at the southwest intersection closest to Sears, at Hollywood Boulevard and Park Road, about to turn onto Park Road toward the mall. That's when a blue 1979 Ford van traveling very fast westbound on Hollywood Boulevard almost struck him. Ron Hickman asked Menacho if he'd undergo hypnosis. He would, and they scheduled an appointment for Saturday.

Timothy Pottenburgh's hypnosis session lasted ninety minutes. He remembered a white man about six feet tall, in his mid-twenties, medium to heavy build (180-200 pounds), with dark brown or black curly hair and a thin mustache, wearing a striped T-shirt. He was standing in the toy department, looking around the Atari games area.

Then he saw a little boy leave the store by the north door, and the man followed him. As the boy walked to the west side of the store, the man ran to the blue van. Inside the blue van was a second white man sitting in the passenger seat. The running man got in the van and drove it to the west side of Sears.

As Timothy and his grandmother walked toward their car, the blue van almost hit them. Then the van stopped by the garden center and its right sliding door opened. Then he saw a little boy [he didn't say for sure it was the same one] standing in the parking lot, and a hand motioning him to come toward the van. The boy did, and was then pulled inside.

Both men in the van wore stocking masks, he said. He also recalled that the little boy wore a red hat. [Reve said Adam wore a beige hat; he wore a red baseball cap in his missing photo.]

Timothy also added details to his description of the van: it was a navy blue, late-model Ford with tinted windows, shiny rib-type mag wheels, a ladder on the left rear and a right-side sliding door with a large rectangular window. It also had a black front bumper, no spare tire on the back, and a Florida license plate. In his first description, it was late-model, shiny, dark blue, with dark-tinted windows, mag wheels, and a chrome ladder in the back.

At a wake in a Hollywood funeral home, a *Miami News* reporter described the chapel with bouquets and Adam's familiar portrait above the altar. Below it, she saw Reve praying over the coffin. "We will get through this. And we'll go on with what we're doing. We are going to make it."

"God gave man free will," said Father Michael Conboy, John Walsh's first cousin, from Rochester, N.Y., who would preside at the service. "Free will to commit good or evil. We can't blame God for the evil that man commits. (Adam) is at peace."

John Walsh took issue with that, he later wrote. "Is this the benevolent God that we have worshipped our whole lives? Is this an all-powerful, benevolent, gentle God who allowed this to happen? Tell me about that one, would you, Father Mike? Explain to me how it is that I'm supposed to deal with this."

Charlie Brennan wrote that fear was gripping the community, especially among parents of young children. School would begin in ten days. "Every person I've talked to is frightened. They're just frightened to death," said a parent, one of two dozen about to discuss security with a elementary school principal. She said they were all ready to put their children in private schools.

Saturday, August 15

Eight detectives were working the case full-time, as well as six officers who'd fielded a thousand phone tips. "Now we're going to get a lot of calls on vans with black front bumpers. Maybe this is our break, I don't know," Fred Barbetta told the *Miami Herald*. Lt. Richard Hynds told the *Miami News* he would try to get a list of every 1979 and 1980 navy blue Ford van sold in Florida. 1981 models didn't come in that color. "We'll run down every one if we have to."

The *Herald* found that Sears in Hollywood Mall hadn't added additional security. "I don't think any blame can be placed on the store," said manager Herbert Gellman. "One thing that's changed is we don't have any announcements for lost children any more. Parents are being more attentive to their children." The manager of a Sears mall in Palm Beach County said the incident had upset his whole mall. He'd even seen a woman shopper clutching a string leash tied to her child's belt.

At 10 A.M., services began at St. Maurice Catholic Church in Hollywood. Newspaper crowd estimates were between 300 and 1,000, including the overflow outside. Adam's casket was shrouded in white velvet and gold trim, empty for reasons of police evidence. A children's' choir, in white, performed.

"There will always be this struggle between good and evil. God forbid, some choose evil," spoke Father Conboy, his voice breaking. "The hundreds and thousands of people who came forward to help John and Reve in their hour of need show that, yes, there are people who are good in this area. Evil will be overcome by good, somehow.

"We are hurt that this has happened to such a sweet, innocent, loving little boy. But he is now with God."

From a poem, he read: "It's time to say goodbye for a while. Do not weep for me. But if you must weep, weep for me because I am once again free. I have returned to the Lord, in the presence of God who is love.

"I am still here when you need me. Just call my name.

"So long for now, Cooter. We'll see you again. We promise."

Adam was too young to need prayers, said Father John Kapellen. "We believe Adam is already in heaven."

A *Fort Lauderdale News* reporter wrote that the only audible crying during the service was by young children. John Walsh frequently bit his lower lip and dabbed at his eyes with a handkerchief. Holding a single yellow rose, Reve looked composed. As she greeted friends and relatives, she smiled guardedly. Toward the end of the service, John took her hand, brought it to his breast, clutched it, then held it to his lips. Reve approached the photograph of Adam and kissed it.

As John Walsh left church, he unfurled a gold-lettered white banner a little girl had handed him during the service, a smaller copy of what hung above the altar. The banner read, If His song is to continue, we must do the singing. "We knew that the word His was supposed to mean the Lord. But to us, it meant Adam," Walsh wrote.

Under hypnosis, Eugene Menacho recalled it was about

twelve-thirty when he drove to Sears with his wife. Eastbound on Hollywood Boulevard, he had a green light to make a left turn onto Park Road, the west border of the mall. While turning in the intersection, a westbound blue van sped past him in the lane closest to the center divider, narrowly missing his car on his passenger side.

Menacho was able to describe the driver: white male, mid-twenties, black hair, thin mustache, olive complexion, not wearing a shirt. He didn't recall anyone else in the van.

He described the van: a 1979 or 1980 Ford, dark navy blue, very shiny, with a rectangular tinted window on the passenger-side sliding door. It also had chrome running boards, shiny mag wheels, a chrome ladder on the right rear, two tinted square windows on the rear doors, a small silver mirror on the passenger side, and two antennas—one on the roof and one on the front passenger side.

He could also describe the interior: black stock seats, black steering wheel, and a wood grain partition between the front seats. He recalled the numbers four-six, or six-four on the license plate, possibly a Florida tag.

At 3:30, both Menacho and Timothy Pottenburgh met with police artist John Valor, of Miami P.D., at Hollywood police headquarters. Over the next two and a half hours, Valor made two drawings that both witnesses cooperated to produce. When they were done, police released both composites to the media.

The biggest difference between the two drawings was mustaches. One was pencil-thin, the other fuller, extending a bit past the suspect's lips. The similarities were in the faces' ovalness. It was hard to say whether they were drawings of the same man.

Dr. Sanford Jacobson, director of forensic psychiatry at Dade County-owned Jackson Memorial Hospital, offered a profile of the person who killed Adam, to the *Miami Herald*.

He was a loner, Jacobson said, but someone who easily

blended into society. His choice of victim was a reflection of his dual self—"somebody they both hate and, in a sense, envy or admire. The weakness of the victim reflects what they remember of themselves. For they themselves might have once been victims of abuse, some of it sexual.

"By doing this to the victim, they identify with the person who aggressed against them in childhood and kind of master their own trauma.

"I've never seen a great deal of remorse in such people that I thought was sincere."

CALLERS TIP POLICE TO DOZENS OF BLUE VANS
—The Miami Herald

At the Hollywood detective bureau, the hotline phone button glowed. Still dressed for his earlier Sunday school class, Det. Ron Hickman told a *Miami Herald* reporter, "Here's a big lead coming in now." Like hundreds of other calls police said they'd gotten by the end of the day, this caller thought he'd seen a blue van matching the more specific description police had released to the media.

The number of every license plate tipsters called in eventually would be checked on the state department of motor vehicles computer. Also, detectives had since asked the DMV for a list of every Ford van registered in Florida—there were about 10,000, and not delineated by color. Meanwhile, tips were also coming in from police elsewhere in the state, as well as other states.

"There's a guy in Miami who has a blue van, and he's been stopped by police ten times," said Sgt. Dennis Naylon. Another reported van turned out to be owned by Sgt. J.B. Smith.

After a few more frustrating weeks, police let the blue van fade as a lead. Perhaps having taken it on the way they did reflected their leadership's early resolution to do anything to solve the case, no matter how daunting the task. But even had they been able to check every Ford van in the region—on their slim assumption the van was a Ford—what good would it have done? How would it have led them to recognize the killer?

In September, lead detective Jack Hoffman met again with the Pottenburgh family, this time while Timothy and his cousin were in school. They said they'd gotten to Sears that day around 11:45, shopped for school clothes for an hour, then as they were leaving for the food court heard a page for a lost child. They ate lunch until 1:15 then the boys' grandmother Carolyn Hudson took Timothy through Sears to return to their car, parked on the store's north side. The blue van incident happened at about 1:25, Carolyn said.

In what became the last mention of the blue van for 10 years, Hoffman wrote in his report, "If Mrs. Hudson is positive of the time, it appears that the incident that Timothy Pottenburgh had witnessed is unrelated to the Adam Walsh abduction."

So instead of merely shelving the blue van lead until some new information arose that matched it, Hoffman determined that it had no value at all. But should he have been conclusive that someone couldn't have seen Adam an hour after Reve began searching for him?

Relying on Reve for incident times that day was problematic. On her first recounting to Hoffman and Det. Ron Hickman, she said that on her way to Sears that morning she'd stopped at Adam's church school, staying just long enough to leave a check for his upcoming year's tuition. From home it was about five minutes' ride to the church, then another five to Sears, but inexplicably she said she'd arrived at the church at 11, then Sears at 12:30.

At Sears, Hoffman found much firmer-grounded times. Angelique Ganas, a young woman working in the lamp department, remembered Reve asking her questions at about five or 10 minutes after noon. She was precise because she had just replaced the regular lamp counter employee, who'd left for lunch. Switchboard operator Jenny Rayner, who'd paged Adam, said her first page was at 12:25. Catalog desk employee Joanne Braun remembered seeing a gray Checker park between 11:30-noon. Reve drove a gray Checker.

And besides the Pottenburgh clan and the 12-year-old boy who'd said he'd played videogames with a child he thought was Adam and had last seen him between 1:30-2 (and whom a police lieutenant believed because he came from a very religious family), still others said they'd seen Adam in the toy department long after the first intercom page. Joyce Sotillo, mother to Andrew Sotillo, 13, and aunt to John Sotillo, 11, who'd both played in a tennis tournament that day at the park next to Sears, told Hoffman the boys had seen Adam play the videogames at 12:45. They were certain of the time because they'd finished their morning match, eaten lunch in the mall, and were due to play again at one. They were almost late because of a videogame incident involving two black children.

Also, 13-year-old James Martin told Hoffman he'd wandered into Sears at 12:45-12:50 after also having lunch at the food court. He played the videogame with a boy he thought was eight when two black boys tried to wrest the controls from the smaller child. He remembered that a female security guard came then the black boys left. James said he left at about 1. When Hoffman showed him a picture of Adam, he said he couldn't be sure that was the same child he'd played with. However, it was five weeks after the incident when Hoffman showed it to him..

Hoffman also re-interviewed Kathy Shaffer, the security guard, who said the fight she broke up happened between 12:30-12:45. She was also sure that neither of the white boys she threw out of the store was Adam.

Another contradiction Hoffman found was that St. Mark's Lutheran church secretary Jackie Wing said she saw Reve come in that morning between 10-10:30. She remembered the check she left, for $90 and signed by John Walsh—but said Adam wasn't with her. And she was positive about that. Later, Hoffman spoke to the church vicar who also said he saw Reve by herself.

When the detectives returned to Reve she insisted Adam was with her. (Later, confronted with the vicar's statement, she recalled that Adam was barely higher than the secretary's desk, and that she'd asked him why he didn't say hello to either the secretary or the vicar.) She revised her times forward to being at the church at noon and Sears at 12:30. But when they told her about the Sears employees' times, she admitted she might have been mistaken, she wasn't wearing her watch that day.

There was another side issue involving Reve. When the police interviewed Jimmy Campbell, a family friend who'd lived with the Walshes for almost all of Adam's life and had been the equivalent of his nanny, he'd volunteered a startling admission: he'd been having an affair with her for at least three years. John had spent a lot of time on business trips and had felt comfortable keeping Jimmy in the house. Jimmy, nearly 10 years younger than John, was originally John's friend.

But the Walshes, or at least John, had apparently grown tired of Jimmy living with them. They'd asked him to leave earlier in the year, and after stalling for a few months, Jimmy had moved out just two weeks before Adam disappeared. He didn't really have anywhere to go, or enough money to get his own place. In those two weeks he'd slummed at his parents' house and with a friend, and slept a night at a cheap hotel and another in his un-air conditioned beach cabana, from where he ran his business, a concession renting sailboats by the day to tourists.

The police made Campbell their prime suspect. In their minds, he might have killed Adam as retribution against the Walshes for throwing him out. This was at the same time they dropped the blue van lead, which clearly didn't connect to Campbell.

When Jimmy had learned Adam was gone, he immediately raced to Sears to help look, and for the two weeks the child was missing had devoted all his time to the search. Along with other Walsh family members and friends, he'd even helped the police answer incoming tips that came to the detective bureau. He'd also moved back into the Walshes' home.

It also came out that on the morning of the incident Jimmy had gone to the Walsh home after John had left for work, and that Reve had wanted him to take Adam to the beach with him so she could do her errands. But Jimmy had said no, perhaps because he didn't want to revisit his babysitter role. He said he went to work but the police couldn't find anyone who had seen him in the middle of the day. Later, two *Miami Herald* reporters canvassing Campbell's hotel found an elderly couple who'd rented a cabana for the season who did confirm seeing him

When Hoffman and Hickman asked Reve if she'd had any extramarital affairs, she said no. But when pushed, she admitted, yes, she'd been having one with Jimmy for three years, but it wasn't serious.

Hoffman later said he'd pressed Campbell harder than he'd ever pressed anyone before. Relying on his desire to help the police any way he could, they polygraphed him twice, hypnotized him once, and kept interrogating him. Finally they confronted him point-blank that he killed Adam. Campbell deeply denied it but didn't convince the police.

When Reve first confirmed the affair to Hoffman and Hickman, they suggested she tell her husband before they told him. Were they right? They believed their mission was to solve the case, even at the risk of further emotional distress to the Walshes. And of course that was their mission. But this was only a week after the discovery of Adam's remains, and days after his funeral service. The affair in itself wasn't relevant, it was only in regards to Campbell as a suspect, and had the detectives waited before threatening Reve by telling John, they might have reasoned out that Campbell wasn't as good a suspect as in their zeal they'd thought. Police and profilers had described the killer as a psychopath, and that was not Campbell. Instead, according to his repeated professions to police, and from all others who knew him, he'd loved the child. He told the detectives, "I was his father, brother, uncle, and playmate."

So on top of all the other calamities that had happened to the Walshes, the police relentlessly pursued Campbell for three months, until finally disgusted he walked out of an interview, and John hired the top criminal attorney in Broward County to write a letter to the police to either charge Campbell or leave him alone. The police never charged him, nor ever quite cleared him either, and he lived the rest of his life with the indelible stain of being a suspect in a never-solved murder case.

The press wouldn't learn about the affair until 1983, after the Walshes sued Sears and Hollywood Mall for negligence and announced it to the media. Again the Hollywood police were to blame, this time for failing to keep confidences. They'd helped the Walshes' attorney by opening the case file for him to see. When the defendants' attorneys learned of that, they demanded equal access, and a judge granted it.

Reading the file they learned of Campbell. The defense then played hardball. During a combative sworn deposition of John Walsh they asked if he knew about the affair on the day Adam disappeared. Walsh answered no, adding, "I've never found that out." Days later the defendants deposed Campbell, who repeated what he'd told police. Since depositions once transcribed regularly become public record for the court file, they offered the Walshes a chance to keep Campbell's hidden if they'd drop their case. They considered that a courtesy; the Walshes considered it blackmail and wouldn't back down. When the judge denied a plaintiffs' motion to seal the depositions they were made public and the newspapers quoted from it. Weeks later the Walshes dropped the suit anyway.

John wrote of his discovery of the affair. Reve, he wrote,

"knew there was no justification. No explanation, no cop-out, no excuse. She had known it was wrong. She had done it anyway. And now there was nothing that could be done except to live with whatever I decided to do. I came to a decision, that some of this was probably my fault too. I told Reve that I would not leave her. And that was the truth.

"It wasn't that this thing was small. It was not a small thing. But compared with Adam's being missing, it didn't even register... It did not mean that we deserved what happened to our son."

6
Dahmer On a Rampage

AFTER HIS SON WAS DISCHARGED FROM THE ARMY in March 1981, Lionel Dahmer didn't learn where Jeff was for months. Lionel couldn't recall exactly when Jeff finally called him, but he thought it was summertime. He was living in Miami, he said he'd been sleeping in the open for a while, but now he was working at a "sandwich and pizza place called the Sunshine Sub Shop" and had earned enough to rent an off-season tourist apartment in a place called the Bimini Bay. Although he was cheerful he offered few details. In a later conversation, he said he was living with a woman, an illegal alien from England who'd offered him money to marry her. Lionel and stepmother Shari urged him not to.

In September 1981, his last call was for money—he was flat broke, he said, with no way of getting more. Refusing his request, Shari instead offered to pay his airfare to Cleveland, where they'd pick him up. She'd have a ticket waiting for him at Miami airport. Jeff got off the plane in excellent spirits— drunk and stinking of whiskey. His clothes were filthy, and he'd grown a scraggly, unmanaged mustache.

On October 7, home merely two weeks, Jeff entered Maxwell's Lounge in the Bath Township Ramada Inn drinking from his own open bottle of vodka. When asked to leave, he refused, and he was bounced first to the lobby, where he didn't leave or stop drinking, then to the parking lot. The bar called Bath Police, and when they arrived, Jeff suddenly turned violent and threatened to kick one of the officers in the groin. He was arrested and charged with disorderly conduct, resisting arrest—it took three officers to restrain him—and holding an open container of liquor. At the Akron lockup, he stumbled out of the police car and needed assistance. In court, he was sentenced to ten days in jail—suspended—and fined $60 plus costs.

His unruly drinking continued. He'd stay in bars, even past closing time, demanding more to drink. Sometimes bartenders or the police would call Lionel to pick him up, since he couldn't drive home. He'd also get in fights, lose his glasses or wallet, and sometimes even forget where he'd parked the car.

Searching for solutions, Lionel proposed a change of scenery. Jeff was sent off to live with his grandmother Catherine in West Allis, Wisconsin, a blue-collar suburb of Milwaukee. The two got along well. Jeff helped with shopping and chores, including mowing the lawn and planting roses. He attended several Alcoholics Anonymous meetings and services at his grandmother's Presbyterian church. In late 1981 he got a job drawing plasma for a Milwaukee blood bank—he'd learned the skill in the army.

Lionel thought his son was improving. But in January 1982 Jeff bought a Colt Lawman .357 Magnum revolver from a gun shop, which his grandmother later found under his bed, frightening her. She told Lionel, and Jeff explained to him it was for target shooting. Lionel quickly took it away. Jeff later said it was one of the few objects he owned that gave him pleasure.

Jeff soon lost his job, and on August 8, 1982, he was

arrested again, in Milwaukee at the Wisconsin State Fair by the State Fair Park Police, for drunk and disorderly conduct. The police report said he "lower[ed] his pants in the presence of approximately 25 people, including women and children." He was fined $50.

Another night he stayed in a department store called the Boston Store after closing so he could steal a male mannequin; he kept it in his closet, dressed, until his grandmother discovered it. Answering his father's question how he stole it from the store, he calmly explained he'd disassembled it at its waist, then put each half in a separate shopping bag and walked out.

He began staying away from home for long periods, even entire weekends. He told his grandmother he liked to go to a mall, nearby, or Chicago. He began hanging around the city's gay clubs, including a bathhouse, where he attempted to pick up men for sex. He'd ask them into a private cubicle he'd paid $7 a night for and offer them a drink—a Mickey. After at least four patrons complained, in 1986, management kicked him out permanently. One victim told the *Milwaukee Sentinel* he remembered nothing after a few sips. "His interest in me didn't seem to be sexual. It seemed to be to get me to drink. Maybe he was experimenting with me to see what it would take to put someone out."

Jeff slept in his grandmother's basement, which had a private entrance, and one morning Catherine saw him with a man who seemed staggeringly drunk, since he fell down several times. Catherine told Lionel, and Jeff told him he and the man had drank too much the night before, and he'd invited him to sleep on a chair, downstairs. They'd drunk some more at the house, then the next morning Jeff walked him to the bus stop and stayed until a bus came.

Another odd incident occurred when Catherine smelled a bad odor one Sunday morning. Jeff explained it came from the cat box, although to her it didn't smell like that. Jeff told his father it was caused by the bleach and muriatic acid he'd used on chicken parts and beef bones he'd bought at the grocery. He'd just wanted to experiment. Months later, on another Sunday when she again smelled something awful, Jeff told her it was from the chemicals he'd used to clean the garage floor. To his father he said he was experimenting again. He'd found a dead raccoon in a gutter and had brought it home in a garbage bag.

"I know it sounds stupid," Lionel wrote in his book *A Father's Story* that his son told him, "but I just wanted to see what the chemicals would do."

"But why would you be adding chemicals to those things?" Lionel pressed him.

"Just to experiment."

"But what kind of experiment, Jeff?"

"Just an experiment. To see what would happen."

"But what would be the point of that?"

"I know it's stupid, Dad, but I just like to experiment."

Yet that 1994 version seems to contradict what both Lionel and Shari told the Milwaukee newspapers in 1991. Lionel told the *Milwaukee Sentinel* that Jeff was about 10 when he'd bought him a chemistry set, and together they'd poured household bleach over some chicken bones. "He wanted to see what bleach would do to whiten them. It was no extensive experimenting at all, just curiosity of a young kid." Shari, not in the family at the time, told the *Milwaukee Journal* she thought that father and son had used road kill, or at least, animals that were always dead. "Because his father's a chemist, Jeff used to take animals and melt them down to the bone," she said. She compared them both to biology students dissecting frogs. She thought Jeff had always done his experimenting while supervised by Lionel.

On January 15, 1985, Jeff ended years of unemployment when he began a $8.25 an hour job on the overnight shift as a mixer for Ambrosia Chocolate Company, an industrial candy manufacturer in downtown Milwaukee.

That didn't stop his erratic behavior, though. On September 8, 1986, two 12-year-old boys told Milwaukee police they'd seen Dahmer masturbating in a park by the Kinnickinnic River, his pants around his thighs. One of the boys asked whether he was having a good time, and Dahmer answered, "Yeah, I'm having a great time."

The boys laughed at him and ran to find a police officer, who arrested Dahmer for lewd and lascivious behavior. He told the officer he'd done it about five times before in the last month, that he knew he had a problem and wanted to get help. In court he pled guilty to reduced charges of disorderly conduct, and was sentenced to a year of probation. Later, to his probation officer he changed his story, he was urinating from drinking beer.

On September 15, 1987, according to his admission in 1991 after his arrest, Dahmer killed again, for the first time since 1978, he claimed. Outside a gay bar he met a 25-year-old man and took him to a cheap hotel room. They drank wildly, and when Dahmer awoke, he found himself atop the man, naked and dead, his chest beaten in and blood on his mouth. But he had no memory of murdering him, he insisted.

The room had been registered under Dahmer's name. Had it not, he wouldn't have worried about disposing of the body, he said. So he bought a large suitcase and stuffed the body inside, then took it by taxi to his grandmother's house. In the basement he had sex with it, masturbated over it, dismembered it including the skull, then left it in a bag for garbage pickup.

In the next few months, Dahmer killed twice more, finding victims in gay bars; one was only 14. He also began keeping skulls as souvenirs. While his grandmother wasn't certain what he was doing in her basement, she did see—and was terrified by—the Satanic-like altar he'd constructed, complete with griffins and black lights.

A 35-year-old patron of Milwaukee gay bars who knew

Dahmer told a Knight Ridder reporter, "He appeared to be a lonely person. Face it, you go into a bar or a nightclub and start a conversation with someone who's not looking at you, who's not buying you a drink—they're kind of desperate for human contact."

Another patron, Timothy Johnson, who spoke to the *Milwaukee Sentinel*, remembered chatting with Dahmer about the disappearance of Tony Hughes, a deaf-mute who was later identified as one of Dahmer's victims. Dahmer replied, "Those people got what they deserved."

A man who described himself as a street minister, Jean-Paul Ranieri, who'd once spoken to Dahmer for two hours while he was drinking in a gay bar, told the *Milwaukee Sentinel* that Dahmer had a Christian fundamentalist view of homosexuality, and believed that AIDS was punishment from God. Although Ranieri had later spread the word for gay men to stay away from Dahmer, he said he didn't look like anyone capable of serial murder. Nor could he tell whether Dahmer was straight or gay. "He looked like a drunk yuppie," he said.

Anxious for privacy—and possibly asked to leave by his grandmother, on September 25, 1988, Dahmer moved into his own apartment, in the city of Milwaukee, close to work. Within a day, at a shopping center he found 13-year-old Somsack Sinthasomphone, from a Laotian family that had come to America to escape its civil war and communist government, who for $50 agreed to come to Dahmer's apartment to pose for photos. After drugging his coffee and Bailey's Irish Cream, Dahmer fondled him. Although under the drug's influence, the boy escaped and stumbled home. His parents immediately took him to the hospital, and when he regained coherence, he led police to Dahmer. On September 27 he was arrested and charged with sexual exploitation of a child involving enticement.

On bail and back living at his grandmother's, Dahmer killed again.

In court in May 1989 on the sexual assault, Dahmer pled guilty. He denied doping the boy and said he didn't realize he was a minor. Blaming his actions on alcoholism, he asked for treatment, which he suggested he'd more likely get outside of jail.

Don't buy it, prosecutor Gale Shelton told Milwaukee Circuit Judge William Gardner, asking him to sentence Dahmer to five years in prison. Dahmer was a "very manipulative" person who'd merely gone through the motions during court-ordered treatment after his prior arrest: "In my judgment, it is absolutely crystal clear that the prognosis for treatment of Mr. Dahmer within the community is extremely bleak... and is plain not going to work. That's absolutely clear from every single professional who's looked at Mr. Dahmer, and the reality is that his track record exhibits that he is very likely to re-offend.

"His perception that what he did wrong here was choosing too young a victim—and that's all he did wrong—is a part of the problem. He appeared to be cooperative and receptive, but anything that goes below the surface indicates the deep-seated psychological problems that he is unwilling or incapable of dealing with."

In response, Dahmer addressed the court himself. "What I have done is very serious. I've never before been in this position before. Nothing this awful. This is a nightmare come true for me. If anything would shock me out of my past behavior patterns, it's this.

"Please give me a chance to show that I can, that I can tread the straight and narrow and not get involved in any situation like this ever again. This enticing a child was the climax of my idiocy. I don't know what in the world I was thinking when I did it. I offer no defense. I do want help. I do want to turn my life around."

Buy it the judge did: "This is the kind of thing that the prosecutor would just ask the judge to throw away the book, and the judge would say ten and ten consecutive and goodbye.

But if there is an opportunity to salvage you, I want to make use of that opportunity." He gave him five years probation, the first year on prison work release. Dahmer was able to keep his job at Ambrosia Chocolate. He was ordered to have no contact with juveniles, and not to hang around schools, playgrounds or parks. The Sinthasomphone family said later they were never informed of the sentence. They would have protested it.

Dahmer never did follow through with a treatment plan. Despite Lionel's written plea to the judge not to release his son until he finished treatment, the Milwaukee County House of Correction released him two months early, in March 1990.

After spending two months in his grandmother's house, in May 1990 Dahmer rented room 213 at the Oxford Apartments. In the next 15 months, until Tracy Edwards escaped, he killed 12 men and boys, aged 14-31. Nine were black; the others were white, Hispanic, and Asian. Most of them were gay, and most had arrest records. Most of them, after they were murdered, were not immediately reported missing.

Dahmer's most notorious murder happened the night of May 27, 1991, involving 14-year-old Konerak Sinthasomphone. To Dahmer's apparent later surprise, Konerak was Somsack's younger brother. On a Sunday evening Dahmer came upon Konerak in Milwaukee's Grand Avenue mall and offered him money to pose for pictures, same as his brother. After he took shots of him wearing a black bikini, Dahmer drugged his drink.

At the time, Dahmer's refrigerator was empty of beer. With his prey unconscious, he left to buy more. But before he returned, after midnight, two 18-year-old neighborhood girls walking on the street saw Konerak "butt-naked". He was dazed, bleeding from his buttocks, cuts on his elbows and knees, frightened, and unable to speak or stand. Then Dahmer showed up, beer under his arm. He grabbed Konerak by the arm, but one of the girls wouldn't let go of the boy while the other ran to call 911 on a pay phone.

When three cops arrived, Dahmer tried to control the situation. He coolly explained (in his later words), "Look, we've been drinking Jack Daniel's, and I'm afraid he's had too much." When an officer asked how old the boy was, Dahmer answered, 19. "We live together, right here at 924 (his address). We're boyfriends, if you know what I mean."

The girls argued the naked boy was obviously less than 19—he had a baby face and no chest hair, but the officers tried to shoo them away, and even threatened to arrest them when one insistently touched the officer's shoulder, trying to get him to listen. Dahmer was stuttering and didn't even know the boy's name, one girl told the *Milwaukee Sentinel.* "Well, his name is, well, uh, his name is Jim something. And they just believed him," said Nicole Childress, 18. Instead, the officers covered Konerak with a blanket and escorted Dahmer as he took him home. They wrote in a police report that Dahmer said his companion's name was John Hmung.

Inside his apartment's living room, the officers smelled what they thought were bowel movements but didn't ask to look around into the other rooms. Had they entered the bedroom, they would have found a body dead three days on the bed. Nor did they bother to run a background check on Dahmer—they would have discovered he was on probation. Konerak still wasn't able to speak by the time they left Dahmer alone with him. Once they were gone, Dahmer strangled him, had sex with his body, then dismembered him and saved his head. As one of the officers left the scene he reported over the police radio:

"Intoxicated Asian naked male (laughter) was returned to his sober boyfriend (laughter)." Later, he or his partner joked that the other was "gonna get deloused back at the (police) station." After the story broke, in defense of the officers, an unnamed patrol officer from the same district told the *Milwaukee Journal,* "A lot of bizarre things happen in that area of the city. People have been known to run naked in the street."

After Konerak didn't come home, his family searched places in Wisconsin and four other states. Days after his disappearance, the family got a phone call: "Konerak is in danger right now," said a man with a deep voice. It was similar to a call Eddie Smith's sister got in March 1991, after her brother went missing the previous June: "Don't even bother looking for your brother anymore," the caller said. When asked why not, he said, "Because he's dead." Asked how he knew that, he answered, "Because I killed him." The family of Ernest Miller got a call in September 1990 from a man who chanted, "Help me. Help me. Help me." Another call was just groaning noises, as if in pain. Dahmer later admitted killing both Smith and Miller.

Meanwhile, Dahmer may have been growing increasingly suicidal. On July 8, Dahmer told his probation officer he was close to getting fired at the chocolate factory because he'd been late and missed work too often. If he lost his job, he said, "That would be a good reason to commit suicide." In fact he was fired six days later, which put him at risk of eviction from his apartment on August 1. It was the fourth reference to suicide in his official files. In August 1990, after being sued by a hospital for failure to pay a bill, and under pressure to pay other bills, he said, "The only way I can see a way out is to jump from a tall building." In 1987 he said "Carbon monoxide. Always an alternative."

On July 22, 1991, a rainy Monday evening, walking with friends in downtown Milwaukee's Grand Avenue enclosed shopping district, Tracy Edwards saw someone he recognized from his twin brother's neighborhood, where Tracy had been staying the last six weeks. He'd seen him shopping before, too, and they'd previously chatted, briefly. Since the man, who said his name was Jeff, said he lived near Tracy's brother, he suggested they share a cab to get out of the rain.

At Tracy's brother's place no one was home, so Jeff

suggested they go to his place, where he had some beer.

Edwards became apprehensive the instant he entered Jeff's one-bedroom apartment. Although it was neat, it stank. Jeff said the rain had backed up the sewers. The front door had double locks, and what turned out to be a fake video surveillance camera was pointed from a corner of the living room toward the entrance. Framed on the wall were black-and-white posters of bare-chested athletic men. Sitting on the beige sofa they opened cans of Bud that Jeff got from the refrigerator. "You should see what I've got in here," Jeff told him. Later, Jeff made him a rum and coke—then kept asking if he was high yet. Edwards took only a sip, thinking it might be drugged.

Sensing that his guest wanted to leave, Jeff tried to divert him by insisting they watch the fighting fish in his lit four-foot wide aquarium. As Edwards told the *Chicago Sun-Times*: "He was talking about the catfish, and how they clean the (bottom) of the tank. A split second later he throws a handcuff on (Edwards's left) arm and (presses) a big-ass military knife right below my rib cage, right below my heart."

"What's goin' on, man?" Edwards cried, sinking into the upholstery as Jeff straddled him, desperately trying to attach the second cuff to Edwards's other wrist. Edwards resisted, and they rolled off the sofa onto the floor. Jeff was about 40 pounds heavier, six inches taller, and strong—he worked out at a Vic Tanny club, Edwards said Jeff told him.

"I want to listen to your heartbeat. I'm going to eat your heart," Jeff said.

"His face was completely changed. I wouldn't have recognized him. It was like he was the devil himself."

At knifepoint, Jeff forced him into his bedroom, where photos Edwards called "disgusting" were posted on the walls. There was also a bolt-lock on the outside of the door, so someone could be kept locked inside. On his VCR, Jeff played *The Exorcist III* (which Dahmer later admitted he'd watched a few times a week, for the previous six months). On the edge of the bed, knife still at his ribs, Edwards tensed while Jeff rocked back-and-forth trance-like for 15 minutes and chanted "uuhhmmm." Then he talked about people he'd killed, and how he hadn't wanted them to leave.

To stall for time, Edwards decided to play compliant, that he liked the idea of being handcuffed. Jeff said he wanted to photograph him, because his body was so beautiful. As the hours passed, five in total, Jeff was alternately Satanic then rational. Back on the couch, knife still at him, Edwards finally spotted his chance when Jeff looked away for an instant. Using a karate move he'd learned, Edwards punched his captor in the face then kicked him in the stomach.

Stunned, Jeff dropped his knife. Dashing for the door, Edwards managed to open its two deadbolts—just as Jeff grabbed his wrists.

Jeff calmly promised that if Edwards would return, he'd remove his handcuffs. Instead, Edwards yanked away and ran down the hallway, screaming for help.

Just before midnight, Milwaukee police officers Rolf Mueller and Bob Rauth, on patrol in their car in a rundown neighborhood near Marquette University, spotted a sprinting black man, a set of handcuffs dangling from one wrist. They were surprised when he changed direction and ran toward them, stopping at their car.

"Which one of us did you escape from?" asked one officer.

Breathlessly the man pointed at an apartment building. "There's this white dude in apartment number 213, he's got a big-ass knife stashed under his bed. He said he was goin' to cut my heart out!"

To the cops the story sounded vaguely like homosexual love gone awry, but they agreed to check it out. At number 213 in the Oxford Apartments, with Edwards, they rang the doorbell.

"Milwaukee police officers!"

Dahmer answered.

"Are you Jeff?"

"Yes, I am. Is anything the matter?"

In the doorway, Dahmer was cool, matter-of-fact, and polite. At six foot, he was big enough to worry the cops if he wanted to make trouble, and there was beer on his breath. Edwards was right; the stench inside was awful. The officers asked Dahmer to get the key to unlock the cuffs on Edwards's wrist. As Dahmer went on his way to the bedroom, Edwards reminded the cops Dahmer had a knife.

Mueller told Dahmer to stop, he'd go in the bedroom himself. On his way, he passed an open dresser drawer. Peering inside, he saw Polaroids of dismembered men—photographed in that same bedroom. Others, taken in the kitchen, were of skulls. Another, taken in the shower, was of a skeleton, hanging. He shouted to Rauth to make an arrest.

Suddenly Dahmer leaped from the sofa screaming like an animal. They rolled on the living room floor until Rauth clamped cuffs on him.

"You're one lucky son of a bitch, buddy. This could have been you," Mueller told Edwards, showing him a photo of a severed head.

Edwards pointed at the refrigerator. "Maybe he's got one of those heads in there," he said, recalling earlier that Dahmer had gotten upset when Edwards had wanted to get his own beer.

Edwards looked scared. Mueller opened the refrigerator...

... and screamed.

Quickly, he slammed the door.

Besides the head in the fridge (next to an open box of baking soda), they discovered three more in a top-opening freezer, neatly tied in triple-wrapped garbage bags—as well as lungs, intestines, a kidney, a liver, and a human heart, the latter of which Dahmer later said he had planned to eat. In the hall closet, an iron kettle held two decomposed hands and a penis, while above it on a shelf were two more skulls.

A sliding door to Dahmer's bedroom had a set of locks—but on the outside, suggesting not security but a prison. On the wall near his bed were photos of naked men. On the bed itself, its black linen and mattress bloodstained, rested a Polaroid camera. Under the bed was a large knife, just where Edwards said it would be. To the side was a sealed blue 55-gallon drum; when the medical examiner's office opened it, they found three headless torsos, preserved in formaldehyde. A further inspection of his dresser drawers found more photos—corpses in various stages, body parts, and graphic homosexual acts, some involving bondage. One showed a man sliced open, neck to groin. There were also gay pornographic magazines and videos.

In a laptop computer box, police found two more skulls and still more photos. The top drawer of a filing cabinet hid three skulls, the bottom drawer a variety of bones. They also found: ether, chloroform, acetone, formaldehyde, ethyl alcohol, gallon bottles of hydrochloric acid, muriatic acid, Clorox, Lysol spray, Odor-Sorb, and Woolworth brand pine solvent; prescription tranquilizers including Halcion; near the sofa, an electric three-quarter-inch drill and a handsaw with five detachable blades. In the kitchen, potato chips, rum, beer, and things unspeakable only because of their juxtaposition: two butcher knives, meat tenderizer, mustard, and barbecue sauce. They also found several dietary supplements sold to bodybuilders, including one called Anabolic Fuel.

When police led Dahmer away, a neighbor said he heard him meowing. Another described it as "a screeching I'll never forget. It was terrible. It almost made me throw up."

"I thought it smelled like dead bodies," a neighbor told *USA Today*. "Never thought I'd be right."

Later, Dahmer said he had no memory of the episode inside his apartment. "The only reason the last guy got away was because I was completely unconscious for at least six hours according to what he said. I have no memory of anything that happened but I was still functioning... I don't know why I blanked out like that... I have no idea why half of my brain just turned itself off, that's what it seems like. I came back to consciousness five minutes before I heard the knock on the door and there were the police. I didn't have time for a cover story or anything."

After their initial stunned reactions, Milwaukeeans began blaming each other for not realizing that a serial killer had been among them. The cops blamed the justice system—the judge who in 1988 had leniently sentenced Dahmer for sexual assault of a minor. The city's blacks accused the cops of racism for poorly investigating black missing persons—most of Dahmer's victims were black. The city's gays protested the same point. Meanwhile, the white racist Aryan Brotherhood threatened to kill Dahmer, prompting tight security at his court appearances.

That night, Dahmer capitulated. Initially declining his right to an attorney, he began narrating to police his reign of murder. He described incidents—he said he didn't know, or want to know, the names of his victims or much about them. That way, in his mind he didn't have to humanize them.

As police fielded calls from people all over the Midwest whose relatives were missing, Milwaukee and other area police combed their missing persons files to see if they could match their photos to Dahmer's. They showed the photos to Dahmer, who claimed several of them.

Dahmer said he'd met some of his victims at shopping areas, but most he found at gay bathhouses and bars in Milwaukee and Chicago, where he'd sit alone, sometimes starting conversations with men. Following the suggestion of a party or $50-100 he'd pay to take their nude photos, he'd lured them all home. Once there, he'd drug their drinks, then, generally, strangle them. He'd have sex with them both before and after.

When Dahmer admitted he cannibalized some of his victims, he said it gave him a sexual charge, as well as a feeling of permanently possessing them.

As an M.O., Dahmer said he preyed on men who were vulnerable and often needed money. Most but not all were gay. Most apparently didn't have cars. Some were runaways. Most but not all had criminal records, some violent. One was a deaf-mute. Usually they were smaller built than he. Some were adolescents, as young as 13.

He said killing was merely the means to an end. To do it, he needed to be intoxicated. For his victims he tried to make the killing as painless as possible.

During consensual gay sex, Dahmer discovered he liked sodomy—but not on the receiving end. His solution was to slip his partner knockout drugs so he could have his way without reciprocating. To make his victims permanently compliant, he experimented; he'd crudely lobotomize them by drilling a hole in their head, then he'd inject muriatic acid into their brains.

He enjoyed necrophilic sex. He'd masturbate over a body or while holding a skull in his hands—it implied control. As well, he'd cut open abdomens and have intercourse.

Perhaps his larger purpose in all of this, he explained, was to create a theatrical occult altar. At a black table in his apartment he wanted to place ten painted skulls on the sides and a full skeleton at each end. He hadn't yet bought a black leather chair for himself. Burning incense, he'd illuminate the room overhead with four blue globe lights, and hang on the wall a blue curtain and a plaque of a goat. He already had a statue of a griffin—a mythical lion-eagle—that represented evil.

In total, Dahmer admitted to 16 murders in Wisconsin, beginning in 1987. The 11 skulls in his apartment were incontrovertible evidence, and the Milwaukee County medical examiner confirmed most of their identities through dental records. From three severed hands the FBI matched fingerprints. Also, Dahmer had kept IDs of two victims. Kin identified victims from Dahmer's photographs. A twelfth, his body never found, was confirmed that way.

Shown additional missing-persons photos, Dahmer claimed four more victims he said he'd killed in Wisconsin, although there was no physical evidence. Three, he said, he'd killed while he was living in the basement of his grandmother's house in West Allis.

But Dahmer's most remarkable admission was the murder of Steven Hicks, in 1978. Dahmer told police that in 1981, when he returned home to Ohio after his military service, he exhumed the bag of Hicks's dismembered bones he'd buried three years earlier, peeled off all its rotting flesh, then sledgehammered them into pieces no larger than a hand. Then, behind his house, he dispersed them into the air, scattering them over a rocky 10-foot cliff in the thick woods as he turned around in a wave, making a complete circle.

After Dahmer drew them a map, police, like archaeologists, cordoned off squares on the 1.7-acre property where they thought they'd most likely find human bones. They found more than two hundred fragments, including three teeth, which forensic anthropologists from the Smithsonian Institution eventually identified as Hicks's.

Around the country police wondered, had he committed murders elsewhere? They wanted to know everywhere Dahmer had traveled to see if they could match any similar fact unsolved crimes.

COPS SAY SUSPECT ADMITS DRUGGING, STRANGLING MEN
—*The Miami Herald*

On Wednesday July 24, 1991, still working the overnight shift as a printer at the *Miami Herald* as he had 10 years before, proofreading the next morning's newspaper before it went on the press, Willis Morgan saw the first photo the *Herald* published of Jeffrey Dahmer, arrested in Milwaukee two nights before. The thumbnail-sized mug shot ran buried in a five-inch wire story on page 16A in all its editions Thursday. (The paper had run the same photo Wednesday morning, also buried, but Morgan hadn't seen it because he wasn't working.) Although the *Herald* didn't say so, the mug shot was from August 1982.

In Morgan's words, he freaked out. He had to be calmed down by his supervisor. *"This is the guy!"* he told his friends.

Morgan's friends and co-workers all knew the story. As they'd encouraged him in 1981 to go to the Hollywood police station—where he'd been brushed off—they urged him to go back. So once again, after his workday ended, Morgan went to the Hollywood police station. This time an officer briefly took his information and left a message for Jack Hoffman

July 26, 1991

Lionel Dahmer considered his son Jeff a liar. He wasn't convinced that 17 murders was the full total.

Like everyone else who knew him, Lionel had no idea Jeff was a killer until his arrest. Immediately he thought back to where his son had lived and made the connection between Miami in the summer of 1981—and Adam Walsh. Calling the tip line at John Walsh's show *America's Most Wanted*, as Walsh recalled it in his book, Lionel suggested that his son had killed Walsh's son.

On July 26, the *Milwaukee Sentinel* had published an interview with Lionel that made news the next two days in papers across the country. It said Dahmer had worked in Miami at a sub sandwich shop. From speaking either to Lionel or Jeffrey, Milwaukee police that day obtained the names Sunshine Subs and the Bimini Bay apartments, where Jeff said he'd rented.

When Hollywood Police checked, they found that 10 years later, Sunshine Subs no longer existed. A Walgreen's had since replaced the Bimini Bay, on Collins Avenue in North Miami Beach. When police contacted the apartment's owners, they said they'd since trashed their records, and the manager who might have recalled tenants had died. Hollywood police also asked Metro-Dade and Miami Beach police if they had any record of Dahmer, perhaps for vagrancy. Neither said they did.

However, according to Hollywood police's estimation, the Bimini Bay had been merely 15 minutes by car from Hollywood Mall.

Quickly responding, Dahmer's Milwaukee attorney Gerald Boyle told reporters his client denied killing anyone else. He quoted Dahmer: "I have told police everything I know." But when Hollywood police asked Boyle to let them interview his client, the lawyer refused. Police speculated, the likely reason. Florida had the death penalty—Wisconsin didn't. Ohio did, but not in 1978, when Dahmer admitted killing there. Nonetheless, Jack Hoffman had Milwaukee police ask Dahmer directly if he'd killed Adam. He answered no.

July 27, 1991

MILWAUKEE MUTILATION SUSPECT LIVED BRIEFLY IN DADE
—*The Miami Herald*

ADAM WALSH KILLING REVIEWED FOR LINK TO DAHMER
—*Palm Beach Post*

July 28, 1991

DAHMER DENIES KILLINGS OUTSIDE WISCONSIN, OHIO
FLORIDA POLICE INVESTIGATE POSSIBLE LINKS TO ADAM WALSH
—*The Birmingham (Ala.) News*

On July 28, 1991, Bill Bowen, living in Birmingham, Alabama, saw his local Sunday paper's Dahmer story and photo, and recalled a peculiar incident that deeply upset him. Later that day he dialed Hollywood Police, and left a message:

In 1981, Bowen had lived in Hollywood. On the day Adam

Walsh was kidnapped, Bowen had been at Hollywood Mall and saw someone throw a small child, shrieking in protest, into a blue van that quickly screeched away.

He now thought the man might have been Dahmer.

On Monday July 29, Jack Hoffman returned calls to both Bowen and Morgan. By coincidence, Bowen was scheduled to fly to Miami that Tuesday on a job assignment to shoot a commercial with then-University of Miami football coach Dennis Erickson. Late in the afternoon, Bowen arrived at the Hollywood police station with his crew. While the others waited in the lobby, Hoffman took his sworn statement.

He brought in a bill from Sears, date-stamped by the Hollywood store for payment received July 22, 1981. That was a Wednesday, as he'd checked on a perpetual calendar, which helped him remember that five days later, a Monday, he'd returned to the store.

He was off work, and he'd returned to kill some time and look for a book. He couldn't recall exactly when he arrived, but he'd parked his blue Olds Cutlass Supreme on the west side of Sears.

What he saw had happened quickly. As he walked a few steps from his car, toward Sears, about forty feet away:

> I heard the racket of a man dragging a boy out by his arms, really manhandling him... I heard the little boy saying, I don't want to go, I'm not going—something along those lines. The man proceeded to pick the boy up, throw him physically into the van that was parked in what I thought at the time looked like a fire lane. And I vividly remember this van screeching off, you could hear the tires screeching as the van took off.

Ten years after the fact, Bowen described the man dragging the child as wearing a dark blue baseball cap and a private's green army jacket—"which I thought was kind of odd for July, it was like today, very hot, very steamy, didn't make a lot of sense." He described the man as roughly the same age as himself—which at the time was 23. He was 5'9" to 5'11", medium build, and had scruff for facial hair. His hair was dirty blonde, collar-length in the back. He'd seen him from the side and recalled his jutting chin.

The child, he said, seemed to be about 5 or 6, with straight hair and a haircut as if from a Chinese bowl, and was wearing a striped shirt, perhaps red and blue. Reve had told police Adam wore a red-and-white striped shirt.

The van, he said, was plain—a "cargo-type van... a commercial-type van". He couldn't tell if it was old or new, but it was in reasonably good shape. He thought it had a Florida tag, with letters either BAC or VAC. And the van's color was blue—navy or dark blue.

Afterward he entered the mall, stayed maybe an hour, then left and didn't think much of it. At the time, he didn't read newspapers or watch TV news, so he wasn't reminded of it until he saw Adam's missing poster at a drive-through Kentucky Fried Chicken in Hollywood.

In 1991 he was surprised to see the *Birmingham News* story that the case had remained unsolved because he recalled reading that someone had confessed to it. When he saw Dahmer's photo, "It hit me like a baseball bat" that it might be the same man he'd seen in 1981.

On Monday July 29, when Jack Hoffman returned Willis Morgan's message from the week before, he didn't ask him to come in and make a full statement, as Bowen would the next day.

Determined not to be dismissed as he had been ten years earlier, Morgan the day before, Sunday, had called *America's Most Wanted's* tip line to leave a message for John Walsh. When no one from the show returned his message (although they did forward it to Hoffman, unknown to Morgan), on August 6 Morgan addressed a handwritten letter to Walsh, in care of the show, which was also forwarded to Hoffman, unknown to Morgan. After introducing himself he wrote:

> I was in the Hollywood Mall the day your son Adam Walsh was kidnapped. A man tried to pick me up in Radio Shack, located at the north end of the mall.
>
> The man was Jeffrey Dahmer. I will never forget his face.
>
> After failing to pick me up he headed south in the mall. I followed him all the way to the toy department in Sears. I went to the Hollywood Police department the very next day!! [It was three days after, Morgan later realized.]

Nearly three full months after Morgan first called police, Jack Hoffman finally took his sworn statement. He wasn't sure of the time, but on the Monday Adam was lost he'd come to Hollywood Mall and went to Radio Shack.

> Browsing the red tag sale table, I noticed somebody staring at me with a big smile on his face, smirk, or whatever, and as soon as I looked at him he says, Hi there, nice day, isn't it?
>
> He was standing in the entrance way and I just took a deep breath and I said, Geez, you know, I gave him a look like, you know, What are you looking at, and I remember he smiled again and came over to me and he just was standing there.
>
> What was really strange is that he said Hi there, nice day, isn't it? again when he came up to me but he said it like he was standing 20 feet away, real loud, but he was standing right on top of me.

Morgan said he didn't answer. Panning the store, he saw only a clerk far in the back. Finally the man turned and left.

119

He described the man as between 20-25, wearing a yellow button-down shirt and faded blue jeans. "I remember when I was watching him, I kept saying I gotta remember this guy and I gotta remember what he was wearing, and I looked at his hair." His hair was dirty blonde and "scraggly," almost touching his collar in the back.

I knew, I had this sense that he was gonna approach somebody. He was intent on approaching somebody 'cause of the way he approached me, so I just wanted to see what would happen when he approached somebody, what their reaction would be... I was also thinking that they might need some help.

He went all the way down to Sears and he turned into Sears and I turned into Sears right behind him. I remember thinking, I wanna keep, I was keeping a distance 'cause I was afraid if he saw me following him, he would get, you know, upset... I remember when he went into Sears, as soon as he entered, I saw him like looking around for somebody but there was nobody there, except the two girls behind the perfume counter.

Morgan said he continued to follow the man into the store, until the man reached a dead end—in the toy department. Fearing he'd turn around and see him, Morgan ended his surveillance.

After seeing Dahmer's photograph in the newspaper, he was certain Dahmer was the man he'd seen in the mall. "Without a doubt," he told Hoffman.

At the *Herald*, Morgan had a friend in the art department pull a July 28, 1991, news service photo of Dahmer in court in Milwaukee. At Morgan's instruction, the friend penciled longer hair on him. He left that artwork with Hoffman, as well as a high school yearbook picture of Dahmer, reprinted by *People* magazine. On the page, Morgan handwrote:

"Keep in mind his hair is combed in the photo. When I seen him he looked like he was living out of his car."

Dahmer's Trial

The trial of Jeffrey Dahmer began January 28, 1992, at the Milwaukee County Courthouse. Although he'd confessed to 17 murders, he was charged with only 15. Of the remaining two, Ohio had one, and without physical evidence Milwaukee wasn't confident enough to charge him with the last.

Dahmer had already entered a plea of guilty by reason of insanity. The contest of the trial would be whether his actions met the legal standard of insanity—did he know his actions were wrong? The difference to Dahmer was whether he'd spend the rest of his life in a secure mental institution or in a Wisconsin state prison. To win, Dahmer needed to be judged insane on only one of the counts.

The defense's strategy was to acknowledge all of Dahmer's horrific acts, as confessed at length to the police. Then they would call to the stand psychologists, all of whom had been allowed access to the defendant. Nobody denied Dahmer was mentally ill. But by citing Dahmer's multiple locks on his apartment door and his interior security system, prosecutors said he knew what he was doing was wrong and didn't wish to be caught.

The defense conceded Dahmer did know right from wrong but argued that his compulsions overrode his rationality. That constituted legal insanity under Wisconsin law, they said.

As the prosecution recounted Dahmer's police confession, a few more details emerged of his version of his 1981 stay in Miami:

At Sunshine Subs a woman from England who was in the U.S. illegally befriended him. She wanted to marry him so she could become a citizen. Her name was Julie, he remembered, and she had long, curly, thick black hair. He was never physically attracted to her, but they did occasionally go out to

121

dinner and take long walks on the beach.

In his closing argument, quoted by the *Milwaukee Sentinel,* defense attorney Gerald Boyle said:

> How would you like at age 15 to wake up and have fantasies (about) making love to dead bodies? What kind of person would wish that on any human being? Who do you tell it to?
>
> This boy who at age 15 or 16 found himself sick... (became) a steamrolling killing machine. This was a sick boy right here. Plenty sick. And anyone who says he's just mean or evil is trying to sell you something that can't be sold. This is sick.
>
> There's no end to it until you destroy everything that is right in life. You destroy yourself. You destroy other people. That's what happened here, an insatiable appetite. He had to do what he did because he couldn't stop it. This is not a matter of choice, not when this pattern is here for these years.
>
> He was a runaway train on a track of madness, picking up steam all the time, on and on and on, and it was only going to stop when he hit a concrete barrier or hit another train.
>
> And he hit it, thanks be to God, when Tracy Edwards got the hell out of that room. Thanks be to God that this madness stopped.
>
> No human being on the face of the earth could do anything worse than what he did... Nobody could be more reprehensible than this man, if he's sane. Nobody. The devil would be in a tie. But if he's sick, but if he's sick then he isn't the devil.

Prosecutor E. Michael McCann followed:

> Cold-blooded planning. For sexual satisfaction.

Your life, your life, your life, for my sexual satisfaction.

What is the price of not trying [to control himself] anymore?... The price for him is... to kill... 'Sorry, Mr. Doxtator [a 14-year-old victim], I want a couple more hours of sexual pleasure. You're going to have to die to give me that pleasure.'

The defense is painting him as a wild man out of control. Not a wild man out of control. Calm. Don't be fooled by him. He fooled the police in Bath, Ohio. He fooled the West Allis police. He fooled the Milwaukee police. He's fooled a lot of people, including the court who gave him probation for sexual assault.

Please, please, don't let this murderous killer fool you.

Under Wisconsin law, to return a valid verdict a jury of 12 needed only to vote 10-2. After a three-week trial, then a day of deliberation, on February 15 the jury voted 10-2 on each of the 15 murder counts that Dahmer was legally sane—prompting loud cheers in the courtroom from the victims' survivors. Dahmer was sentenced to 15 consecutive life terms in prison, with no parole eligibility for 936 years.

In the months after Dahmer's conviction, the FBI's Behavioral Sciences Unit asked Dahmer to talk to them so they could draw his psychological profile, and he agreed. As Walsh recalled in his book, in August two Wisconsin-based FBI agents asked, "John, what the hell is going on with the Hollywood police department? Dahmer's lawyer has quit him. We've interviewed him on all kinds of unsolved cases around the country. We can get you in to talk to him. We can get the HPD right in. Where the hell is this detective? What if Dahmer was the guy who abducted Adam? Why the hell hasn't someone been up here to investigate it?"

Walsh called Jack Hoffman, who called one of the FBI

agents. He told Hoffman that Dahmer would talk to him. But, Walsh wrote, Hoffman told him Hollywood police had already spent a great deal of money on the investigation, and had none budgeted for travel to Milwaukee.

"You know what?" Walsh replied. "I'm making a pretty good living on TV these days. I'll pay your way to go talk to Dahmer."

Apparently he never had to. But first, to resolve the issue of Florida's death penalty, Walsh asked Mike Satz, the Broward state attorney, to write a letter for Hoffman to carry stating that if Dahmer admitted Adam's murder, he'd waive the death penalty.

In his letter to Satz, Walsh wrote that he understood "two credible witnesses" had come forward that placed Dahmer inside Hollywood Mall on the day Adam disappeared:

> I have discussed the situation with my wife Reve, and we both concur that it is acceptable for you to offer whatever concessions you deem necessary in order for the Hollywood police to question Dahmer.
>
> We are not vigilantes nor are we obsessed with vengeance, but after ten years of heartache and the nightmare of wondering why and who took Adam and if they would ever strike again against our family or our two beautiful new children, we need to know something. I know Dahmer will never get out of prison and I believe he will receive justice in the next life as well. At least knowing whether he did it or not would be some consolation.
>
> Many people in the criminal justice system and the public have forgotten that Jeffrey Dahmer started out as a pedophile, kidnapper, and torturer of young boys and committed the ultimate travesty to a family. After being released on parole for the kidnapping and molestation of the youngest son in the family, in an act of cold-

blooded brutal revenge, he kidnapped, tortured, and murdered the other son in that family. He certainly fits the profile of someone who might be capable of murdering a beautiful six-year-old boy.

Carrying Satz's letter, Hoffman flew to Wisconsin to ask the most notorious serial murderer in American history if he'd killed Adam Walsh. Accompanied by Milwaukee-based FBI Agent Dan Craft, Hoffman began by asking Dahmer what he did when he first arrived in South Florida:

DAHMER: Okay, I was discharged six months early from the service for uh, drinking too much. I didn't want to be discharged early, but they did. So when I arrived in, I think it was South Carolina, from Germany, they processed me out and told me they'd give me a plane ticket to anywhere in the United States that I wanted to go. I didn't want to go home right away because I didn't feel comfortable explaining to my folks why I was out six months early. So I decided that Miami, Florida, would be a nice warm place to go. They flew me down there. I stayed, I arrived I think at the end of, the very end of March, I think.

He said he flew into Miami airport, found a room at an oceanfront hotel on Collins Avenue in Miami Beach—he couldn't remember exactly which, then a week later ran out of money: "I didn't think very well ahead, didn't plan ahead very well. And so for about a month or two months I had to live most of the days—sleep literally under the mangroves of the beach, and take a shower once or twice a week in a hotel room."

After about two months, he said, he finally got a job at Sunshine Subs, in a strip mall on Collins Avenue. He worked there, off the books, he said, from April to September 1981.

Asked about his work there, he said, "I had all types of positions, cashier, cook, cleaner." At the same time, he also collected state unemployment insurance. He had a bank account at its peak worth a thousand dollars in a bank he couldn't remember the name of "right next to the sub shop." By May, he said, he had enough to rent a one-room furnished apartment in the Bimini Bay motel, a few blocks from work, for $400 a month.

He worked 10-12 hours a day, morning to night, "every day, almost every day, once in a while I'd get one day off on the weekend." He said he didn't have a car. To leave the beach, he used buses.

His supervisor at Sunshine Subs was Ken Houleb, he spelled out the name—a white man then about 65. He didn't make any friends there or anywhere else, except perhaps a co-worker, a 28-or-so year-old English woman with an accent. He couldn't remember her name. She'd been working there when he started, and was concerned about being deported for lack of a green card. When her boyfriend came from England, he took her and Dahmer to some bars in Fort Lauderdale. The entire six months, that was his only time out of Dade County, he said.

Because Bill Bowen had said the man he'd seen was wearing an army fatigue jacket, Hoffman asked Dahmer whether he'd kept any of his military clothes when he got to Miami. No, he said.

Willis Morgan had said Dahmer's hair was longer in 1981 than in his 1991 news photo. Asked its length in 1981, Dahmer said it was the same as it was at present. "Never had it longer than this."

Out of nowhere, Dahmer made an odd association of infamous crimes. "I remember lying in a hotel room—that was one of the times I had a hotel room—and I remember seeing on the news that, that you know, missing boy Adam Walsh, and that was the same time the president was shot, around that time, too, so I remember both those stories."

It couldn't have been the same hotel room. John Hinckley shot Ronald Reagan March 30, 1981. Adam disappeared July 27, 1981.

Continuing, Hoffman asked if he'd ever been to Hollywood Mall.

"The only mall I went to was the Omni Mall," he said, referring to an enclosed mall on the north edge of downtown Miami. "Never went, wouldn't even know where to find the Hollywood Mall."

HOFFMAN: I asked this gentleman, I said, what was the encounter that you are speaking about? And he said, Well, I was at this store inside the mall, and the person that he believed to be you...

DAHMER: Uh-huh.

HOFFMAN: ... came up to him and tried to pick him up, had a conversation, asked him, Isn't it a beautiful day outside, and started following this gentleman. He got a little leery and he continued to walk through the mall and you followed him and eventually he lost you somewhere inside the Sears mall. [Morgan had said the reverse, that he'd followed Dahmer.]

DAHMER: Uh huh.

HOFFMAN: That's my purpose for being here. You at no time were never in Sears? Or ever in Hollywood, Florida?

DAHMER: Absolutely not... I didn't have the place to go back with anyone where I felt comfortable with anyway. I remember sitting after work one night right on Collins Avenue and there was this guy from Canada, and uh, he tried to pick me up—which is a switch—and I didn't, I didn't want anything to do with him 'cause my place was a mess and I just didn't feel like going back. So, no, I wasn't into picking up people or starting relationships with anyone then.

DAHMER: Then this gentleman who came in from out of state had spoken to us. He also, after seeing accounts of you on the news and also in the newspaper—he brought down this newspaper from Alabama with him—and he said that he remembered that he parked his vehicle in the parking lot and he was approaching the store, he saw some child apparently having problems with a male.

DAHMER: Uh-huh.

HOFFMAN: He described the male, you know, similar to you.

DAHMER: Coincident.

HOFFMAN: Excuse me?

DAHMER: What a coincidence, huh?

HOFFMAN: And the thing that stuck out in his mind is that here it was the middle of July and this gentleman was wearing an army fatigue jacket.

DAHMER: What year was this supposed to be?

HOFFMAN: Eighty-one, when you were down there. And he said that the boy was saying, I don't want to go, I don't want to go, and this man was struggling with him and eventually threw him into a vehicle.

DAHMER: Uh-huh.

HOFFMAN: And the vehicle took off. I said, did you see this gentleman's face and everything? All he said was, I saw his profile, because he saw you from an angle. I said, well, who do you believe it to be? And he said, I saw this article on the news and I saw the newspaper and I got a flashback and I believe it to be Jeffrey. Now we want to know if you had anything to do with the abduction of Adam Walsh.

DAHMER: I didn't. You heard all the false leads about I supposedly had done something to some women in Germany, that was proven to be just bunk... And people have said they seen me in Arizona and in California...

never been there. I can't prove that I didn't do anything to them but the biggest thing I can say is, why would I have admitted to half of them [his confessed murders] when they would have known nothing about, and then leave him [Adam Walsh] out?

Dahmer had admitted five murders for which his apartment held no evidence, but that was still less than half his seventeen.

HOFFMAN: That's what Dan was explaining.

DAHMER: I told Dan that I wanted to clear my conscience of everyone. So, it wouldn't make any sense to be trying to hide that.

HOFFMAN: You know, as an individual, even me, I would be embarrassed of something that I've done in life, you know, I might divulge certain things, but there are some things that I would keep secret, you know, maybe take to my grave with me...

DAHMER: Well, I don't want to do that. So that's why I spilled everything when I was hopeless to hide anything anymore.

HOFFMAN: And like I said, that's why we're up here, and you know, and I had to ask you right out if you had anything to do with the kidnapping and murder of Adam Walsh.

DAHMER: Nothing. Nothing.

DAN CRAFT: One of the things that did impress me last week when we were talking was your openness and honesty about this, you remember, we've talked about this, and then I'd ask you, and I shared this with Jack, if you would have done that, would you tell us? And you said, Absolutely. And then I said, why? And you had a good reason, it's like you said...

DAHMER: No secret, there's no point in trying to hide it anymore, you know.

CRAFT: The devil's advocate, I mean, those people that we always have to answer to, they said, well, he's afraid of the death penalty. Florida has the death penalty.
DAHMER: I would welcome the death penalty. In fact, if that would get me the death penalty I'd, I'd admit to it, you think it would?
HOFFMAN: No, we don't want you to...
DAHMER: I don't want to go on rotting away in this place... I'd be more than happy to get it over like that.

After praising Dahmer for being forthright, Craft suggested he was embarrassed to admit he killed a child. "Never went after children," Dahmer said. "My interest was in older adults of bar age, and all of them that I met I thought were bar age." That included Konerak Sinthasomphone, who was 14.

A week after the interview, Hollywood Police received a curt letter from a Philadelphia attorney who said he now represented Dahmer in his appeals, telling police not to again speak with Dahmer unless he or a designated attorney was present. He also threatened legal action against Hollywood unless they gave him a copy of their taped interview, and chided Hoffman for not warning Dahmer of his Miranda rights.

Rather than the letter intriguing Hoffman to keep going, a month later, in a report for the case file, Hoffman wrote he'd dismissed Dahmer as a suspect:

> Since Dahmer's arrest by the Milwaukee Police and the taking of his confessions, no other unsolved murder cases have surfaced linking Jeffrey Dahmer to them.
>
> This detective and Special Agent Dan Craft were in agreement that if Jeffrey Dahmer committed the Adam Walsh homicide, he would have confessed to this crime.

After a lengthy time in segregation, Jeffrey Dahmer asked to be put in the general population of his prison, Columbia

Correctional Institution in Portage, Wisconsin. On November 28, 1994, assigned to clean bathrooms in the gymnasium area, he was found in a staff bathroom, bloody with massive head injuries. Rushed to a local hospital, he died an hour later. Another inmate, one of the work crew, was charged with his murder and later convicted. He was Christopher Scarver, who had once told a psychiatrist that he was the son of God.

"Now is everybody happy?" Dahmer's mother, Joyce Flint, asked a sympathetic *Milwaukee Sentinel* reporter. "Now that he's been bludgeoned to death, is that good enough for everyone?"

7
The Drifters

"I'VE DONE ME SOME BAD THINGS, JOE DON."

Bad things indeed, the voice confessed from the wrong side of the food pass-through. A prisoner in a rural Texas county jail, in June 1982 Henry Lee Lucas scrawled a pathetic note to his guard Joe Don Weaver, "I've been killing ever thing I can for the past ten years. I am to say a bout X different people." The "X" was his scratch-out of a number because he didn't seem to know what it was—a hundred? Three hundred? He thought he'd committed murder in every state in the lower 48.

Glass-eyed as a result of a childhood knife fight with his brother, in 1960 he'd killed his mother, strangling and stabbing her with a penknife after she'd accused him of having sex with his stepsister. He was in the Texas jail only for carrying a weapon, as a convicted felon—but Texas Ranger Phil Ryan suspected him in the murder of an 80-year-old named Kate Rich, who'd hired him as a handyman. Now admitting his crime, Lucas said that during a drive in September 1982 he'd stabbed Rich dead then had sex with her. Using a two-by-four, he crammed her body into a drainpipe.

Lucas also admitted that a month earlier, in August 1982, he'd killed his 16-year-old, slightly retarded lover Frieda Powell, who was orphaned in 1981 when her drug-addicted mother overdosed. A juvenile home either released her into the custody of her uncle Ottis Toole, or Henry and Ottis had helped her escape. One way or the other, Lucas took her alone on a road trip to California, then Texas, where after an argument he said he stabbed her on the side of an interstate.

On videotape, Lucas said he'd had sex with her dead body, beheaded her with an ivory-handled meat-carving knife, then "I cut her up in little teeny pieces and stuffed her in three pillow cases. All except her legs." He scattered her remains over a field. Using his descriptions of locations, Ranger Ryan found body parts. He was charged with both murders.

"I know it ain't normal for a person to go out and kill girls just to have sex with them. No matter how much trouble I try to prevent, I always end up in it," he said, almost charmingly, like a psychopathic Oliver Hardy.

Detectives and reporters beat a path to Lucas's jail door. Lucas listened to fact presentations of open murder cases and answered whether or not he'd done them. Often he said yes.

Only a few homicide detectives were skeptical. In July, two Oklahoma Bureau of Investigations inspectors wrote that Lucas wanted them to describe their murders. When instead they asked Lucas to tell what he knew, he was vague. When they did describe a case to Lucas—and he confessed to it—it turned out the inspectors had invented it from whole cloth. For Texas Ranger Ryan's part, he doubted that Lucas had murdered anyone besides Rich and Powell.

That didn't stop Lucas from confessing. In August, Lucas told Jacksonville sheriff's detective Jesse W. "Buddy" Terry that he'd killed "all over Florida," including twice, maybe four times, in Miami—with his pal Toole. By himself Toole had committed a homicide in Jacksonville—an arson that killed a middle-aged man.

Ottis Toole was then in Florida state prison serving 20 years for an arson of two abandoned flophouses in his Jacksonville neighborhood the previous May. He'd been arrested when two 16-year-olds, in police custody a week after the fire, said he'd used a gallon pickle jar to pour gasoline on the buildings. Earlier in August, Toole had pled guilty.

Confronted by Terry, Toole admitted the fatal arson, which occurred in January 1982. On September 8, Terry charged him with the first-degree murder of 64-year-old Nicholas Sonneberg, a boarder in the torched rooming house.

Quickly, the detectives who'd lined up at Lucas's cell raced to book appointments with Toole. Ottis was a scary-looking guy, agreed most law enforcement agents who met him. He was tall, husky, with bad teeth and thin, balding brown hair. His eyes were disconcerting, and his mannerisms were effeminate. He described Lucas as his homosexual lover. He said sometimes they killed together. Other times Toole killed alone, all over the country.

On September 22, Jacksonville police announced at a press conference they believed that Lucas and Toole had murdered eight women, ages 18 to 76, who they'd picked up in Jacksonville between 1979-81. They were shot, strangled, or stabbed. The mastermind was Lucas, yet Toole would become the focus of police interest in the murder case of Adam Walsh.

Born in Jacksonville in 1947, the youngest of nine, Ottis Elwood Toole was shy, simpleminded, and clung to his mother—who herself suffered from mental illness, wrote a psychiatrist who examined him in 1983. He had a sister who'd attempted suicide and a brother who'd been institutionalized. His mother had kicked his father, an alcoholic, out of the house when Ottis was seven, ordering the children never to utter his name.

His schoolmates called him "retard," and in fact, he failed first grade. Struck in the head by a rock, he'd since suffered seizures and for years had been prescribed anti-convulsive medication. As a small child, his sister liked to dress him as a girl and later she coerced him into incest. At six he set his first fire, in a field. He dropped out in the seventh grade, largely illiterate, a loner. As an adolescent he nightly drank a half-pint of whiskey, several six-packs of beer, and used a spectrum of drugs and marijuana. He graduated to burning buildings; while watching them ablaze he would masturbate, fantasizing about sex. A racist, he often targeted homes belonging to blacks.

In drag, his legs shaved, he wandered streets and bars at night to pick up men while trying to hide his missing teeth. He was arrested propositioning an officer in a pornographic theater. He was a window-peeper and an obscene phone caller. He also had arrests for carrying a concealed weapon and transporting stolen cars across state lines.

He married "to see how it was," but it only lasted four days because his sister told his bride he was gay. In 1977 he married a woman 23 years older; they consummated the marriage but he didn't enjoy it.

Toole met Lucas at the Jacksonville Rescue Mission in 1976. By '78, Lucas had moved into Toole's mother's house, where Frieda Powell, then 12, also lived.

After his mother died in May 1981, Toole said he would lie beside her grave and sometimes would feel the ground move. Asleep or awake, he sometimes heard voices he thought might be the Devil. They told him to kill himself, and once he tried by overdosing on pills. However, the examining psychiatrist in 1983 wrote, "He has no homicide thoughts and he is not given to violence."

His native intelligence tested average, and despite trouble thinking, his cognitive abilities were intact. But on his admission, his memory was poor. Asked in 1983 who was President, he answered Johnson.

Was Toole dangerous? Opinions conflicted in his Jacksonville neighborhood, Springfield, where the city's early elite had built Victorian manses amid oaks, now shabby, decaying shells, subdivided and cheaply rented.

"Brutal" is what one neighbor called Toole in the *Florida Times-Union*, of Jacksonville. "The man was dangerous. He wouldn't think twice if he had a disagreement to take a two-by-four and knock you in the head with it."

"Ottis was a big liar," another neighbor told the *Sun-Sentinel*. "One day we were sitting on a porch talking about somebody. He said, 'you want me to get rid of him? Well, I'll kill him in a house and set the house afire.'" Nobody took him seriously, he said.

On Monday night October 10, NBC premiered a movie simply called *Adam*. It was based on the Walshes's story, and had their cooperation. The network's promos showed a cheerful family in polo shirts. Daniel J. Travanti, of the hit show *Hill Street Blues* played John, JoBeth Williams played Reve, and child actor John Boston was Adam.

The same day it aired, the *Miami Herald* sent a reporter to Monroe, La., to cover a three-day conference at a Holiday Inn of 90 homicide detectives from 19 states and the FBI to see if Henry Lee Lucas and Ottis Toole's admissions matched any of their cases.

Scorekeeping rather than skepticism held the day. Even Texas Ranger Phil Ryan said Lucas had detailed about 150 killings. Already he'd been charged with ten and had led detectives to four bodies. Police said they had enough evidence to charge him with seven more, plus they'd connected Lucas and Toole together to another 97.

"If there was ever an argument for the death penalty, it's Lucas," said Ryan. "He's a demon," said a Louisiana detective. "I've been a policeman for 26 years and I've never seen anything like this guy. He's atrocious," said a Mobile lieutenant.

By himself, Toole was claiming 65 murders, some including decapitation and dismemberment. That's what he told Steve

Kindrick, a sheriff's detective from Brevard County, on Florida's space coast. To speak to Toole, at the Duval County Jail, Kindrick had patiently waited his turn. On the morning of October 10 he got his allotted hour. When it ended, Toole asked Kindrick if he was from Fort Lauderdale. No, Kindrick said, that's Broward County—not Brevard.

"Are you sure?" Toole asked.

Kindrick asked if he was expecting someone from Fort Lauderdale. "You get into something there?"

"Yeah, I did."

Toole had casually talked about killing until he mentioned Fort Lauderdale, Kindrick thought. When he spoke afterward with Buddy Terry, he suggested that Toole might have been talking about Adam Walsh.

Terry was just about to leave for the detectives' conference, but first he dropped in on Toole, who asked Terry if he'd ever been to Fort Lauderdale. He had. Had Toole? Yes, he said. Something had happened there two or three years earlier he wanted to talk about.

The next morning, Kindrick called Hollywood police and told Jack Hoffman that Toole might have been talking about Adam Walsh. Hoffman called Terry and left a message.

Monday, October 17

KILLER'S CONFESSIONS LEAD INVESTIGATORS
ON TRAIL OF MURDER
—*The Miami Herald*

MONROE, La.—The horrors crafted by Henry Lee Lucas and Ottis Elwood Toole remain incalculable.

No one knows how many women were abducted, raped, murdered, and mutilated by the short, unkempt one-eyed drifter and his blond pyromaniac lover. Not even Lucas...

At the conference the next day, Terry had told its hosts, Monroe Lt. Joe Cummings and Sgt. Jay Via, that Toole had told him he'd have something big to say when he returned. Investigating the murder of a 16-year-old Louisiana girl, the two detectives spent the day in Jacksonville talking to Toole.

When Toole told the detectives he was reluctant to talk about killing blacks, because blacks in his prison might kill him if they knew, Via asked, was he was similarly reluctant to talk about killing children?

Toole smiled. "You are talking about the kid that got his head cut off around West Palm Beach, Florida."

Toole explained: he was at a shopping center near West Palm Beach when a six- or seven-year-old was abducted, taken to a remote area and decapitated. He said the child's head was later thrown into a canal near Fort Lauderdale.

Who killed the child? Via asked.

Henry Lee, said Toole.

Figuring this was what Toole had teased Terry with the week before, the detectives asked Terry into the room. Once again, Toole's demeanor changed.

With the intent to get a child, he told them, he and Lucas had gone to West Palm Beach. Outside a department store, saying they had candy and toys inside Toole's white, black top old Cadillac, they enticed this boy.

Once in the car, they drove south toward Fort Lauderdale, the whole way tormenting and threatening the boy. After an hour, they found a dirt road leading into a swampy, wooded area. There they killed him. Using a machete or bayonet, they cut off his head, then chopped his torso into pieces and scattered and buried them throughout the same woods.

But they kept his head. Leaving, they continued driving south. Arriving at or near Fort Lauderdale, they threw the head into a ditch or canal. Then they kept going south, to the Florida Keys.

Yet the next day Toole was singing a different tune. By the

time investigator Paul Ruiz of Travis County, Texas, which includes Austin, met with Toole for his appointment, he'd heard the story. So Ruiz bluntly asked, have you killed any children?

"I don't think I could kill a kid, you know, little kids like 7, 8, 9, 10 years old. I may, and could have killed 14, 15, 16 year olds."

Ruiz asked if he'd told anyone about killing and decapitating a child in Florida. Toole laughed. "I wouldn't do that, not no little kid. I could kill someone 14, 15 years old, and it could have been in Florida," but "if I killed any I wouldn't know the exact location."

Eight days after Jack Hoffman's message, Buddy Terry finally called police in Broward—but not Hollywood. He was referred to Hollywood, where he left a message. When Ron Hickman returned it, Terry said right then he was talking to someone who'd said he'd killed a 6-10 year-old boy he'd snatched from a Fort Lauderdale-area Sears mall. Immediately, Hickman and Hoffman arranged to fly to Jacksonville to speak to Ottis Toole.

Arriving at the Jacksonville Sheriff's Office at nine P.M., the Hollywood detectives had to wait until Toole was finished talking to investigators from another police agency. Finally at ten, Buddy Terry introduced them to Toole then stayed.

Audiotape rolling, Hoffman read Toole his rights. He said he understood them and declined to have an attorney present, although he wouldn't sign a document saying so.

Toole quickly admitted that he and Lucas had traveled to Broward County. But details were short. "I ain't really sure on the month. See, I always get jawed up on months all the time." He did think it was a couple years earlier.

Hoffman pumped questions. Did anyone know they went to Fort Lauderdale? Did they use credit cards? Did they have a reason for going? No. Did he remember the route they took?

"I say, went down A1A."

That sounded wrong. A1A, the famous scenic beach road, from Jacksonville to Fort Lauderdale was 350 miles of local traffic.

Toole said they stayed two nights. In a motel? No, they slept in their car.

Did they know anybody there? Had any police stopped them, or their car, or had either gotten medical treatment while there? Again no.

Toole did say he remembered the mall where they took the child. "There was a Sears." What time of day was he there? "It could have been in the afternoon, or it could have been a little bit later. 'Cause I don't keep up with the time when I'm somewhere."

In the absence of Toole's own ideas, Hoffman resorted to multiple choices:

"Do you remember coming down a main road, the interstate, A1A, or what road you used to get to this mall? Do you recall anything like that? Was it close to an interstate or the turnpike?"

"I'd say it was pretty close to A1A."

A1A was the easiest answer to eliminate. All the way down the Florida coasts, the better shopping, at the bigger malls, was inland. The right answer was near interstate 95.

"Well, what else?" asked Toole, impatiently. For him it had already been a long day.

Hoffman asked the reason why he and Lucas went to that mall. Toole answered, without credit cards he wasn't able to buy anything, he just liked to window shop.

"Did you go inside the mall?"

That question tipped off that Hoffman's mall was enclosed—it wasn't a strip mall.

"I looked at all kinda stores. There was a Sears store, there was all different kind of drug stores, and wig shops and furniture shops and..."

Any grocery stores in that mall? "Like Winn-Dixie?"

Another lob. Florida had two major supermarket chains, one already named. The second was Publix—on the north side of Hollywood Mall.

Still, Toole missed it. "I say, there could have been one there."

Did he go into Sears? "Umm, no, I didn't go into the Sears store. I went in some of the other stores. But I could have went in it, came back out and forgot I went in it. I do that sometimes." Asked if he was drinking or intoxicated that day, he said yes. "I drink quite a bit. I pop pills, I smoke pot."

Outside the mall, Toole said he and Lucas saw a kid exit a Sears door and run through the parking lot, banging on cars, including theirs. Then they "snatched" him.

Asked to describe him, he said "Ah, he had blonde hair and kinda curly, I'd say it could have been curly or wavy or in between. I'd say it wasn't no straight-bodied hair. And, ah, he had on a pair of dungarees and a blue shirt and I know he had a, he even had a pair of [mittens] on."

Mittens? In July? The police department's transcription of the interview read "smitten"—a typo. However, in Hoffman and Hickman's report two weeks later, they wrote he said "sneakers".

Mittens or sneakers? If Toole said, "he even had a pair of sneakers on," that didn't make sense. Besides, Adam's mother said he was wearing rubber beach sandals, green shorts and a red-and-white striped shirt. As for his hair, no one had described it as curly or wavy.

Hoffman followed with a question about the weather that day. Toole answered by recounting the month, something he'd just said he wasn't good at remembering.

"I'd say that was somewhere around close to the first of the year, somewheres right in there." That further increased the chance Toole said "mittens," although even in January, mittens on children are rarely seen in South Florida. North Florida is different.

Hoffman asked if the child had resisted him.

"He kinda raised hell wanting to get out of the car, but when we put the windows up on the car nobody gonna hear anybody yelling anyhow, you know. They figure, well, you got a kid in the car and the kid's cutting up anyhow."

"Did he tell you his name?"

"No, he kept telling us all kinda different names. One time he told us his name was Jim, one time he said his name was Tom and Joe and all that shit."

Returning to roads, Hoffman asked which ones they used to leave the scene.

"I'd say went out on A1A... and then we, ah, some kind of turnpike or something we got onto."

"Florida's Turnpike?" That was the only turnpike in the state.

"Yeah, we got on it for a little while and then we got off of it and then got back on A1A... I call it turnpike, I say it was about the same thing as a freeway to me."

Florida's Turnpike used a ticket system to determine tolls. Hoffman asked if he passed a tollbooth to enter the highway. "It could have been, I'm not really sure about that shit."

Prompted by Hoffman's question "Did you travel northward?" Toole said they drove north toward Jacksonville, an hour or so on that road. But the day before, to the Louisiana detectives, Toole said he'd continued south, toward the Keys.

Traveling northbound, Hoffman asked, what happened next?

"Well, Henry says find somewheres and turn off. We turn off and got on, like, we went down a dirt road down there and ah, he said he couldn't hold the kid, and so, ah, he got the fucking bayonet out of the car and ah, I held the fucking kid and Henry chopped the fucking kid's head off."

"With the bayonet?"

"With the bayonet."

Toole described the bayonet as about a foot and a half long, like a machine. Hoffman asked how many blows it took.

"I think maybe 'bout three or four times. If you catch somebody right, shit, you can chop the head off in two or three times, you know."

"Yeah. Was he laying on his back or stomach when you chopped his head off? The kid. When you held the child down."

"I had the kid down and his face was down. 'Cause I know I was getting that fucking blood all over me."

Toole said they chopped up the boy the same place they killed him, "dug holes toward the swamp area, and kinda scattered out the pieces, and kept some of 'em, we put 'em in the car." Those were the child's head and arms.

Hoffman asked about his clothes. Toole said they pulled them off, then as they drove, "throwed [them] out all over the side of the road." At the same time, "we threw different parts of the body all out, out of the window, out of the car all up and down the road." The head too, it was Lucas who threw that out.

Hoffman didn't get a straight answer to why they kept the head at all, nor where they buried the torso. But asked if all this happened the same day, Toole answered, "Same day."

As for the murder weapon and the shovel they used to dig a grave, he said he'd put them in his mother's house in Jacksonville then muttered something about the house falling down.

Did Toole see anything unusual about the boy, or his face?

"No, the kid was a pretty-looking kid."

"Anything unusual about his teeth, crooked teeth?"

"No, he was a nice-looking kid."

The missing front tooth—Toole missed another softball.

Buddy Terry had his own questions, starting with whether Lucas used the child's head for sex.

"Yeah, he fucked the fucking head."

"Did you?"

"No, 'cause I don't look for blow jobs for sex."

Terry asked where they stopped for gas, whether it was a service area on the turnpike or elsewhere. Toole thought it was at an off-brand "outlaw station, a station way out." Then Terry asked if when they left the highway where they threw out the head, they had to pay a toll.

"I'd say it was no toll booth, it was something like, ah, see in my, my mind a toll road, I mean you kept saying turnpike, a turnpike in my mind is about the same thing as a freeway."

"Yeah. But did you have to pay money to get off this highway you were on?"

"I don't think so." Again Toole missed the prompt.

"But you're not sure," Terry said.

"No."

"It's been some time ago now. Is this the first child that you and Henry picked up?

"Oh, we killed some older than that, you know."

"No, but I mean a six-year-old child like this, seven years old."

Now Toole knew the child's correct age, thanks to Terry.

"First, first one. I ain't never, never got messed up in killing any kid that young."

Next, Terry offered Toole chances to revise his description of the boy's clothing—another prompt to Toole that he didn't have it right. But after he again missed his obvious hint, Terry began arguing with him.

"Now when you described the clothing to myself and Detective Hickman, okay, are you just trying, you know, I know you're meaning to tell us the truth, but is it possible you're not sure about the clothing?"

"No, I'm sure about the clothing."

"Why are you so sure about the clothing? What makes you so sure that you remember the clothing that the child was wearing? Was there something unusual about the clothing that you remember?"

"No, there wasn't nothing unusual about the clothing, he had on a pair of dungarees and a blue shirt, light blue shirt," Toole repeated.

"Ottis, don't tell him what you think..."

"I ain't tellin' him what I think, I ain't telling him..."

Had he heard about this murder in the news? Hoffman asked. Toole said he never paid attention to the news—which may have explained why he'd thought Johnson was still president. How about in jail, the week before, had he seen a TV show about missing children?

"Not with the guys in the cell. When the news comes on they just switch it off."

"It wasn't a news program, this was a movie, nine o'clock movie last Monday, a week ago last Monday."

"No, I didn't."

"Did you ever hear anything during the past few years about a person by the name of Walsh?"

"Walsh?"

"Yeah, Adam Walsh."

"Adam Walsh? Was he blonde-headed?"

"Excuse me?"

"Was he blonde-headed?" Toole inquired.

"It was a child."

"Was he blonde-headed?"

"Yeah, sandy-colored hair," Hoffman confirmed, now answering Toole's questions.

"Was his hair kinda curly or wavy like that?"

"I think his hair was fairly straight if I'm not mistaken," said Hoffman.

"It could have been because he had hair tonic on his hair, you know, ah, it was kinda, he was kinda sweaty a little bit."

"Was he wearing a hat?" Hoffman took back control of the

questioning. No. "Did he have a hat with him?" No.

After briefing Toole what a highway mile marker was, Hoffman opened a photo album and showed him a crime-scene photo of the Florida's Turnpike near where the head was found.

"Now this is what I mean by a turnpike," Toole said.

Hoffman tried to get him to say that the picture looked like the roadway he and Lucas were on when they took the child.

"Yeah, almost."

Toole said they'd stopped the car when they threw out the child's head. Hoffman pointed to another photo, of a canal along what he said was the same highway. When Toole said he would recognize the child, Hoffman showed him Adam's "missing" picture.

Toole paused. "I don't think so. No, I don't think that's the kid, though."

"You don't think so?" said Terry. "You'da had no problem remembering who this kid was, or do you think you were just too intoxicated to remember at the time. You're not intoxicated now, we know that."

"It could have been 'cause I was too fucked up in the head, you know. I ain't really sure."

Hoffman asked how many people he'd seen Henry kill. "I'd say, a couple hundred."

"But like you said, you told Detective Terry you only remember one incident of a child being taken from a Sears mall."

"What was this kid tooken from?"

"This was in the Sears mall," answered Hoffman.

"He was taken from a Sears mall?"

"That's correct. And for the record, you did not identify the photograph from the flier that we have on a missing child in the Adam Walsh case, and that was the Adam Walsh child, and you're telling us that you don't recognize those photographs as being him."

"Maybe that was because I was drunk and I ain't drunken now."

Hoffman showed Toole a photo of Adam's head, fished from the canal. Toole took a long time to gaze at it. "Since the kid's head's wet, it does kinda look like the kid some."

"But you're not a definite hundred percent positive?"

"Umm, because the kid was sweaty in the parking lot, and his hair was all sweaty."

Again Toole paused for a long time. "See, it looks more like the kid than them other pictures 'cause his hair is more, it ain't, ah..."

"Yeah..."

"... probably about the same, you know what I mean."

Hoffman went on to tell Toole the abduction took place in July 1981, and asked for ideas how they could document where he was that month.

Toole said after his mother died, on May 16, 1981, he soon after left for Texas with Henry and Toole's niece and nephew Frieda and Frank Powell. About the end of June, beginning of July, they returned to Jacksonville then they traveled in Florida. He might have been in Fort Lauderdale then, he said, but there was no way to prove it.

Back to logistics, Hoffman asked how long they drove after leaving Sears parking lot until they got to the highway. (30 blocks west on Hollywood Boulevard was the turnpike entrance, three blocks east was an I-95 entrance.) Was it 3-5 minutes, or 10? Toole thought 10. They made no stops between abducting and killing the child, and the murder scene was close to the highway, although he wasn't sure if he could see passing cars from it.

Hoffman asked if either he or Lucas kept a memento of the child's killing, like a piece of clothing, or a shoe. Toole said no. "Was he wearing socks, the child?"

"He was wearing socks. I'll say he was wearing socks."

Hoffman asked, "Do you know where the clothes are?" Terry: "This was two years ago, you say you take drugs and pills and smoke marijuana so possibly you're also not a hundred percent positive of what you recall of this murder. You know, it's been two years and you've been under the influence of drugs and things like that. Is it possible you're confusing it with other murders also?"

"Could be possible."

"But there's no doubt about you and Henry abducting the child from the Sears mall a couple years ago. That you're a hundred percent positive."

"Yeah, a hundred percent positive," Toole echoed.

At 11:49, the detectives ended the statement. But the evening was hardly done.

8
The Drifter's Story Drifts

ONCE THE INTERVIEW WAS CONCLUDED, Detective Terry checked records on Henry Lee Lucas and discovered that Maryland State Police had arrested him on July 22, five days before Adam was reported lost. He'd remained in custody until October 7, 1981.

Terry confronted Toole, and Toole promptly changed his story:

"Uh, Lucas wasn't with me, I was by myself." He alone enticed the child into his car, Toole said as the tape rolled again, 50 minutes later. "And after I get somebody in the car with me I can lock all the doors and the windows on the driver's side." He'd since sold the car, he said, to a junkyard in Jacksonville.

When Hoffman asked again if Toole could remember the clothing the child was wearing, this time Toole said he couldn't, and Terry berated him.

"See this boy and see what you did, you think about it. What you did."

Toole repeated his story that he told the child about the

candy and toys in his car. "He did say his momma and daddy was in the store and..."

Hoffman stopped him. "Both his mother and dad? Think about that now."

"Well, maybe I didn't even ask him was his parents in the store, you know..."

Hoffman asked the direction in which he left the mall. "We showed you a photograph with a mile marker 130 on it," said Terry. "And you said that looked like the turnpike, I believe." The turnpike or I-95? Hoffman pressed. "We've already gone this far, let us have the rest of it."

"Come on now," said Terry. "Look at me and tell me the truth. We've been honest with each other for a long time. Which one, were you on the turnpike or I-95?"

"On the turnpike."

"Are you sure of that?"

"Yeah."

"You had to get a ticket at the tollbooth, and you got a ticket." "What was the boy doing when you got a ticket? Hoffman asked.

"Aw, he was yellin'."

"What was he yellin'?"

"But I told him to shut up, you know."

Right or left when he left the mall? Toole said right, which Hoffman assumed meant westbound on Hollywood Boulevard But before the turnpike was a traffic circle where a military academy kept a campus. Hoffman guided him through it.

"I don't mean a complete circle, maybe around a half-moon circle, or did the highway just go straight there?"

"I'd say some of it was kinda..."

"Curved," Hoffman finished his sentence.

"Curved," agreed Toole.

Guided through another choice, whether it took 10 or 15 minutes to arrive at the turnpike, Toole chose 10.

"Okay. So the first thing you did was get a ticket to get on to the turnpike. Which way did you go on the turnpike, north or south? Did you go back towards Jacksonville or did you go south of Fort Lauderdale, Hollywood?"

Toole admitted he didn't know north from south—or east from west.

Terry: "Did you go back from where you came?" Yeah. "Comin' back home?" Yeah. "Or did you go the other way?"

"I ain't really sure."

"Look at me."

"My mind is gettin' stuck."

"Look at me. When you left, where did you plan on going? Did you plan on going back home?" Yeah. "Alright, did you go in the direction to go back to Jacksonville, or did you go the other way?"

"I could've went the other way."

"Ottis, look at me. What did you do when you left the shopping center? Which way did you tell me you went? Just think. Which way—where did you tell me you were going? Where did you tell me you were going? Come on now. Now you know which way you were going, 'cause you told me and you told Detective Ruiz where you were going. Which way did you tell us you were going? Where did you tell us you were going? Were you going home, or were you going to Miami?"

"I was going back, goin' back to Jacksonville."

Both Terry and Hoffman pumped him to remember something—anything—about where he said he pulled off the turnpike. Was it farmland? Was there a lake? A pond? Was it soggy?

"I'd say it was a soggy road."

Was there an overpass nearby? "I can't remember. I really can't."

"Look at me. Look at me," insisted Terry. "No more lookin' at the ceiling."

"I know what you're tryin' to do..."

151

"I'm not tryin' to do nothin," Terry asserted.

"I know what..." Toole tried to say.

The browbeating continued. They got Toole to say the child may have been unconscious after he slapped him, so when he dragged him out of his car it wasn't hard to chop off his head.

It took about four blows. "I laid him face down and I chopped his head off."

"Did he ever move?"

"I'd say his body kinda, kinda shimmied, kinda shaky." Following that, he cut up the remainder of his body and scattered the parts.

Terry: "Right in the area where you killed him, right?" Hoffman: "Did you just throw it like this, or did you just take it and throw it out a good distance?"

"A good distance.

Terry: "Did you put any of his body in the car? Did you put any part of the boy? Look at me. What did you put in the car? Did you throw anything out of the car window while you were driving? Did you throw any part of the boy out of the car window while you were driving?"

"Yeah, his head."

"Did you bury any parts of the body in the area where you chopped his head off? Did you dig any holes, or did you just scatter the parts of the body?"

"I scattered it all out."

"Just layin' on the top on the ground," said Terry. Yeah.

Toole said he left the child's clothing at the murder scene, but put the murder weapon on his front seat floorboard and the head on the front seat.

Hoffman asked how far it was from the murder scene to where he dumped the head. Failing an answer, Terry asked how long he drove until he got to "the place where you threw his head into the water or canal?"

Hoffman: "How many minutes?" Terry: "Ten minutes, an hour, a half-hour were you drivin'?"

"I ain't really sure of the time."

Terry: "Thirty minutes, forty-five minutes?" Hoffman: "Two hours?" Terry: "How long do you think you were drivin'? How many minutes do you think you were drivin'?

"I'd say, about a half-hour."

Hoffman suggested, if they would take him to the turnpike, might he remember locations? No.

Hoffman then asked Toole why he'd said earlier that Lucas had committed the murder.

"Well, I was gonna try to get him convinced it was him, I don't wanna savisty myself."

"You don't want what?"

"I was gonna try to get him savisty and hang his ass more than what he's hung." Toole couldn't come up with the words "publicize" or "publicity."

"Oh, you wanted to get him in trouble. Well, we know for sure he was in jail at the time of Adam Walsh's abduction, and you're the only one who did this crime, is that correct?"

"Yeah."

Then he asked why he killed the child.

Toole paused. "When I asked him would he come back to Jacksonville with me and he said no, that's when I said, well, I thought, I didn't want to kidnap him, I didn't want to get turned in on kidnappin' charge 'cause he woulda recognized me and so, I ended up, I ended up killin' him."

Terry asked if he thought the head would ever be found. "I wouldn't think it would."

Hoffman asked, did he realize he threw the head into water? Toole's answer suggested he thought the area was a woodland swamp. However, the canal where the head was found was clearly a waterway, without tree cover.

More problems: Toole admitted he lied when he said the

child had been wandering Sears's parking lot, banging on cars. Rather, he and the boy had talked for fifteen minutes before he entered Toole's car.

Hoffman showed him the photo of the severed head. Was this the child?

Toole paused.

"Don't tell me what you think, I want to hear you tell me what you know to be the truth." Terry: "If you know in your mind and your heart, okay, that that's the child, or it's not."

Toole still didn't answer. Terry: "I think he wants to tell us the truth." Hoffman: "Is that the child you abducted from the Sears Mall?"

"I'd say, I'd say it was. I'm pretty sure that's the kid."

Terry: "Not pretty sure, Ottis, either you know it's the child or you don't know, okay?"

Hoffman again showed him the "missing" photo. "Is this the boy you took from the mall?"

"The other pictures, the other pictures look more like him than that one does."

Hoffman returned to the severed head photo. "Is this the child?"

"Yeah, I'd say, yeah, that's him."

"Alright, for the record, he has identified the photographs of Adam Walsh." The statement ended at 1:53 A.M.

Toole had said he'd never registered his Cadillac, but a woman named Faye McNett had sold it to him. Using motor vehicle records, Buddy Terry found it at a Jacksonville used car lot. He took Hoffman and Hickman there.

It was a white, four-door, 1971 Cadillac Sedan de Ville with a black vinyl roof and black leather interior—just as Toole described it, except he'd gotten the year of manufacture wrong. But it didn't have power door locks, which Toole had said he'd used to imprison the child. It did have, on the driver's side, power windows and a power window lock control. So unless the child was unconscious almost as soon as he entered the car, he would have been able to open a door anytime the car had stopped.

Testing the car using the chemical luminol, the Jacksonville sheriff's crime lab found "a trace of bloodstaining" on the floorboard carpets—both sides of the front, and the left side rear. Further tests were needed to tell whether the blood was human. Police then took custody of the car to examine for fingerprints and to let agents from the Florida Department of Law Enforcement vacuum for fiber and hair evidence that might match Adam Walsh. Later, the FDLE crime lab reported that there was not enough blood to allow for further testing, nor did any hair or fiber samples match.

Also, Hollywood police requested permission from the Florida circuit court in Jacksonville to transport Toole to their crime scenes. The court consented, and so did Toole.

Hollywood Police sent their own small plane to Jacksonville to pick up Toole, Hoffman, Hickman, and Terry. Arriving at nine A.M. at Broward's North Perry Airport, they were met by a van, which drove them east on Hollywood Boulevard, past the turnpike entrance, Military Circle, and then to the police station.

Although Sears in Hollywood Mall was directly across from the police station, Assistant Chief Leroy Hessler suggested they take him to another Sears then show him Hollywood Mall.

With Toole in the front passenger seat, the van left for Sears in the Broward Mall in Plantation, about twenty minutes north. Arriving, Hoffman asked Toole if this was the store. No, Toole shook his head, definitely not.

When they returned to Hollywood Boulevard, just off I-95, Toole said the area looked very familiar. Hoisington drove into the east side mall entrance, then did three-quarters of a circle around the parking lot before coming to the west side of Sears—where Timothy Pottenburgh said he'd seen a man in a blue van take a child he thought was Adam.

Alongside Sears, Toole said this mall looked more like the place where he'd found Adam. But he wasn't sure.

During lunch at the police station, Toole asked to again see the mall across the street. This time they parked alongside Sears's north entrance—where Reve had parked. After five minutes, Toole said yes, this was the right mall. He'd seen Adam exit the west side door and stand near the bus benches. That's when Toole parked his car, walked toward him, and told him about the candy and toys. Once Adam was inside his car, he said, he locked his doors, turned right on Hollywood Boulevard then drove about ten minutes to the turnpike. (Unknown to Toole, the detectives had already discovered that Toole's car didn't have power door locks.)

Det. Larry Hoisington drove the route. As they again passed Military Circle, then the turnpike tollbooth, Toole affirmed this was the road he'd traveled—he remembered the school within the circle and getting a toll ticket. Passing the toll entry, the road split; southbound to Miami, northbound to Orlando. Hoisington chose northbound.

Two hours north of Hollywood, Toole said they were approaching where he'd killed Adam. It was near Mile Marker 126—four miles south of 130, where the head was found. Of course, two nights earlier, the detectives had shown Toole a photo of the sign.

A problem left unanswered was why Toole, supposedly returning to Jacksonville, would have stayed on the turnpike north of the Fort Pierce exit. There, the turnpike veered northwest into the center of the state toward Orlando. Signs advised northbound travelers, including to Jacksonville, to exit at Fort Pierce for I-95, the free road.

Passing a construction site, Toole told Hoisington to stop. He said he remembered pulling into this area, then driving about three hundred yards. Everyone got out. A fence blocked a gravel road entrance. Hoisington said he'd driven the turnpike every weekend in the summer of 1981, and recalled that here workers had mixed asphalt for road repairs. At the time, there was no fence. As they looked, a state trooper stopped. He confirmed that construction workers had been there that summer.

Strolling, Toole repeated he thought this was where he'd decapitated Adam—although he wasn't certain. He'd buried the rest of the body here, then put the head on the floorboard behind his driver's seat, intending to keep it. (Before, he'd said he'd put it on the front seat.)

After driving north about ten minutes, he changed his mind. He pulled his car to the edge of the road, walked onto a wooden dock area, or bridge, and tossed the head into a canal.

They next drove to Mile Marker 130, then walked to the drainage ditch where the fishermen had spotted Adam's head. This was where he'd thrown the head into the water, he said, off that wooden walk bridge. It was the one in the crime-scene photo.

Returned to the construction site, Toole tried to find the place he buried the remainder of the body, while the detectives scouted for signs of dug-up ground. Two hours later, nobody had found anything. To explain his poor memory, Toole said he was extremely intoxicated when he killed Adam.

At 6:10, in the near dark, the detectives decided to go home. They'd look more on Monday.

Back in the detective bureau that evening, Ron Hickman asked Toole why he said Lucas killed Adam. Toole answered that the detectives didn't tell him he was in jail. Then he added that he'd heard about a story in the newspaper that Lucas was going to write a book about his murders. Since Lucas seemed to want publicity—sublicity, Toole called it—"I said well, I'll give him something where he can get some sublicity."

Next Hickman asked why he changed his statement about chopping Adam's torso into small pieces and scattering them.

Again Toole referred to a newspaper story about Lucas, that he'd pointed police to dismembered bones they'd found in a wood stove. He was copying the story of what Lucas said he did. He denied decapitating any other victim, or chopping up their bodies. "I ain't never, I wouldn't take all that time."

To Hickman's last question, why he confessed to this crime, Toole said because this victim was so young. His murders with Lucas didn't bother him, but this one did.

"Okay, so everything you did indicate now is the complete truth as you know it to be?"

"Yeah."

"And you are the individual responsible for the abduction and murder of Adam Walsh, is that correct?"

"Yeah."

Hollywood Police Chief Sam Martin was going to wait until Saturday morning to hold a press conference, but *Sun-Tattler* publisher Ed Wentworth asked him to do it that night. The paper published Saturday mornings but not Sundays, so a Saturday press conference wouldn't make it into the paper until Monday afternoon.

Martin and Wentworth were friends. So even before the detectives had finished, the press conference started, at 10:30. It only made the announcement more dramatic: the case was solved. The killer had confessed and was in their custody.

"Toole killed Adam Walsh by himself," declared Assistant Chief Leroy Hessler. He had Adam "outside the city before Mrs. Walsh knew he was missing." Referring to Toole's other confessions, some with Lucas, Hessler said, "I've heard details of some of these homicides, and they make Charles Manson look like Huckleberry Finn."

Toole was not yet under arrest for the murder, he said. Monday, at the State Attorney's Office, they planned to charge him with kidnapping—they wouldn't charge him with murder because they didn't have evidence of the remainder of the body. But they expected that would happen.

The press was stunned. Someone asked, did they know where the body was? Would they say how Toole said he killed him? They wouldn't answer. Had he seen the TV movie? No.

Since they were relying strictly on Toole's confession, how could they be sure it was real? "Certain statements this man has given us have convinced us," said Martin, adding that only the killer could have known those things.

Away from the press conference, Hickman and Hoffman asked Buddy Terry, on tape, whether he'd slipped Toole any information he'd gotten from them.

Terry answered he didn't have much information. Once Toole began talking about the murder of a boy in the Fort Lauderdale area, and someone in his department mentioned the name Adam Walsh, all else he'd learned was the child had been taken from a mall and his head was found in a canal.

He added that he'd known Toole eighteen years, and had confirmed ten other homicides Toole had recently confessed to.

Hickman asked, in Terry's experience, had Toole ever confessed to a crime he didn't do? "No, sir, he will not."

"WE HAVE ADAM'S KILLER," HOLLYWOOD POLICE CLAIM
—*The Sun-Tattler*

A family friend of the Walshes, Les Davies, commented "It's more sickening and disgusting than I ever could have imagined, assuming that what he told the police is true. My God. That [Toole and Lucas] killed someone in every one of the forty-eight states, it underscores all of what [John Walsh] has been saying."

Appearing later at the Hollywood police station, without Reve, John Walsh's eyes teared. "My heart will be broken for the rest of my life. I will always miss Adam. It will always be a nightmare." He didn't know the evidence against Toole, but said detectives had told him Friday afternoon they were "99.9 percent" certain they had the right man. "We pray the criminal justice system will not break down, and Adam receives justice."

Did he feel any compassion or pity for his son's killer?

"I don't, because I know the reality of what happened to Adam. He was a beautiful little boy, and there was no justification for doing that in any realm of human thought that I can think of."

Sunday, October 23

MANY QUESTIONS REMAIN IN ADAM WALSH'S DEATH
—The Miami Herald

The doubts emerged slowly Saturday, but police remain convinced that Ottis Elwood Toole killed six-year-old Adam Walsh...

Unlike Hollywood's top brass, Jack Hoffman wasn't cheerleading the case. Without talking specifics, he admitted they had no evidence beyond the confession that Toole had even been in South Florida when Adam was killed. And, he added, a beheading didn't fit Toole's pattern. "There are certain aspects of the investigation that do raise some doubts."

Buddy Terry contradicted him, to the *Sun-Sentinel.* "Everything [Toole] has told us so far has been confirmed."

Florida Senator Paula Hawkins told the press in Jacksonville Sunday that information not yet made public convinced her Toole was Adam's killer. Her source: John Walsh.

In Monday morning's *Miami Herald,* Chief Assistant Broward State Attorney Ralph Ray said his office would present evidence to a grand jury as soon as possible. But later in the day, after Hollywood police met for ninety minutes with Ray and State Attorney Michael Satz, official comments to the press were decidedly lukewarm.

"Yes, we have a case. But we have some work to do," said Chief Sam Martin. "They are carrying on with their investigation," said Satz.

Translation: the prosecutors told the cops they didn't have enough to present to a grand jury.

In Jacksonville, Alfred Washington, an attorney previously appointed to defend Toole's murder charge in the arson case, discounted his client's Walsh confession. "It appears that Toole and Lucas are in a race" to confess to the most murders. He said Toole previously had confessed to many things that hadn't checked out, and in this case, Hollywood had only a "naked confession." "Unless they can come up with some other evidence, I think it's going to be difficult to make a case."

In an editorial the next day, the *Miami Herald* doubted Toole's tale:

The nature of that confession meshes with the dreamlike unreality about Adam's disappearance. Just as many found it hard to believe that a bright, reliable first grader could vanish from a suburban Sears store, many now find the confession by admitted murderer and arsonist Ottis Elwood Toole unbelievable. So far no physical evidence seems to place Toole in the Hollywood region at the time of the killing. If his confession is false, it would not be the first time that an unbalanced personality has responded to prolonged emotional publicity about an unsolved crime.

9
The Drifter Recants

TO FIND MORE EVIDENCE, 25 searchers began digging at turnpike Mile Marker 126 on Tuesday, October 25. Police described the area as marshy and thick with vegetation, about seventy-five yards east of the turnpike, on private property. Three FDLE technicians used a device to examine whether ground had been disturbed, but had no luck. At three P.M. they quit for the day.

Wednesday they brought more sophisticated equipment that could penetrate the ground with radar. With it mounted on the back of a pickup truck, searchers identified seven soil disturbances or foreign objects—all the size of a body. At seven o'clock, in the dark, they decided to leave the excavation of those spots until Thursday.

Should those seven places yield nothing, St. Lucie County Sheriff's officers were ready to get down on their hands and knees and dig up the entire 1,800 square foot area, the *Sun-Sentinel* reported.

Closing the day, Chief Martin told the *Miami Herald*, "We've run all up and down the turnpike, and this is the only place it could be. He describes the location perfectly. So far as we are concerned, we are looking in the right spot."

On Thursday, as a backhoe excavated four inches at a time, the Grave Team followed, sifting with rakes and shovels. Then they repeated the procedure until they'd gone down two feet, but they found nothing.

Detectives were growing restless. "I've seen every scoop of dirt that came out of there, and there's no body there. If he was there, we would have hit on his bones somehow," St. Lucie Sheriff's Det. Steve Williams told the *Sun-Sentinel.*

In the same effort to collect evidence, Hoffman began trying to track Toole's movements in 1981. Could he document where he was on July 27? In a short time, he patched together this timeline:

After his mother died in May, in June he and Lucas took Toole's niece Frieda Powell, then 14, and her brother Frank, then 13, to Texas, California and Virginia. On June 15, Lucas and Toole were documented at a Houston blood bank.

They returned to Jacksonville by June 19, the day Toole's brother Howell said his 1972 blue Ford truck was stolen. On June 30 and July 1, in Wilmington, Delaware, Lucas signed for Traveler's Aid vouchers totalling $25.00. On July 8, Delaware State Police in Wilmington told Howell they'd found his truck, abandoned and burned. In a Jacksonville police report dated July 15, Howell blamed Ottis and Lucas for stealing it.

On July 22, Lucas was arrested by police in Cecil County, Maryland—about 25 miles southwest of Wilmington—and charged on a two-year-old warrant for stealing a pickup truck from one of his own relatives. Maryland state social services took the children into emergency custody and soon returned them to Florida. But Toole wasn't with them.

Hoffman called Wilmington and got a lead that Toole had gone to Newport News, Va. He knew that when Lucas and Toole went on the road, they often tried to get money from the Salvation Army. Calling their office in Newport News, he got a hit; Toole had been there Friday, July 24, requesting money to return to Jacksonville. In fact, they'd given him a $71.93 check made out to Greyhound for a one-way bus ticket.

The woman who wrote the check had left the agency, but Hoffman found her at home. She remembered; she called someone in Jacksonville who said he'd hire him when he returned. She recalled the time of day as about 11:30 A.M.

Hoffman then called Greyhound to get bus schedules that were in effect back then. Toole would have needed to take a bus from Newport News to Richmond, which took two hours, then transfer to a bus to Jacksonville, which took between 14½–17½ hours.

The Newport News information presented new questions: After he got the bus ticket, did Toole immediately go home? Did he quickly leave again for Hollywood, arriving at the mall by Monday at noon? If he was broke, what money did he use for gas?

Hoffman's captain had asked him to fly back to Jacksonville to ask. Arriving, Buddy Terry took him straight to the jail. Toole remembered the Salvation Army check for the bus ticket. Taking it, he walked directly to Greyhound and stayed until nighttime when the bus left. He didn't get off at any stops before Jacksonville. That suggested he arrived midday or evening Saturday, July 25.

Asked what he did after getting home, Toole said he either saw his wife, Novella, or went to Southeastern Roofing, where he worked. Hoffman asked whom he worked for there. Toole said John, he was certain because he worked at his house, possibly within a day. Company time sheets would prove it. When he was broke, John would sometimes advance him $20 to get through the week.

Hoffman asked how long he thought he stayed in Jacksonville until he went somewhere else.

"Been a pretty good while. 'Cause I don't go anywheres on

no 15 or 20 dollars, or something like that."

From reviewing the interview transcripts, Hoffman returned to something Toole had said, that he'd put the murder weapon, the machete, in his mother's house. But he'd also mumbled about the house being destroyed.

Toole interrupted. "But I got to thinking more. I done burnt my mother's house down."

"That's my point! If your mother's house was burned down, you couldn't have hid the murder weapon in your mother's house, correct?"

"Correct."

"So now you have to tell me what you did with the murder weapon."

"Shhh, that's why I'm tryin' to give you all these statements, I'm not really sure that I really did kill Adam Walsh."

Toole also remembered that when he arrived home, he rented a room for himself and Novella in Betty Goodyear's rooming house. That was also when his brother Howell "beat the shit out of me" outside a convenience store for stealing his pickup truck. Toole said he filed a police report at the time. He also mentioned that when he was in Newport News, he'd been in a hospital.

Searching police records, Hoffman and Terry found a report dated Friday, August 1, 1981, 4:10 P.M. Just as Toole said, the sheriff was called to a convenience store in his neighborhood, and found him rubbing a red spot on his face. Howell had just hit him and threatened to kill him with a pistol, he said.

One of the only important case fact the detectives hadn't told Toole in their interviews was the date of Adam's disappearance. Now, with dates established that Toole apparently came home on the bus, July 25, and a clear date that he was in Jacksonville, August 1, plus Toole saying he thought he stayed home for at least a while to make some money because he was flat broke, Hoffman returned to Toole and told him the date, July 27.

"So only thing, if I didn't really kill Adam Walsh, I would have to have been working the Monday on the 27th."

"That's correct. If I could verify you were working at John's, then you didn't kill Adam Walsh and you made up a whole story here."

"Yeah, that would be what it would be if I didn't, ah..."

For a moment it looked like the whole charade was going to end. But instead Hoffman reversed course, asking him how he could "know so many things about this homicide? How do you explain how you abducted the child, how you took him out to a location, how you laid him down, how you chopped his head off, how do you explain that?"

Then Terry jumped on him. "Look at me. You told the man something that only three people knew, the person that did it, the police and medical examiner. This thing has been eatin' at you a long time, hasn't it? But you told people other than me that you did it—Ottis?"

Toole stumbled to explain. He figured, by confessing to so many murders, he could get in a prison cell near Lucas then get him to say what happened to Toole's niece Frieda Powell. "I still ain't sure she's dead, and that's the only way I could get him to bring out the truth on it."

"Ottis, were you lying today? Are you sure you didn't kill Adam Walsh? Now come on now, let's don't do this way. Look at me. Look at me. Ottis."

Toole began to cry. "My mind ain't gonna take much more of this shit."

Toole kept insisting he didn't kill Adam. If he had, he said, he would have been able to show where the body was. But Terry continued to press. How did he know to tell the Brevard County detective there was a boy taken from the Sears mall, and ask him if he was from Fort Lauderdale?

"Made it all up."

"You were right on the money, you told me a young boy between six and ten. I mean, making it up, that's a little difficult to understand. You were exact on the other murders. These other agencies were able to prove the murders that you confessed to. They got the bodies, everything you told 'em. Ottis, look at me. We've been pretty truthful with each other, ain't we?"

"Yeah."

"Have you ever lied to me?"

"I don't really know if I have at all, now."

"You're digging yourself a hole, Ottis, and you're not gonna get out of it. You know that. You know what you're doing. You want me to tell you what you're doin'?"

"What?"

"You're trying to go to a mental hospital."

Toole began crying again. "I don't believe that shit."

"You don't believe me? Huh?"

"My fucking life, I, I, can't stand it!!!"

Terry ended the interview. It was 10:30 P.M. Hoffman told Toole they'd talk again in the morning, then left the interview room. Terry stayed behind. Minutes later, outside the room, Terry told Hoffman wanted to talk more, because just before, he hadn't told the truth.

At 10:42 P.M. they began again. This time Toole clearly recalled he got off the bus in Jacksonville on a Saturday just before noon. He went to John Reaves's roofing company and opened the gate with his keys.

The Cadillac was there; under the car seat he kept his tools—a shovel and a machete. He drove to his mother's house, burned but still standing, and took from underneath it the about $300 he'd buried in a tin can. He took the money, bought gas, then got on I-95 south, then much later, the turnpike. He drove straight before stopping "in Miami at Biscayne Bay," where he turned tricks whenever he came, for $25-50.

Toole said he got to the shopping mall that Monday before

noon and window-shopped. When Hoffman asked if he entered Sears, his answer progressed from "I coulda" to "pretty sure" he did. He couldn't remember which departments he'd been in—Hoffman had never told him which one Adam had been in.

Outside the store, he sat down on a bench for ten to twenty minutes talking a little boy he described as being between 6-10.

"Did he tell you his name?"

"Yeah, he told me... yeah, he told me his name. He told me his name was—he told me his name was Adam."

Perhaps the last remaining thing police hadn't tipped Toole in the past week was what Adam had been wearing. Hoffman asked.

"No, I wasn't really, really payin' attention too much to what he was wearin'."

Did he mention where his mother was?

"He told me his mom was in the store shopping."

"Did he say what his mother was shopping for? Any particular item?"

"No. Not exactly."

Toole said he asked Adam if he liked sports; he'd answered he liked baseball. Hoffman recognized an opening; if Toole knew the answer, it might have proved that he really did meet him. Did Adam mention his favorite sports team?

"He said he was playin' on some kind of little league team or something."

The right answer, Hoffman knew, was the Fort Lauderdale Strikers soccer team. As a family, the Walshes often went to their matches. Toole's idea of baseball could have come from showing him his missing photo.

One more chance: did Adam tell him what baseball position he played? "He did, but I, I forgot what it was."

In the first days that Adam was missing, his father had called him an all-star right fielder.

The rest of the statement was a description of how Toole

got Adam in his car—he didn't need power door locks because the kid wasn't going to jump from a moving car anyway—followed the same route police had shown him, stopped somewhere on the turnpike to beat and choke him until unconsciousness after he'd gotten wild, parked off-road at a place similar to where police had shown him, and used both hands on a bayonet and chopped off his head.

He wrapped the head in the child's shirt, dug a hole a foot deep between the road and a ditch, then buried the body but forgot to include the head. Instead he put it first on the back seat then a back floorboard, then on the front passenger seat, then drove away.

He didn't have sex with Adam, alive or dead. Five or 10 minutes later, driving, he spotted a wooden bridge, stopped then threw the head in the water. It sank. He kept the shirt. Returning home, a week or so later he sold the murder weapon at a flea market for a few bucks.

Hoffman tried to wrap it up: "Now in this statement, this final statement..."

"This is the final statement."

"This is the complete truth," Hoffman tried to establish.

"The complete truth, the whole—whole thing."

"And you're telling myself and Detective Terry here that you're the individual responsible for kidnapping and murdering Adam Walsh on July 27, 1981, from the city of Hollywood?"

"Yeah."

"And nobody else is responsible for that kid's death."

"Nobody else."

The statement ended at 11:41 P.M.

Thursday, October 27

POLICE: SUSPECT DESCRIBED DETAILS
OF ADAM'S MURDER
—*The Miami Herald*

When he confessed to killing six-year-old Adam Walsh, Ottis Elwood Toole gave what police called a flawless description of the child's clothes and the place he was abducted.

Because Toole had said he was hospitalized in Newport News, Hoffman called a police detective there to see if there were any records. There was: on July 22, 1981, Toole was admitted to Riverside Hospital's emergency room, and the next day was put in the psychiatric unit for depression. He was discharged July 24.

Working the street, Hoffman found the John that Toole was talking about, his former boss John Reaves. He remembered someone called from Newport News to ask if he'd hire Toole when he returned home. Checking records, Reaves found that Toole's last day of work for him was June 4, 1981.

Betty Goodyear recalled that Ottis and his wife had moved in sometime in August 1981. She offered to check her receipts. She said Ottis always had money, he was never broke.

At Southeast Colorcoat, roofing foreman Mack Caulder said Toole had access to tools, knives, and a machete. He also knew that Mrs. McNett kept the white Cadillac on the grounds. John Reaves Sr. said Toole had a key to the company compound since it was his job to clean the grounds. He remembered a machete with a brown wooden handle but couldn't find it.

A machete did show up at Spencer's Motors. Spencer Bennett said he'd known Ottis for twenty years, they'd traded cars together. Two or three years earlier, he recalled, he found a blade in one of those cars—he didn't remember which. He showed it to the detectives: a wood-handled machete sheathed in a green web, its handle wrapped in black electrical tape, its blade rusty and tarred.

The detectives asked to take it. Bennett said he didn't need it back. When the FDLE crime lab later examined it, they found a trace of blood, but not enough to test further.

LONG TRAIL OF BLOOD
POLICE STUDY CLAIMS OF LUCAS AND TOOLE
—*The Sun-Tattler*

Ottis Elwood Toole has been linked to more than 100 murders. He has yet to be convicted of any.

Police now concede the (Walsh) case may never go to trial because investigators haven't been able to find evidence to support last week's confession by the suspect.

On Saturday, October 29, Assistant Chief Leroy Hessler seemed apologetic for trumpeting the confession too soon. They anticipated the story would leak once Toole returned to Jacksonville, he explained.

Yet the *Miami Herald* quoted a police spokesman who held the line that Toole was their man. "Toole did it. He is the suspect and we're 99 percent sure he did it. He just knows too much not to be the one."

Back in Hollywood on Monday, October 31, Hoffman and Hickman continued their search for footprints Toole might have left anywhere. In Jacksonville they'd called Salvation Army branches, Traveler's Aid stations, the state welfare department, hospitals, pawnshops and missions. In South Florida they added blood banks, police agencies that wrote parking tickets, and the state division of employment, looking for payroll records under Toole's social security number from 1981 to 1983.

They learned nothing—except it would take longer to search all the parking ticket records.

Later, to discover Toole's state of mind during his time in Newport News, police acquired his hospital records. A priest had brought Toole in after a parishioner found him in a bathroom of their church hall. To the priest, Toole was disoriented, rambling that he'd been in New York and needed to return to Jacksonville. The priest thought he was possibly suicidal.

Riverside Hospital admitted Toole to its psychiatric unit. On admission, he was "disheveled, though pleasant and cooperative." He said that since his mother had died in May, he'd been hitchhiking, sleeping outdoors or in vacant buildings. He denied having suicidal or homicidal thoughts. But the next day, July 23, he was claustrophobic and on the verge of tears. He hallucinated his mother's voice speaking to him. The next day, against medical advice, he left the hospital. His discharge report said he was not considered acutely psychotic, suicidal or homicidal at the time.

Tuesday, November 1

WALSH SUSPECT RECANTS CONFESSION
TOOLE DENIES EVEN HAVING SEEN MURDERED BOY,
ATTORNEY STATES
—*The Miami Herald*

The attorney was St. Lucie County Public Defender Elton Schwarz, who, claiming jurisdiction, had contacted Toole and then sent an attorney and investigator to Jacksonville. Toole then agreed to let Schwarz's office represent him. "The man, in my opinion, is not psychologically right," Schwarz told the *Sun-Tattler*. He seemed willing to confess to crimes whether or not he actually committed them.

In response, Toole told a detective he wanted to speak to Buddy Terry. Afterward, Terry began a taped statement. First Toole said both his legal counsels had told him not to talk to him, but he wanted to anyway. "The [public defender] is trying to get me to say I ain't guilty on the Adam Walsh case... I really know myself that I really did kill Adam Walsh, but the lawyer I got from Miami [he meant St. Lucie], he's trying to tell me I didn't kill Adam Walsh."

"Are you telling me you didn't make any statements to the effect that you didn't kill Adam Walsh? That your attorney did? Or did you make any statements?"

"I didn't make any. I didn't say anything on tape, or start anything that I didn't kill Adam Walsh."

As the Hollywood detectives could find no evidence, even they grew sick of Toole.

Several weeks later, on November 19, he told Jack Hoffman, "Everything I told you about the killing, about chopping his head off and all, that's true, and the mall, all that's true. When I chopped his head off, I started to dig a hole, but then I didn't dig a hole, I put it in the, there was a, I had some blankets in the back of the car, and so I wrapped him in some blankets and put him in the trunk of the car, and I drove back to Jacksonville, and I cremated his body here in Jacksonville."

In the backyard of his mother's house he used to burn trash in an old gutted icebox. Late in the evening the same day he abducted Adam, he loaded wood in the icebox, then the boy's body, dumped gasoline over it and set it ablaze. He hid the shovel and the machete he'd used under the house, went to sleep in his car parked at the house, then the next morning took the burned remains and the trunk's blood-soaked carpet to the city's north dump.

Hoffman asked why he'd said before he'd buried Adam near Mile Marker 126. He answered, he was just "fucking around with the police department."

Six weeks later, FDLE did a cursory dig of Toole's mother's house backyard and found, about a foot beneath the surface, a pair of children's light green shorts. Reve had said Adam was wearing green Adidas shorts the day he disappeared. FDLE then scheduled a full backyard excavation.

Operated by a city of Jacksonville public works employee, an eight-foot wide bucket dragged dirt two inches deep. They repeated until they got down six inches. Amidst a great deal of junk, they found a pelvis, two bones and a toddler-size yellow rubber beach sandal. Later, the Duval medical examiner determined all the bones were animal.

Another flip-flop occurred on January 6, 1984. In the Jacksonville homicide department, Hoffman passed Toole, who again wanted to talk. Without Buddy Terry in sight this time, Toole blurted out that he'd lied about killing Adam. Hoffman looked at his lieutenants Smith, Naylon, and Banks. They decided to put him back on audiotape.

After again advising Toole of his right to an attorney, which he declined, Hoffman asked why he was giving this statement.

"Ah, I didn't, ah, I didn't kill Adam Walsh."

"You didn't kill Adam Walsh?"

"No."

Hoffman asked why he'd stuck to his initial story all this time.

"Ah, I was trying to hang Henry Lucas at first, but, ah, I found out he was in jail, and, ah, and so I changed it three or four different times, I did."

After his first statement, "I didn't know if I could change it back or not. That's why I kept telling different stories about it, 'cause I didn't know if anybody would believe it or not. I didn't know how to turn it back around, but I didn't kill Adam Walsh."

Toole added, he didn't leave Jacksonville between July 25-30, 1981, the week after he got home from Virginia.

"Okay, is this your final statement referring to the Adam Walsh case?"

"Yeah."

"And is this statement the complete truth?"

"The complete truth."

"And you're telling me you're not responsible for the abduction and murder of Adam Walsh?"

"No, I ain't."

Returning to Hollywood, the detectives showed the green shorts and yellow beach sandal to the Walshes. They said they definitely weren't Adam's.

On May 18, 1984, for his 1982 fatal arson, the state of Florida sentenced Ottis Toole to death. But on June 10, 1986, while sitting on Death Row, he got a re-sentencing hearing, at which time the state declined to ask for a reinstatement of the death penalty. Instead, a judge sentenced him to life in prison, with a minimum non-parolable sentence of 25 years. In 1991, he pled guilty to four murders committed during a December 1980 robbery of a gas station near the Florida panhandle town of Campbellton. He was given four consecutive 25-year terms, without parole. Equivalent first-degree murder charges were lodged against Lucas, which the state declined to pursue since he was still on Death Row in Texas.

Although Toole confessed to perhaps hundreds of murders, those were the only ones that ever stuck.

10

"He's Still Out There"

IN OCTOBER 1988, WITHIN DAYS, the Broward Mall Sears store, Disney World, the *Orlando Sentinel*, the *Lakeland Ledger*, the sheriffs of Broward County and Holmes County (in the state's panhandle), and John Walsh (by then the host of *America's Most Wanted*) each got handwritten letters signed Ottis Toole, postmarked Starke, Fla., the town that encompassed the Florida state prison where he was held. Most recipients passed their letters on to Hollywood police.

Each message was individual, but they all carried the same theme. Sears received this:

> Dear Sirs,
>
> In 1981 I kidnapped, raped and murdered a little boy by name of Adam Walsh. I snatched that little boy right out of a Sears store down in Hollywood, Fla. I don't recall the address exactly but you know the one I mean. When I got done raping the boy I cut off his head and disposed of his nude body.
>
> I am now making a deal with the magazine to tell

my story of how I snatched, raped and murdered this boy and some others. I like to snatch them from stores like Sears, in fact Sears is my favorite hunting ground for little boys.

I'm getting paid big money for my story and as you know I've never been charged for the murder so I get to keep it all.

One major part of my story is about how I hunt for little kids in stores, and of course everyone wants to know how I snatched the little punk out of SEAR'S store in Hollywood. The cockteaser Adam Walsh was in that store when I snatched him away.

My friend suggested to me that Sears might pay me NOT to tell how I grabbed that kid Walsh and others out of Sears stores here and in other states. I can omit saying the NAME of the store, say only it was a dept. store. Like that. Of course it was a Sears store, everyone knows that already, but for some money I'm willing to downplay my activities hunting kids in Sears, and also I know Walsh could sue you for millions of dollars when I tell how easy it was to grab that sweet little boy's ass right out of the store. I'm a boy lover. I love to fuck them and then I kill them.

If you want to make a deal I'll be very agreeable for a fast check but since my story will be told soon you'd better rush a lawyer to see me. I'll talk to no polices, no State lawyers, only a Sears private lawyer. If you turn this letter over to the police I'll be talking about how easy it is to grab kids out of Sears for a long time. You know, everyone wants to hear how I get them and rape them and kill them and chop them up into little bits. I do my shopping for juicy little kiddies at SEARS. See what I mean?

We can talk about it.

See you soon. Bring money.

Sincerely,
(signed) Ottis E. Toole
090812
P.O. Box 747, Starke, Fla. 32091

The *Orlando Sentinel*'s letter was a solicitation to sell the story, asking for "your best CASH offer promptly." But John Walsh's letter was the worst. It offered to tell him where Adam's bones were so he could have a good Christian burial, but only after Walsh paid him $5,000 up front and $45,000 after he found the remains. "Now you want his bones or not? Tell the cops and you don't get shit. Sincerely, Ottis E. Toole."

Days later, the FDLE received a letter in the same handwriting, only neater, a bit effeminate, and without grammatical errors and misspellings. It introduced the writer as Gerard Schaefer, an inmate in a cell next to Toole.

Schaefer wrote that Toole admitted to him the Walsh murder as well as others. His confession was detailed, including the blade he used to cut up Adam's body. He'd eaten some of the boy's flesh, but he could show police where his bones lay. They weren't at the city dump.

As a witness, Schaefer wanted a deal for himself, to be negotiated through his legal counsel. Plus, he wanted the reward for information leading to the conviction of the killer. Hollywood Police didn't bite. Instead, the Broward Sheriff's Office, after consulting with Hollywood, assigned two homicide detectives to speak with Schaefer and Toole.

Gerard John Schaefer was one of Florida's most notorious convicted killers—and since his imprisonment among its most annoying. In the early 1970s, he'd been a police officer in two Broward jurisdictions—and fired, twice.

Then the sheriff of Martin County, north of West Palm Beach, hired him as a deputy. On duty, to teach two girls about the dangers of hitchhiking, he'd driven them to the woods, handcuffed them and tied them to a tree, then threatened them with bizarre sex acts.

For that Schaefer was arrested. While in jail, police found in a remote area the butchered remains of two teenage girls from Broward. One girl's father had written down the license plate of the car of the man his daughter had been seeing. It was Schaefer's.

Searching Schaefer's mother's house, police found links to four other murdered teenage girls, plus unpublished stories of grisly mutilation murders of women that seemed to match evidence found at the crime scenes. Schaefer was convicted of murder in the first two cases, but was sentenced to life because the state's death penalty had been reinstated only four days before the girls went missing. From prison Schaefer sold his stories in a mail-order book called *Killer Fiction*, maintaining that they were, indeed, fiction.

At their interview, Broward detectives Richard Scheff and Tony Fantigrassi saw that Schaefer tended to prompt Toole. Toole said he would testify in court that he'd killed and dismembered Adam with a bayonet and a black plastic-handled straight knife. Buddy Terry had the knife—he'd seized it from his car, he said, and the bayonet was hanging on a wall as part of a display in the home of his sister Vinette Syphurs, south of Jacksonville.

Adam's hacked remains, he said, were wherever he'd thrown them in a ten-mile stretch of canal alongside the turnpike near where he'd left his head.

The detectives found Syphurs, who'd moved. She said she did have an antique Japanese army bayonet on her wall, but it had never left her house. Had Ottis removed it for any period of time, she would have noticed. The next day she found it in storage and gave it to local police, who forwarded it to the Broward detectives. It eventually reached the Metro-Dade police crime lab, which had already processed Adam's skull. They couldn't find enough similarities to prove that the bayonet had been used on Adam.

"One can readily detect the ease with which Toole, a brain-damaged and troubled man, can be manipulated by others," Scheff wrote in his report. "Ottis Toole now appears to be under the influence of Gerard Schaefer, who may be using Toole for his own purposes."

Soon after, the warden at Starke placed Schaefer in solitary confinement for four months, then transferred him to another state prison.

On June 26, 1991, the retirement of Hollywood police Maj. J.B. Smith, a sergeant when Adam disappeared, prompted a *Miami Herald* story. Even 10 years later, leads were still arriving, he said. He reiterated past police statements they'd eliminated Toole as a suspect. "Ottis Toole is probably the most complete investigation we've ever done to prove that somebody didn't do it."

If the case was going to be solved, he said, it would be through a tip, perhaps from someone who had been afraid to come forward. "I don't know of any homicide that's this old that's going to be solved because of legwork."

A week and a half later, on a Friday, an hour before Jack Hoffman was to start two weeks off, a man named William Mistler called to say that when he saw the story about J.B. Smith, he'd become upset that Toole had never been charged with the murder—because he'd seen him take Adam from Sears.

At the time, he said, he didn't realize it was a kidnapping. He thought a family member was putting the child into his black-over-white four-door Cadillac. Adam hadn't resisted. In the west-side parking lot near the garden shop, he took Adam from the sidewalk then drove off.

Mistler said he'd gone to Sears in Hollywood Mall that day to buy camping equipment. Returning to the store later with his wife, he remembered intercom pages for Adam Walsh. That afternoon he took his family on vacation for a few days. Back home, reading that the kidnapper had a blue van, he didn't call police because he never put it together that in fact he'd witnessed the abduction.

Nor did Mistler call police when Toole first made news because he figured he'd been arrested, and therefore police had other witnesses. From then on, until he read the story about J.B. Smith, he never realized Toole hadn't been charged.

Hoffman asked Mistler to call him his first day back from vacation. They next talked on July 29, two days after the publicized tenth anniversary of the murder. Most provocatively, Mistler said he got to Sears that day between 10 and 11—and that Toole's car was a rusty white Cadillac.

As he was driving the lot near the garden shop, Mistler described a woman driver creating gridlock in front of him. That was when Toole pulled up next to him and left his car, his door open.

They locked eyes for a moment. He was shabby, wearing a filthy T-shirt the color of a manila envelope, stained with what looked like spilled coffee. He was about six-foot, 130 pounds, with crossed eyes, uncombed reddish-brown hair and a beard.

He walked a few steps to the curb near a five-year-old boy standing near the store entrance. Mistler couldn't describe what he was wearing. Kneeling down to the child's eye level, they talked. Mistler didn't know whether to be concerned, because a woman and her teenage son were nearby, but then they left.

Mistler described Toole as an "old man... a grandfather-type guy." But in 1981, Toole was 34. Also, in 1983 he was noted as weighing 200, not a bony 130. Newspaper and TV stories had also shown his car, an old white Caddy.

Mistler said he didn't know whether to intervene. "What am I going to say?" 'Where are you going with your grandson?' And if he says no, what am I going to pull out, my Sears credit card and tell him I'm an official Sears customer, I can arrest you?"

Mistler began to cry. "I made the wrong call, I didn't

know. I kept looking for Adam to give me some sort of signal, any kind of a signal, he never..."

He said he watched Toole guide Adam into the front seat of the Cadillac. The back was crammed full of gardening tools. He'd wanted to jot down the license plate number, but he didn't have a pen. He thought he remembered it was a Florida tag.

He then totally forgot about the incident until he returned to Sears about three the same day. At a cash register, his wife saw a woman very upset with a man. His son recognized him: "That's Adam Walsh's dad." He knew Adam from the playground. They'd also heard Adam's name on the store intercom.

The Mistlers left on a camping trip that afternoon. Coming home, following the story in the newspaper, he didn't associate what he'd seen because police were looking for a blue van.

Hoffman asked Mistler if he would consent to be polygraphed. He would. The result was inconclusive, and at Hoffman's further suggestion, Mistler agreed to undergo hypnosis. That session took place on September 20 after a failed first attempt six weeks earlier, stopped because Mistler again had gotten emotionally upset.

Adding to his description of Toole, Mistler said he had a two-week-old beard, weird eyes, greenish teeth, dark pants and brown shoes.

Previously Mistler hadn't been able to describe the child's clothes. Under hypnosis, he said he was wearing a ball cap and white shoes.

Reve had said Adam was wearing a captain's hat and yellow rubber sandals. In his missing photo, he wore a baseball cap.

Nonetheless, based on Mistler's statements, Hoffman and his supervisors decided to re-interview Toole.

Still at the Starke maximum-security prison, Toole immediately denied he killed Adam, and admitted he'd lied to police. He said when he returned to Jacksonville from Virginia in July 1981, he never again left the city.

He'd lied about killing Adam, as well as so many others, because detectives would feed him, give him cigarettes, and take him out to their locations. He knew specifics about murders he hadn't done because Buddy Terry had fed him facts from other agencies' case files before they interviewed him.

Gerard Schaefer had done something similar. He approached Toole about writing a book about his and Lucas's confessions, to include the Walsh case. On the outside he had a woman who knew how to sell it, and if he'd sign over rights, she'd give him money monthly.

Toole said he told Schaefer he didn't kill Adam, but Schaefer told him, Confess to it anyway, it'll sell more books.

One last final time, Hoffman asked, did you murder Adam? No, said Toole, he didn't.

Hoffman wrote: "Based on the interview with Ottis Toole, it is this detective's opinion that Ottis Toole was being truthful and sincere about his noninvolvement in the Adam Walsh homicide."

In local media interviews, John Walsh also dismissed Toole as a suspect. To the *Miami Herald*, for its tenth anniversary story, he said, "My personal feeling is that [Adam's killer] is one of these predatory serial pedophiles, but I don't know. I hope he gets brought to justice one day because they just don't kill one kid and stop."

Asked by *South Florida* magazine in July 1992 who he thought killed Adam, Walsh replied:

In my heart, I think a child serial killer got him. A lot of people still think Ottis Elwood Toole did it. But he and Henry Lee Lucas confessed to a lot of murders they didn't do. It's a great ploy for convicts: They read about a murder and they're in solitary. They call the police, desperate to clear a murder, and they say, 'Fly me there and buy me a pizza,' and they get out of their cells for two days!

In an interview with the *Palm Beach Post* on November 6, 1994, he added, "I figure whoever killed Adam is probably still killing, if he's still out there."

11
Cold Case

IN AUGUST 1994, AFTER 13 YEARS ON THE CASE, police removed Jack Hoffman and reassigned it as a cold case to Det. Mark Smith, with instructions to review the entire file with a fresh eye.

After a full read, Smith came to some conclusions: he dismissed the theories of retribution against John Walsh as well as the Jimmy Campbell "love triangle." Campbell, he wrote, "had neither the opportunity nor the motive to carry out this act."

He didn't dismiss Ottis Toole outright. Even if the killer wasn't Toole, Smith thought, he might be "someone like him."

One of the reasons to review the case was an advance in crime lab technology. In 1983-84, the FDLE's Jacksonville crime lab had determined the presence of blood on the carpet of Toole's car, as well as on a machete. Now DNA could be identified from bodily fluids, and samples could be matched.

In January 1995, Smith ordered retesting of all the physical evidence. First he called John Walsh to see if he'd approve, and he did. The carpet had been cut into seven samples. In the

Hollywood Police evidence room, Smith found the machete and one piece of carpet—but it wasn't bloody. Calling FDLE, an agent involved in the original testing told him he'd returned the bloody samples to Buddy Terry in May 1984.

Smith then called Terry, who in a step toward retirement was now a bailiff at the Duval County Courthouse. He couldn't remember getting the carpet samples back.

On his way to personally deliver the machete to the DNA lab in Greensboro, N.C., Smith stopped at the Jacksonville sheriff's office and got permission to search their evidence room for the carpet samples. With Terry's help, they looked—but didn't find it. Later, Smith found an FDLE document proving they'd returned the samples to the Jacksonville sheriff's office.

In March 1995, the DNA lab reported results on the machete: no detected DNA of human origin. The sample was either too old, or the previous tests had used up all the blood.

Smith tried to find the Cadillac itself. From motor vehicle records he found its last owner, Siree Safwat, who knew that Lucas and Toole had driven it. But Safwat had junked it sometime in the late '80s, in Jacksonville.

At the same time Smith was reviewing the case, Jay Grelen, a reporter from the *Mobile Register,* in Alabama, was also interested. His connection to the story was tenuous. In 1981 he'd copyedited stories about Adam's disappearance for a Baton Rouge newspaper, then worked at the *Denver Post* in 1985 just after they'd published a Pulitzer Prize-winning series of stories exposing the burgeoning missing-children advocacy industry spurred on by John Walsh, who after Adam's death had dedicated himself to lobbying Congress and state legislatures for new laws to deal with child abductions. The Walshes had created one such agency, the Adam Walsh Center, which later merged with the National Center for Missing and Exploited Children, which Walsh had helped to obtain federal funding.

The *Post* stories said the groups had grossly overstated the number of children abducted and murdered, stirring a "national paranoia." They traced it back to Walsh, who they quoted testifying to Congress, "This country is littered with mutilated, decapitated, raped and strangled children." Using statistics that the crusading group Child Find admitted to the newspaper were "pulled out of a hat," Walsh and others had said that 50,000 American children a year were being taken by strangers and that up to half of them were being murdered. The FBI, however, stated that the actual number of child stranger abductions nationwide in 1984 was 67. Although there were huge numbers of police reports of missing children, they overwhelmingly concerned runaways. Non-custodial parents had taken the remainder.

Through their vociferousness, missing-children groups had changed parenting in America. At the reminder of what had happened to Adam and others, they'd scared parents into never letting their young children out of their sight or control in public areas or even playgrounds. Ubiquitous shrill school educational programs similarly frightened children to scream at, run away from, or otherwise reject the approaches of any stranger. In 1991, John Walsh seemed to apologize for the overstatements. He told the *Miami Herald*, "There were so many misconceptions and bad information. We thought there were tons of stranger-abducted kids. And there weren't. I didn't know about troubled runaways and custodial cases. What did I know? I was a broken-hearted father out there battling."

One of the *Denver Post* reporters on the series later told Grelen he'd examined the facts of the Adam Walsh case but never wrote anything. He offered Grelen his old file, and Grelen was able to convince his Mobile editors to let him spend months on the story, although there was no local angle. In May 1995, Grelen wrote that he thought police would be happy, and John Walsh grateful, for a newspaper's extended investigation, and that they would cooperate with him.

"I was wrong on all counts," he wrote. The Walshes

refused to speak to him, despite repeated attempts to contact them. He even went to Washington for a taping of *America's Most Wanted* and still got nowhere. Nor would Hollywood police let him see the case file. A week before his stories were published, the *Register* sued the police in a Broward County court citing Florida's public records law. It read that police had to allow public inspection of all their case reports and work product, exempting only those in active investigation "with a reasonable, good faith anticipation of securing an arrest or prosecution in the foreseeable future."

After 14 years, that did not describe the Adam Walsh case, argued the *Register*. Quickly, the *Sun-Sentinel* and *Palm Beach Post* joined the suit. They suggested that a press examination of the files might stimulate new leads.

Grelen wrote that his pursuit became clear to him the night he researched old newspaper stories on microfilm in the Broward County main library. When a photograph of Adam's eyes met his, "I connected with a person, a real little boy who died an unimaginably horrible death... That night, Adam's eyes seemed to ask for help."

But because he couldn't read what was in the case file, Grelen mostly rewrote what had already been reported. Aside from the newspaper archives, his best source seemed to be the attorneys who had defended Sears and Hollywood Mall, who *had* seen the case file. Much of his writing was critical of the Walshes, including that in 1981, investigating their background to consider possible revenge theories, police had heard rumors which they couldn't confirm.

The attorneys shared with him a police report that the local press had not previously reported. Three days after Adam's disappearance, Michael Monahan, then 20, the son of Walsh's business mentor John Monahan as well as a close friend of Jimmy Campbell, had been charged with aggravated assault on a 19-year-old at a skateboard park about 10 miles north of Hollywood. The victim thought he'd recognized his unique skateboard, recently stolen, in Monahan's possession. They'd tussled over the board, the victim wrested it away, then he ran into the skateboard shop and locked the door behind him. Enraged, Monahan broke down the door with a machete blade, waved it within inches of the victim's head, took back the skateboard and threatened everyone else in the shop.

Hollywood police had made the possible association between Adam and the machete. They gave it to the Broward Medical Examiner. On testing, the connection was inconclusive. After that, police dropped Monahan as a suspect. In the years since, however, Monahan had been convicted in federal court with co-defendants for extortion over a Mafia-style loan. Days before his trial was to begin, in Tampa, the victim had disappeared and was found in a drainage ditch, shot five times in the chest. Murder charges were never brought.

John Monahan similarly refused Grelen's interview requests. He told Grelen, "Neither you nor the police are going to find the killer" of Adam.

But the *Register*'s public records suit forced the police's hand. In June, in court, they argued for keeping the case file closed because they were still actively investigating it. They said Mark Smith, in his six months of review, had identified a new suspect although they didn't name him, and added that John Walsh also opposed disclosing the file. The judge ruled for the police but left open the door for the newspapers to later renew their suit.

Who was the suspect? Hollywood police attorney Joel Cantor said they now believed more than one person was responsible for the murder. One suspect was from very early on, the other had been mentioned in the past but never interviewed. After that interview, he said to reporters outside court, "We can bring [the investigation] to fruition in the near future." He seemed to be referring to Campbell and Michael Monahan. In his 1983 deposition, Campbell had admitted that after leaving the Walsh home, when he'd spent a few nights at the apartment of Michael's brother John Monahan, Jr., Michael had slept there at least one night.

But later in the day Hollywood's own press spokesman contradicted its attorney, apologizing for any "misinterpretation that there are exciting new revelations or breaking news in this homicide investigation." John Walsh told the press something different still, "There is a suspect, [and] the suspect is a stranger."

The new suspect *was* Michael Monahan, said Grelen, interviewed days later by the *Miami Herald*. It was ironic, he thought, that John Walsh had made a television career from publicizing unsolved crimes, but he opposed letting the press see police details from his son's case.

Michael Monahan was then free but on federal probation. When he saw a newspaper story connecting him to a criminal investigation, he called his probation officer, as required. The probation officer called Mark Smith, who scheduled him for an interview the next day. Smith wrote in his report that it was Grelen's theory that Monahan killed Adam as a favor to Jimmy Campbell. For himself, Smith discounted it in the absence of other evidence or more specific motive. A machete swing at someone over a disputed skateboard did not by itself indicate a propensity to murder. Besides, Smith wrote, the machete blade had previously tested negative against Adam's remains. (Grelen had written it tested inconclusively.) Monahan was then a landscaper, which explained his possession of it.

To the *Sun-Sentinel*, John Walsh seemed protective of his friends. He said the police had told him Monahan's upcoming interview was "just routine. They wanted to make it clear that Michael Monahan has never been a suspect nor is he a suspect right now. The focus is still on a stranger. They can't tell me who, or any of the details, because they don't want me or the media to compromise the investigation."

At his interview, Monahan offered Smith little, excusing his poor memory by saying, "You know, I'm not the sharpest tool in the shed." He remembered little about the skateboard incident, and little more about the day Adam disappeared besides that he was driving with his girlfriend in her car when they heard the news on the radio. He said they drove to Hollywood Mall and found one of John Walsh's friends, who suggested they hand out "missing" fliers. Maybe that was the day after it had happened, he rationalized. He said Campbell was his best friend, and doubted that Jimmy had anything to do with the murder.

Two days later, Smith spoke to Monahan's girlfriend at the time, Chris Fehlhaber, now married and named McGuire. She remembered the radio news of the disappearance and helping search, but also wasn't sure if they'd heard it the same day it happened. Although she'd recognized Monahan's violent streak and knew he'd gotten in trouble with the police—she didn't know about the skateboard incident—she didn't think he could ever abduct or hurt a child, much less Adam.

To a *Herald* reporter, John Monahan blew up at Grelen for suggesting Michael may have murdered Adam:

> It's my son, and I don't think he's capable of doing anything like that. He may be the suspect in the mind of this renegade reporter who's in this thing for personal gain.
>
> Let this schmuck try to go out and help capture one hundred of America's Most Wanted. Do you think at this juncture after fourteen years that any further publicity will help in any way? It will only damage. Who has a better capacity to find someone than John Walsh of *America's Most Wanted*?

On June 30, Hollywood Police Chief Richard Witt wrote the *Herald* that Michael Monahan had been ruled out as a suspect. Their recent follow-up interview with him "confirmed that he did not have the opportunity to abduct or murder Adam Walsh. This has been independently supported by other witnesses."

12
The Case File Opens

IN SEPTEMBER 1995, the *Mobile Register*, *Palm Beach Post*, *Sun-Sentinel*, and later the *Miami Herald* re-filed their suit to open the Walsh case file, just three months after Broward Circuit Judge Leroy Moe had ruled they could do so. In response, Hollywood Police attorney Joel Cantor told the judge the department still had "some extremely major issues" remaining to investigate.

In October, Judge Moe this time handed police a deadline: six months. Unless by then prosecutors could bring the case to a grand jury, he'd open the file.

John Walsh told the Associated Press that as long as the police investigation wasn't hampered, he wouldn't oppose the opening of the files.

As the February 16, 1996, deadline approached, Hollywood Police kept in touch with Walsh, but gradually a breach emerged. On January 23, Walsh's attorney told the press "impressive developments" had recently occurred in the case. But a police spokesman responded, "I think the meaning of 'impressive developments' is open to interpretation."

By February 7 the rift was out in the open. To the *Miami Herald*, Chief Richard Witt criticized the original case detectives for becoming too close to the Walshes and their friends. They shouldn't have let them into the detective bureau to hear information or answer tip hotlines. One of those answering phones was Jimmy Campbell. "They were involved in every stage of the investigation. That is just not professional. It creates a distraction. Police officers are supposed to be like scientists. You need to leave your emotion outside the ring of your pursuit. You're supposed to be objective." That didn't mean to say he suspected the Walshes in the murder, he added.

On *CBS This Morning*, John Walsh responded in a blast:

"The chief of police in Hollywood, Florida gave up on the case. This is heartbreaking." Walsh added he strongly believed that Ottis Toole might have killed Adam, but the coming publicity from the release of the files would prevent his prosecution. That contradicted what he'd said in past years about Toole, as well as the release of the files.

Even blunter in his criticism of Witt for not charging Toole was *America's Most Wanted* executive producer Lance Heflin: "It was a great opportunity, and he bungled it. [Witt] may well be the poster boy for shoddy law enforcement."

In a February 11 letter to the *Miami Herald*, Walsh insisted "the Hollywood Police Department has made it unequivocally clear that the murder of our son resulted from a stranger abduction." He also said he'd never profiled Adam's murder on his show because he'd been asked not to.

The stage moved to the Broward state attorney's office, where Walsh hoped for a more sympathetic ear. After Walsh met with Chief Assistant State Attorney Ralph Ray, the office filed a last-minute emergency motion to block the files' release. "In reviewing the file we noticed things that, in our opinion, should still be done," said Ray.

On their editorial pages, the newspaper plaintiffs cried foul against both the state attorney and Walsh. The *Miami Herald* noted that *America's Most Wanted* "tries to solve old cases by shedding new, public light on them." The *Sun-Sentinel* called Walsh's opposition "curious."

The Walshes entered their own motion. In an affidavit, they said Chief Witt told them on January 16 he planned to publicly identify Adam's killer at the time the file was to be released.

Witt denied that claim, however. At that meeting, he said, "They presented things that I thought were nonsensical. I think they're focusing on a statement I made that they took out of context. The new findings presented to the Walshes in January were determined by them to be valueless.

"John Walsh is looking for some kind of unequivocal statement that says neither he nor his wife had any part in the death of their son. I don't know why they want that. But they are emotionally upset by certain members of the media pursuing a poor man's Oliver Stone-style plot."

The *Sun-Sentinel* reported that police had just re-interviewed Ottis Toole. They had, in December 1995. As he had the previous June, Toole again maintained no involvement. Witt confirmed Toole was still a suspect, "but there are other places we are looking." The *Herald* quoted Witt saying there was at least one other person besides Toole "who needs to be closely pursued." He wouldn't name names.

Witt's administrative assistant Paul Dungan told the *Herald*, "This case is like putting a jigsaw puzzle together. Right now, there's a lot of missing pieces. Some of those pieces will never be found. But sometimes, like with a jigsaw puzzle, even with pieces missing you can tell what the picture is."

On February 16, Judge Moe ruled, open the files. In open court, Moe said no one had proved to him that an arrest or grand jury presentation was imminent, or that his action would jeopardize any future arrest or prosecution.

In the courtroom, Reve Walsh asked to speak but the judge denied her. Outside the courtroom, she had no comment for the press. The Walshes made a written statement instead: "We are gravely wounded and bitterly disappointed that a judge in Florida has decided that a newspaper's demand to see the police file in our son's case is more important than finding his killer.

"Now, details previously known only to the police and the killer will be known to all—making it almost impossible to find out who the real murderer is."

By telephone from New Orleans, where he was shooting a segment of *America's Most Wanted*, Walsh told the Associated Press:

"I'm absolutely heartbroken. My concern is we may never, ever get a successful prosecution of this case. I think it's a travesty." He also told the *Sun-Sentinel*, "I've had investigators tell me that this is the most active this case has been in fourteen years and now a chance to prosecute someone has been taken away. Everybody wants to cover their political asses."

Ever harsher was George Terwilliger, the Walshes' attorney: "What you saw in court today was a contest between justice for a six-year-old boy who was brutally murdered and the insatiable appetite of the media for these files. Justice lost. The only thing that releasing the files might reveal is that Hollywood police are the biggest bunch of bungling idiots since the Keystone Kops. The Hollywood Police Department gave up on a notorious homicide investigation because they were running scared from a bunch of newspapers."

Walsh told the *Sun-Sentinel*, "I don't fear anything in those files. I don't care what's in those files as it relates to my family."

POLICE FILES ON ADAM'S DISAPPEARANCE
GIVE SUSPECTS, LEADS, BUT NO CONCLUSION
—*Sun-Sentinel*

ADAM WALSH FILES POINT TO 1 MAN
—*Palm Beach Post*

As reporters started reading the microfilmed file's 6,700 pages, their first problem was perspective. Case details, many previously reported, others not, failed to answer the big picture question: Was the solution to the murder somewhere in the file, overlooked?

If it was, reporters quickly realized, it was well buried.

Looking for mere police errors was easier. From the first day, the top story was the lost bloody carpet samples from Ottis Toole's white Cadillac. It took days for reporters to plow through everything. Front-page and lead-newscast stories of excitement faded to disappointment.

Three months after the release of the case file, Fox TV canceled *America's Most Wanted*, after nine seasons and more than 400 criminals apprehended with the help of their tips. The network claimed ratings had sank; Walsh said they'd risen to its highest in four years. Regardless, the "economics" of the show "weren't working," they told him.

On September 21, as its final segment, they would do the story that had always been on everyone's mind, but they'd never broached—Adam Walsh.

"This was a very difficult thing to do. Nobody wanted to push John to do this," producer Lance Heflin told the *Miami Herald*.

The segment's production and narration would be independent of the show. The reporter was John Turchin, a personal friend of Walsh's who worked for WSVN-TV, the Fox affiliate in Miami.

Turchin told the dramatic story about the abduction, the Walshes' grief, that Adam's head was found two weeks later, then said that Hollywood police had announced Ottis Toole's confession two years later, although it never led to his arrest.

"But is Toole really the killer? Despite a massive investigation, some say the Hollywood police so badly handled the case and the evidence that to this day, we still can't answer that question."

Turchin interviewed Chief Witt: "The city of Hollywood and its police department lacked the experience to conduct an investigation of this magnitude."

It was surprising to see Witt on the show, considering what Heflin had said about him. The month after the file was opened, the city of Hollywood had fired him over a hiring scandal, and he'd since been installed as chief for Golden Beach, a tiny, wealthy nearby Dade County municipality.

Turchin described that Reve took Adam to Sears and left him for a few minutes to play video games. "Minutes later, Reve returns. Adam is nowhere to be found.

"Where did he go, and why wasn't he where his mother left him? The truth is this: a security guard threw him out of the store."

Then Turchin interviewed the security guard, Kathryn Shaffer, who'd never before given a press interview:

> For fifteen years of my life, a day has not gone by that I don't think of Adam... I approached him and said, look, this isn't allowed here, are your parents in the store? And the little black boys told me no. So I pointed to the end of the hall, and I said you need to leave, exit these doors.
>
> Then I asked the two little white boys, who I assumed were together, and I said, are your parents here? And the older boy told me no. And so, I assumed they were together, and I sent them both out.

It was agonizing to see Shaffer consider herself partly responsible for Adam's death. But even more agonizing was Turchin's unambiguous conclusion. He didn't report that in August 1981 she'd told Jack Hoffman she was sure she *hadn't* ejected Adam. In 1995 Mark Smith had re-interviewed her, and although she'd changed her mind she still was only "85%" certain she'd sent out Adam. Turchin also didn't mention that the time of the incident didn't seem to match when Reve said she left Adam at the game.

Next was William Mistler, who'd told police he saw Toole put Adam in his white Cadillac at Sears. *America's Most Wanted* was famous for dramatizing re-creations of crimes, which gave witnesses' versions the feel of fact. Now they showed what Mistler was describing:

> When he gets to the front of his car, his head stops and he locks eyes with me. At that time, I couldn't believe what I was seeing. I can't take my eyes off him, because this is the weirdest-looking guy I've ever seen.
>
> He walked over to the curb, got down like a catcher would, and got eye-to-eye with Adam, and their faces were maybe two-and-a-half feet apart. And then they got to where the open [car] door was, and Adam just stood there, and Ottis took him from behind and just like picked him up where his feet would be on the seat, and then Adam walked across the seat.
>
> And I didn't really think anything wrong with that because I did that with my kid dozens of times, you know.
>
> He wasn't afraid of him, and I was looking for the fear in his eyes. I was looking for crying, but nothing, he was a perfect gentleman. It was just like he was walking with Grandpa, or something.

Turchin explained Mistler's confusion, that police had said that Adam's abductor had used a blue van, not a white Cadillac. "But two years later, when he saw Ottis Toole's picture on the tube, he called the cops."

MISTLER: I jumped up out of bed instantly there, and I ran over to the TV, but before my feet touched the ground, I knew who this guy was.

TURCHIN: It was the guy you saw.

MISTLER: It was the guy in the white Cadillac. He wasn't in a blue van.

TURCHIN: Mistler was later hypnotized, and given a polygraph exam, which he passed.

Turchin then asked Mark Smith, "Do you have any reason to believe that [Mistler] lied to you?"

"No," said Smith.

There were a number of facts that were wrong, however.

First, Mistler did not go to police in 1983, as Turchin reported. He waited until 1991. Second, Mistler's polygraph was inconclusive. Also, when Mistler said, "It was just like he was walking with Grandpa, or something," that differed from what he'd told Hoffman: the man actually looked like a "grandfather-type guy," or, an "old man." In 1981 Toole was 34. Also, Mistler had described a man 70 pounds lighter than Toole's weight. But the most glaring problem Turchin left out from Mistler's narrative was time. He told Hoffman he'd arrived at Sears that day between 10-11 A.M.—up to two hours earlier than when Reve was likely at the lamp counter.

"Detectives say Ottis Toole first became a suspect in October 1983 when he began bragging of the murder of Adam Walsh to cellmates."

That was also wrong. Toole's first mention of the case was to a Brevard County sheriff, and Toole didn't then name Adam.

Introducing the tale of the missing blood evidence, Turchin said around 1983 crime labs had showed there was blood on the Cadillac's carpet. That was true, but Turchin didn't say that the blood was never proven to be human.

"But what's considered by many to be the most crucial evidence in the case was sold to a junkyard. Simply put, police let a 4,200-pound piece of evidence slip through their fingers. How could this happen?"

In fact, after the car had been fully tested in 1983, it was properly returned to its owners. The real problem was the lost carpet. With a lack of physical evidence, Turchin reported, all that remained was Mistler's memory and Toole's confessions—which had to be regarded in the light of his recantations.

However, "there are investigators who believe Ottis Toole is guilty of murdering Adam Walsh, and others who believe he has been involved in so much, his story is a compilation of many crimes."

Turchin left unmentioned that other detectives thought Toole had invented almost everything he'd ever admitted to.

Then Turchin reported the most surprising statement of the entire segment:

"All agree, however, that Ottis Toole is still the prime suspect."

Mark Smith: "I think it's safe to say Ottis is a strong suspect."

In summary, the segment led viewers to believe that police had Toole's confessions to investigators and inmates, and a security guard who'd ejected Adam from Sears to a place where Mistler saw Toole put him in his white Cadillac. But absent the ability to retest the lost blood evidence, the case could not come to court.

Richard Witt: "Cases get solved. Sooner or later, they get solved. Prosecution may be an entirely different matter."

Turchin asked viewers, if they knew any facts at all about the case, to call the show's hotline, 1-800-CRIME-TV.

KATHRYN SHAFFER: My life is changed. I'm now a trauma nurse, which I think stems from remorse or some deep-seated guilt inside of me, saying that I want to help preserve life instead of help destroy life.

TURCHIN: Certainly the case of Adam Walsh is not unique, but if there was ever a face that launched a thousand ships in the battle for children's rights in America, it was the face of Adam Walsh. Ever since they lost their son, John and Reve Walsh have been fighting a war with the only weapon they have—the name, the sweet face, the inspiration, and the brief life of their murdered child, to prevent other parents from joining this very select, very devastated group of survivors.

The segment ended with recently discovered old home movies of Adam playing organized T-ball. He mugged for the camera, wearing the same shirt as in his famous "missing" picture. Across his chest was the name of his team's sponsor:
Campbell Sailing Rentals.

September 24

Ottis Toole is dead, reported WSVN-TV in Miami, John Turchin's station. "This means the murder might never, ever be solved," said anchor Rick Sanchez.

Turchin reported the story: "Now we may never know if Ottis Toole was Adam's killer. It is devastating news for Adam's father."

He taped John Walsh on the phone: "You know, this is just another setback. I mean, this is just another heartbreak. You know what this means for my family, now John? No closure. No closure. I mean, maybe, maybe, if Ottis Toole did it, they could convict Ottis Toole. But the door is slammed on the ability of Ottis Toole to tell someone—non-law enforcement personnel—that he killed Adam."

Turchin asked Mark Smith what effect Toole's death would have on the case. "The easiest thing right now would be for us to fold up the tent and go home. That wouldn't be fair. That wouldn't be fair to the family, and it wouldn't be fair to the criminal justice system.

"(Maybe) somebody has been holding back all these years, maybe for fear of Ottis Toole, or not wanting to put him in the electric chair, whatever. Maybe now that person or persons may come forward. In the negative, we didn't get another shot at him, to speak with him."

Turchin: "But Ottis Toole did speak to John Walsh, through the mail. In 1988, Toole mailed Walsh a letter, demanding $50,000. In return, he would tell Walsh where Adam's remains were buried."

On screen, Turchin showed a letter in Gerard John Schaefer's neat handwriting. Turchin didn't mention Schaefer.

Then, John Walsh deemed the case solved. Ottis Toole murdered his son:

"At least, Adam's killer and a child killer is not on the streets. He's in another place. I truly believe that you're held accountable for your actions. I truly believe that Ottis Toole will get his in the next life."

Turchin said that Toole had died on September 15, of cirrhosis of the liver. After waiting four days for someone to claim his body, the state decided to bury him in a prisoners' cemetery.

Sanchez had one more bit of news: an hour earlier, Fox TV had reinstated *America's Most Wanted* on its schedule.

Next morning, the *Miami Herald* reported that Fox did so after getting "bombarded" with 7,000 letters from fans, law enforcement agencies, and 37 state governors.

Peter Roth, the new president of Fox entertainment, called the public outpouring "enormous." "Never before has a TV program made a such a clear and significant impact on people's lives. Quite simply people have told us that this program made them feel safer."

That evening, WSVN rebroadcast excerpts of a 1984 interview its reporter Patrick Fraser had done with Toole.

"That Adam Walsh case isn't, it ain't true. I didn't do that case." He explained how he knew so many details about Adam's murder, even though he didn't do it:

You can go the whole way through a whole case and tell them you don't know nothing about it, and [you wait five or ten minutes and] you can double-back, and you pick up different little details in it, like beer cans, cigarette packs, trash by the side of the road, or something like that, the way the road is, or something like that. There ain't no way you can miss on it after you're done looking at all the pictures.

They don't pay attention to that, 'cause they just want to clear the case, and they don't care how they clear it, as long as they clear it.

13
First Person

I HADN'T BEEN HERE WHEN THE MURDER HAPPENED. In 1978 and 1979 I was a reporter for the *Hollywood Sun-Tattler*, even sometimes assigned the police beat, but I'd left the area in 1980 and didn't return until late -'83. What siren-songed me to it in 1996 was its open case file. I'd already written three true crime books which had heavily depended on public records for their start, but when I'd gotten to them one case already had been resolved by arrests, another by convictions (both cases had been resolved possibly incorrectly or inadequately, as it turned out), and a third was awaiting trial but records had already been disclosed to defense attorneys in the legal discovery process. A long-unsolved murder with the same investigative detail available was a rare bird indeed. And it was in my backyard.

To begin, I bummed a case file copy from a friend at a local TV station and read it on public library microfilm readers. Then I found and copied every printed news story I could. Digital storage of local newspapers had not yet begun in 1981. I had to hand search in library microfilm the *Miami Herald* up to 1983, the *Sun-Sentinel* to 1986, and everything in the *Sun-Tattler*. I then weaved it all together with the police chronology.

The first detective I spoke to was someone I respected from Metro-Dade Police who I'd dealt with on a past story, who asked for anonymity. He'd met Toole, whom he said was creepy: "He scared even me." He'd listened to both Toole and Lucas confess about two dozen murders they said they'd committed in Dade. Toole's information didn't match any open cases. But although he knew that Lucas's confessions elsewhere had become as discredited as Toole's, one of Lucas's did match one of his cases.

Police in Texas holding Lucas sent him information that Lucas had described killing two girls near the Everglades in 1979 or 1980. He was specific even to how the girls were left tied, and the Indian-type jewelry found on their bodies. When he showed Lucas a photo lineup of 30 women, he selected the two victims. A Dade grand jury indicted him for the crime, but since he was on Texas's Death Row, no one in Florida expected a prosecution.

When Jack Hoffman first arrived in Jacksonville to see Toole, the Metro detective was already there. The two detectives had previously worked together in Dade, and in Jacksonville they went out for beers. Days later, when Hollywood Police announced that Toole had killed Adam, the Metro detective was surprised. He called Hoffman, who was "beside himself." Hoffman told him, "Man, it was all politics. I had no part of that."

By chance, my next step turned up a new development in the cold case. When Mark Smith had reopened the case file he'd gotten help from Phil Mundy, an investigator from the Broward State Attorney's office. I managed an introduction to him, but he didn't say much.

Days later, I got a call from Christina Spudeas, a friend who was a defense attorney and had been a Broward prosecutor. She'd just heard from her former secretary, Doreen, whose dad was Phil Mundy. When he mentioned meeting a writer; she recognized my name. Doreen's married name was different so I'd never made the association. Doreen said her father had taken the investigator's job after he retired as a detective for the Fort Lauderdale police, but instead he'd been working as hard as ever, traveling most of the last two weeks. Combing the file, he'd found a new witness, an older woman who'd lived near the Walshes and knew them to say hello.

She'd been to Sears that day and saw Adam at the video games behind a bunch of children. She also saw a man talking to him. Then she went to the lamp department, saw Reve, and told her she'd just seen Adam.

Hearing later in the day that Adam was missing, she became upset and wanted to tell police, but her husband pooh-poohed it. She never did go.

But two years later when police announced they had Toole, she saw his mug on TV news and recognized him as the man she saw talking to Adam. Then she did tell Hollywood police. She said they took her name and phone number but never called back.

After finding her name and phone number in the file, Mundy was the first law enforcement person to talk to her. He said she described Adam accurately, and said the man had a weird grin. Around the same time the Metro-Dade detective was investigating Toole's other confessions, Phil also had interviewed Toole and remembered his odd smile. Of all the people he'd ever met working homicides, Toole was the only person who'd truly scared him.

Before Toole died, she said, Phil was ready to ask the state attorney to indict Toole for killing Adam. He felt he had absolute proof Toole was in Broward on the day of the abduction, and was 100% convinced he was guilty.

It took a month to arrange a meeting with the grizzled Phil Mundy. He was 57, with wavy-thick blonde hair combed back. Behind gold-framed eyeglasses were the sharp blue eyes of a younger man. He looked like he'd been a boxer, and wasn't afraid of holding his ground. But his days of chasing suspects on foot were clearly past.

He still wouldn't tell me much beyond that the case was coming to the "end of the line" in a few months. That's when he would present his conclusions to Chief Assistant State Attorney Ralph Ray and tell him, "If you disagree, find another detective."

Then he'd ask Ray for permission to talk with me.

But once he laid the ground rules, Mundy jumped the gun a bit. Three weeks earlier Henry Lee Lucas had told the press Toole had showed him Adam's body, so I asked Mundy's opinion. "Lucas is full of shit," he said. Nor did he need to meet with him to know. Lucas doesn't know where the body is, he said, and only wants a trip to Florida, a chance to escape, and a delay in his death penalty.

Five weeks later, Mundy relented and told me, the target is Toole. But they hadn't found the body.

When Toole died, John Walsh had railed about Hollywood's failure to offer him a deathbed confession. Mundy said it didn't happen because the last time Mark Smith interviewed him, a few months before he died, "he wasn't really with the program."

As if Toole had ever been with the program. Toole had played games with the police from day one, Mundy said, so he saw no reason to think he wouldn't also have at the end. "The guy gave different accounts—you can toss a coin to which you believe."

Still, Mundy was furious when he heard Toole had died. Had he stayed alive, he thought he had enough to win a grand jury indictment, although he admitted the case had a chance of losing at trial. "State attorneys love when you bring them an ironclad case—but the reality is you can't do that all the time.

"I think you have to ask yourself, is this case going to get any better in the foreseeable future? Witnesses are going to forget, die."

In the Broward courthouse office of Brian Cavanagh, a homicide prosecutor I'd also written about previously, I saw on the phone a man who had the intense look of a detective. It took him an unusual couple of minutes to introduce us. When he did, he said later my eyes lit up. It was Mark Smith.

Months earlier, in a *Sun-Sentinel* interview, Smith had refused to discuss the case. But in comfortable surroundings, he talked with me freely. Later, outside the courtroom while he was waiting to testify, I compared notes with him and realized we thought alike on a number of observations.

On Monahan, we agreed no physical evidence connected him, and the machete incident was a stretch. On Campbell he said there were still some in the police department who thought he did it. Smith wasn't among them. He thought they should have embraced Campbell rather than accused him.

Ever since I'd heard Phil Mundy had evidence that Toole had been in Broward on the day Adam went missing, I'd been trying to guess what it was. Had he found a parking ticket for Toole's car? Hoffman's reports in 1983-84 showed he'd searched municipal and county ticket records in both Dade and Broward. However, he never wrote that he finished the project.

No, they didn't have a parking ticket, Smith said. Contrary to Mundy's assertion, he led me to believe they had no new ideas where Toole had been those six missing days. In fact, Smith disagreed with Mundy that Toole was guilty—or at least that there was enough evidence to have gone to a grand jury. Instead, Smith concurred with me that Toole's interview transcripts showed that the detectives had prompted all his accurate statements of facts. Also, Smith knew of no other evidence that Toole took or killed children.

Phil Mundy's estimate of two months to conclude his research turned into a year. It still wasn't finished when he told me that John Walsh, with a co-author, had written his own book about the case, and that Ralph Ray had consulted with them. The book, *Tears of Rage*, was announced for release later in the month, September 1997, and I wanted to know what Ray had told them.

On that basis, Ray granted me his time, with Mundy present. Ray had a southern accent—increasingly rare in these parts—and made easy-paced conversation—equally rare, and equally welcome. He was in his 50s, with a receding hairline.

Like Mundy, Ray favored Toole as the prime suspect, but since he didn't think the case was complete, he didn't want to open the new investigative records. He denied offering much new information to Walsh because "it would run the risk of prejudicing what we're doing."

"If we decide that Toole did the crime, we'll still never know—there will never be a jury deliberation because he's dead."

Again I found myself debating. When I suggested that Toole's statements on tape seemed prompted, he answered, "That is one argument—a damaging argument in a criminal trial. Though I'm not saying that's true."

When Ray said they put more credibility in the statements Toole made until the police, in their van, took him from Sears, I mentioned that in Toole's first statement he apparently said Adam was wearing mittens. Ray conceded that detectives around the country had been over-anxious to solve other crimes by letting Toole take credit for them.

Again I asked what evidence they had that Toole was here at the right time. Ray said they had none—"not yet"; what they had was "in the nature of corroboration," that Toole was familiar with Broward County. He would only describe that evidence as "little subtleties that come out; by themselves, they may not mean anything. In the general picture, they do have significance."

"We ask ourselves, Why would a guy coming from Miami stop at Hollywood Boulevard and go to Sears—20 miles north, when he's going home to Jacksonville?

"We have no crystal ball, there's a lot of questions."

He also seemed to criticize the original lead detectives, saying that had things been done "that should have been done, that were not done, our results might be corroboration."

What did he think of William Mistler as a witness?

"I'd like to say, 'That's it.' But we can't."

I asked if they'd been ready to indict Toole when he died. He said no.

"I don't know if we've exhausted everything. But we've done everything we can think of. We may never know for sure."

He was still receptive toward possibilities other than Toole. "I'll tell you what—you never know when a witness comes out of the woodwork."

"Problem is, you've got to make a decision on Ottis Toole first—either include him or exclude him. Anybody else has a built-in defense. That's why we took the tack we took. Either corroborate the things he said, or dispose of them.

"There's more questions than answers, unfortunately."

In the case file there was a document apparently missing. Reve Walsh had been polygraphed at the State Attorney's office in 1981 by an investigator named Carl Lord, but the narrative of her interview were absent. I'd asked Mundy to look, but he'd answered he couldn't find it. Lord was long since retired and living out of state, so Mundy suggested I call him.

Relaxing as soon as I mentioned Mundy's name, Lord volunteered information of which I'd had no clue: the Fort Pierce medical examiner, to whom the severed head was first brought, found evidence of sperm in a cavity in the head. He couldn't remember exactly where, but it wasn't necessarily in the mouth—it possibly might have been in the neck area. That information had never been released, he said.

I was shocked. Apparently Lord thought the opening of the

file closed the case, so it wouldn't be a breach to disclose something like that.

"I still think it was Ottis Toole—or Michael Monahan," he said. In 1981, Monahan had refused to take a polygraph, he said—something else that wasn't in the case file. "We tried to get him in the worst way. He ran away from us.

"He had the opportunity and the inclination." His motive: "Trying to punish John (Walsh) and his father (John Monahan)."

"I knew John Monahan from the Hollywood Beach Hotel [across the beach highway A1A from the Diplomat]. I liked him. He had a lot of trouble with that kid."

What about Reve's varying timeline? "I think she was like foggy. She lost track of time. I don't think she ever knew, legitimately, her times that day."

Lord called Ottis Toole "a very viable suspect. He was a psycho, nutty as a fruitcake. He was really a loony. The two of them, Toole and Lucas, had the IQ of what, a blister?" But Toole was cunning, letting the cops feed him details. "That was his style, a game he was playing: Tell me what I did, and I'll tell you if I did it. That was his fun. I had a feeling he knew what he was doing."

"I think Toole was the model for Hannibal Lecter, in *Silence of the Lambs*. Except Toole wasn't intelligent. Toole looked through you. I don't have to tell you, eye contact is very important in an investigative interview. Guys who are lying to you look down so they think you can't tell.

"Toole had a glazed stare. He was scary. He was a screwball, I don't think he could have been polygraphed."

Carl Lord thought Jack Hoffman would speak to me, so invoking his name I left a message at Hollywood police. Hoffman was now a sergeant on road patrol, but he was willing to talk, and it wasn't hard to hear the hurt in his voice. In his opinion, I asked him, during his interviews had Toole ever volunteered anything original that wasn't prompted? No, he said.

How about off-tape, during pre-interviews? Again no.

When he learned Toole was dying, Hoffman said, he visited him, even before Mark Smith. Still hopeful Toole might finally admit the murder and provide the real facts instead Hoffman got one last denial.

I told him that Ralph Ray and Phil Mundy still considered Toole the prime suspect. Hoffman criticized them for thinking that, even in good conscience. Since 1984, he said, nothing new had been added to the case against him.

That was the moment I tried to drop in what I thought I wasn't supposed to know—that sperm had been found in Adam's head cavity. He stopped me short. "That's the first I ever heard of that," and as lead detective, he said he would have known. I told him my source—Carl Lord. Hoffman said he didn't know how Lord would have known that. He called it false information.

I moved on. He didn't think Mistler was credible. If he was, he agreed, the abduction had to have been around 10 A.M.

He'd long ago eliminated Monahan as a suspect because his time was accounted for. On the other hand, he'd never eliminated Campbell because his time was never accounted for, despite what the *Miami Herald* reporters found.

And as to the impending release of John Walsh's book, he said neither Walsh nor his co-author had ever asked to speak to him.

14
John Walsh's Rage

IN *TEARS OF RAGE,* JOHN WALSH'S ARGUMENT—rant, in some places—was that Toole killed Adam and the Hollywood police blew the case. To make this case, he relied on many of the witnesses and statements that others had dismissed or discounted.

Who was right? Walsh took Toole at his inculpating words, ignoring his many problems. He didn't criticize Buddy Terry for supplying information. Hoffman was incompetent and predisposed not to find Toole guilty. The strongest witnesses for Toole were Mistler and the person Phil Mundy had rediscovered. But even more malignant than all the bumblers at Hollywood P.D. were the South Florida press—for invading his family's grieving space on the night Adam was confirmed dead, for their attitude over the years in trying to dig up dirt on them, and then their *coup de grace,* opening the case file.

During Toole's confession to a Denver area murder, Walsh wrote, "The Colorado detective's mind was completely blown. He knew full well the case that Toole was talking about. And every one of those details was true."

That detective, in Littleton, Colo., may have thought that at the time. Colorado indicted Toole for the murder, which occurred August 3, 1981, seven days after Adam's disappearance. But after Hollywood police discovered a Jacksonville police report dated the afternoon of August 1, 1981, documenting Howell Toole's assault on Ottis, Colorado dropped its charges.

Nor did Walsh think Buddy Terry had done anything wrong.

[Terry] had known Toole for nearly two decades now, and had never once seen him confess to a crime he didn't commit...

Mundy and Mark Smith both looked into the allegation that Buddy Terry had fed information to Toole in hopes of lining up a book deal. It was a serious charge, one that, if true, could shed doubt on the whole investigation.

What they found was that Buddy Terry was a good cop who, back in 1983, had basically been trying to help everyone out. Terry was the one who had led Hoffman and Hickman to Toole's white Cadillac. Terry was the one who had learned about Henry Lee Lucas's incarceration at the time of Adam's murder. It may have been fair to say that Buddy Terry had been a little overzealous. But it was clear that he had been wrongly accused, perhaps out of sheer jealousy on the part of other cops. There was not a shred of evidence to suggest that Buddy Terry had tainted the case.

Later, to me, Terry also denied giving Toole any case information from the Hollywood detectives. In sympathy with his position, it seemed the detectives had done that themselves. I also asked him about book or movie rights. He denied wanting them, nor did he know how that allegation started.

(In 2008, Smith and Mundy's 1996 interview with Terry became a public record. Terry said that at Toole's suggestion they had signed what he described as a handwritten document for book and movie rights. However, he denied he ever had a real book deal. Mundy also interviewed John Nelson, Jacksonville undersheriff in 1983, who said he'd learned from a Dallas detective that Terry had already entered into an agreement with a Texas author to write the book. Nelson said Terry admitted to him his agreement with Toole but said he'd merely been "playing around" with Toole and denied anything improper. Nelson had Terry transferred out of the detective division.)

Walsh also omitted Toole's initial statement of the time of year when he said he'd kidnapped Adam, and particularly that he'd probably said the child was wearing mittens. After Toole guided Hollywood police onto Florida's Turnpike (or had police guided him?), he wrote Toole "suddenly" recognized the area around mile marker 126 as close to where he'd buried Adam. Yet Walsh didn't say that Hollywood police had already shown him a picture of mile marker 130.

Walsh offered a possible solution to the problem:

> It never seemed to occur to the cops that the most maddening part about Toole's confessions—his inconsistencies and fuzzy recall—might actually have a reasonable explanation. Any normal person would certainly remember having committed a homicide. Factor in his heavy drinking and drugging, and it makes sense that he might not be able to remember exactly what he had done with the body of one victim out of the hundred or so killings that he had been a party to.

Of course, corroborating proof was slim on those admitted hundred or so killings that he had been a party to.

Walsh thought Mistler was a valuable witness but didn't

mention his statement that he'd been at Sears in the 10 o'clock hour. Nor did Walsh write that Ralph Ray as well as Jack Hoffman had dismissed Mistler.

Then came the only real news in the book: specifics about Phil Mundy's rediscovered witness. Walsh called her Mary H. She was 76 when either he or his co-author had visited her earlier in the year in Central Florida. However, Walsh wouldn't print her full name, he said to keep her privacy intact from the media's intrusiveness.

She'd called *America's Most Wanted* after it aired its segment about Adam. She said in 1981 she was living in Hollywood, not far from the Walshes, and she knew Adam. On several occasions, another neighborhood little boy had pointed him out to her.

Around noon on the day Adam was lost, she'd gone to Sears to buy a lamp—"I had seen in the paper that they were having a lamp sale," she said. She'd bought one the Saturday before, and was returning to buy another. She still had the lamp in her living room.

Passing the computer games in the toy department, blocking the aisle in fact, she saw three kids playing and a younger child, about six, off to the side. She thought that boy was Adam. Talking to him in a low tone, holding his interest, was a man: "He didn't look like somebody that a little child would be talking to, or who would be working in the store." He was "sunburned, and he looked kind of shady." When he moved, to let her pass, he grinned. "The one thing I noticed was that he had big round freckles across his face. And he had a big gap in his upper front teeth." His hair was "shiny" and "laid real close to his head." When she passed him, on the back of his head she saw a round bald spot. He wasn't tall.

Although she was no longer certain what he wore, she mentioned a red shirt, blue pants with heavy stains from white paint or caulking, and dirty sandals. Even from a few feet away, he smelled terrible—like beer and onions.

217

As Mary H. passed, the child's attention never left the man. The boy was pale, slim, had a thin face, and was neatly dressed in shorts, possibly blue, a long-billed cap that was a little big on him, and rubber beach shoes.

Leaving the toy department, Mary H. entered the lamp department, empty of customers except for a woman who seemed to be waiting for something. She was slim with light straight hair parted down the middle, probably in her 30s. After Mary H. shopped for lamps, finding none she liked, she again passed the toy department but this time everyone was gone, the game turned off.

Later that day, neighbors told her a little boy named Adam Walsh had been lost at Sears. "I said, well, I'm sure I saw him in the store. He was talking to somebody, but I didn't know him."

She said her husband had been away for a few weeks on vacation, so she was home by herself. Because the police seemed to have an idea of who'd taken the child, she figured others must have seen him as well. When her husband got home, they took a car trip to Washington, D.C. Returning via Florida's Turnpike, they spotted a blue van. Conscious of the police alerts, her husband even tried to follow it.

When Adam's head was reported found, she was scared: "I was afraid to go out. I didn't know if the guys who had done it were caught or anything. I knew the guy had seen me, and I didn't know that he didn't live around here somewhere."

She said at the time she wrote notes of what she'd seen— she did that sometimes because occasionally she has difficulty speaking to people. She showed them to her husband and wanted to give them to the police, but he said, "Why don't you leave it alone? The policemen will do their job." The notes are gone now, she said. When she left Hollywood, she threw out all her old notes.

But she said she never forgot the incident, or the man in the store. When she saw his photo on Walsh's show, she said she reacted, "My God, you mean he's still living? And they didn't get him?" Not long after, she wrote Hollywood police a letter, which included an apology. When a policeman [apparently Mundy] interviewed her, she picked out Toole's photo from a lineup.

Walsh wrote: "Mary knew she probably should have come forward sooner. But she didn't know any detectives, and had never met any policemen. She is the kind of person who would never have had any reason to."

Then Walsh added that Mary and her husband had tried to tell her story to police just after Adam's head was found. They went to the Hollywood police station, "but there were so many people over there. So many telling things that were no help. And the police had other jobs to do."

Outside at a bench, she said, people were waiting in line to see an officer who looked annoyed, tired, and disbelieving of everything. Looking down at the floor, away from her interviewer, she said, "I decided not to tell it. I guess I just chickened out."

Walsh wrote that he'd fought to keep the case file closed because he thought it would jeopardize any future prosecution.

> Instead it showed what a disaster the investigation was right from the start. How filled with laziness, stupidity, and arrogance. It showed that there had never been a chance of convicting Adam's killer. Not from day one.
>
> At the beginning, the Hollywood police wanted it to be Jimmy Campbell. If it had been, it would have made for one great headline: *Wife's Lover Killed Adam.* There was just one problem with that theory, though. It wasn't true. And that marked the beginning of a bad situation for all of us.
>
> Once Campbell and the rest of us passed those polygraphs, the cops should have bored down. They

should have said, There's the possibility of a stranger abduction here. Even if they were 100 percent sure that the family was involved, in those critical first days they should have been more willing to focus on other things, too. They should still have run a parallel search.

Two years later, when Toole confessed, instead of regarding him as the most logical suspect, the Hollywood police basically ruled him out.

Then Walsh hypothesized what he thought happened. Home from Newport News, without Lucas, without money, Toole knew he could turn tricks in Miami, where the pay was better. "Aimless, weird, and angry... while he is down there around Lauderdale, somewhere in his sick brain he decides to get himself a new traveling companion. A pet. A little kid."

After he talked to Adam at the video games, he saw him again outside, alone. "And you tell him you have a new video game over at your house around the corner. Why, not even three blocks away..."

Why was Ottis Toole never indicted for my son's murder?

The simple answer is that it was because the Hollywood police never presented it to the state attorney's office for prosecution.

That statement is absolutely not true. They did that Monday after their Friday night press conference in 1983, announcing Toole's confession.

The more complex answer is tougher to figure out. It involves conjecture and speculation, and—ultimately—a judgment.

It's not that the HPD cops were simply lazy or stupid. Maybe they honestly believed that he didn't do it. Maybe they were sick of the case. Maybe, once they heard about James Campbell, they didn't think we were worth the effort. Maybe they thought, Toole's in prison anyway. What's the difference?

If someone doesn't see what is hiding in plain sight right in front of them, there must be a reason for that. Maybe a combination of ego and arrogance. Pride—the worst of the seven deadly sins.

What astounds me is how the truth was always out there, just waiting to be seen. And of how many refused to see it: the cops, the courts, and especially the media. Aren't journalists supposed to be the guardians of truth? They certainly worked hard enough to have the case file opened up. And then, after that whole battle, what did they do with it—except flip through it, looking for dirt?

Walsh listed the detectives who thought Toole was guilty: Buddy Terry, Joe Cummings, Steve Kindrick, Paul Ruiz, Joe Matthews, Mark Smith. Plus Phil Mundy, who told him, "Toole's your man. I'm absolutely convinced of it."

Yes, Mundy thought it was Toole. But Mark Smith had told me he differed. Cummings, Kindrick, and Ruiz were all out-of-town cops only tangentially involved in Adam's case. Matthews had been a polygraph consultant to Hollywood at the very beginning of the case, and uninvolved in Toole's investigation except to later help review the file. He'd since become Walsh's friend. As for Terry, only Walsh seemed to care what he thought these days.

I wanted to know what the detectives and others involved thought of the book. First was Jack Hoffman. We met at the Denny's Restaurant across from where the now-defunct *Sun-Tattler* once stood.

He was in his early 50s, with combed-back thick dark hair with some gray. He was sunburned, well built, and wore

Hollywood police's dark blue uniform, short sleeves, with a radio on his breastbone.

I showed him a copy of *Tears of Rage*, which had just reached some bookstores. I told him Walsh thought Hollywood Police had blown the case against Toole and that he held Hoffman personally responsible.

Hoffman's first response was, it was unfair for Walsh to select his facts in presenting his case.

Although he'd failed to document Toole anywhere between July 25 and July 31, 1981, he did prove he was in Jacksonville those bookend days. The head was found August 11. "Where did Ottis Toole keep this child for two weeks?" he asked sarcastically. Furthermore, when they brought Toole to Hollywood, "he didn't know where the hell he was going." On directions and yes or no questions, he continually contradicted himself. The detectives had to keep asking, "Which is it, Ottis?" Even Henry Lee Lucas had told Hoffman that Toole didn't have the personality to do murderous things by himself.

What really happened was that every time Toole would say his confession was a lie, Terry would say "Let me talk to him alone." Then ten minutes later, Toole would reverse himself again. Still, Toole was never ruled out.

When I pointed out that Mundy believes it was Toole, Hoffman bristled. "That's Mundy's opinion. Ask guys who worked the case—J.B. Smith, Hickman. Is this going to make John Walsh feel better—that he has confirmation about Toole through Mundy in State Attorney's Office? I'm not comfortable with it."

As for Walsh's portrait of his family, he commented, "John Walsh wants to show that he and Reve were like *Ozzie and Harriet* back then. The truth was far from it."

At the time, did John know Reve was having an affair? Maybe not, he said. After Campbell told it to Hoffman, it was his decision, with others, to tell Reve she'd better inform John because they were going to tell him themselves the next day. He said John later thanked him for handling it that way.

The fact was, he said, "This department never had a case of this magnitude before." They made many mistakes—the worst, in his opinion, was giving the family access to the detective bureau.

He agreed that tips were lost, as Walsh wrote. "I didn't know half the tips coming in. There were splits and factions in the force. There were 30 different detectives going in different directions, and not all of them reporting back. There was no case management—with all the different [brass] involved in the case."

That extended even to who should have handled the case—Indian River County. "We had the kidnapping, but usually it's the jurisdiction where the crime scene is that gets the case." But Indian River didn't want it and Hollywood did, thinking "if we solve the case, we'll look great."

As for the decapitation, Hoffman believed that the head was disposed of just before it was found. It was easily identifiable, there was very little decomposition. Besides, he said, had it not been found quickly there were a lot of alligators in the area that might have eaten it.

"We're not any closer today to solving the case than we were 16 years ago. Homicides are solved by physical evidence and eyewitnesses. This case didn't have a crime scene [the canal was a secondary crime scene] or reliable eyewitnesses. How do you solve a homicide like this? Without these things, you don't solve it.

"We did our legwork on Lucas and Toole. John Walsh may not have been happy with our results, but my job is to solve cases, not make people happy."

We discussed a few passages from the book. He said he wasn't familiar with Mary H., but Toole had told police he was only outside Sears—Mary H. said she saw him inside.

About 45 minutes into the conversation, a radio call came.

Leaning his neck toward the receiver mounted off his shoulder, Hoffman took it, excused himself then rushed out.

Later in the day, I reached Mark Smith by telephone and asked him about the book.

Did he know Walsh wrote that Smith thought Toole was guilty? No, he said. Walsh's co-author Susan Schindehette had called him but hadn't asked that. If she had, he would not have said yes. Smith went on to note that he'd talked to Schindehette only after his superiors had okayed it—and he gave her no new information.

When I began telling him what Walsh wrote about Mary H., he stopped me. To my surprise, he said, "It isn't accurate." He wouldn't elaborate.

As to Buddy Terry, he'd talked to him, but didn't think he'd tainted the case. Nor was he a strong force on Toole. "But was Terry in way over his head? Oh, yeah."

I moved on to Hoffman's thinking, that because the head wasn't badly decomposed, it might have been ditched just before it was found. Smith disagreed. He said Broward medical examiner Ronald Wright had thought Adam had been dead at least ten days—"but he gave no opinion how long he was in the water." Among medical examiners, Smith said, there's dispute to whether decomposition slows when the head is detached. "There's no way any doctor can give an opinion, 'No way it was in the water for 14 days.' But if you wanted, you could search for and find a doctor who would say 'No way.'"

What about alligators around that canal? That area is not teeming with gators, he said.

And of the sperm found in Adam's head? "Carl Lord is wrong."

The next day, I talked to Ralph Ray. Since Mary H. was no longer a secret, I wanted Ray or Mundy to discuss her with me. Ray wouldn't, but unlike Walsh and Mundy, he didn't think her statements were that helpful. "Such an identity is certainly suspect"—because it came 16 years later. "That's the problem. It's like Mistler's story—why do you wait 10 years before you come forward? In a trial scenario, witness identifications are attacked every day." He added that specific descriptions so many years later are similarly suspect.

To Hoffman's point that Toole never told police he was ever inside Sears, Ray responded, "We don't know of what version, if any, of Toole's that we believe." At various times he said he'd left the body by the turnpike, burned it in a refrigerator at his mother's home, or took it to the dump. Police had extensively searched sites along the turnpike and in his mother's backyard, and all results had been negative. "I don't think any one thing is conclusively going to make it Toole," he said. Although he thought Toole the prime suspect, "that doesn't mean he's the only suspect."

When I said that Walsh gave differing stories of how he first heard Adam was missing, Ray pointed out that an author Walsh was "not under oath. I don't know if there's a such thing as literary license."

In the meantime, John Walsh continued to make news. On September 15, 1997, he appeared on *Regis & Kathie Lee*. Walsh took the occasion to rail again against the newspapers that petitioned for the opening of the case file:

WALSH: I personally don't think they cared about solving the case, I think they were hoping that now that I was a TV guy—there might be something in there, we all know about tabloids.

Well, the saddest, heartbreaking thing about that for me is that when those files were opened, I lost that battle, so did the DA's office, the judge said first time in the history of this country, an unsolved capital murder file was turned over to the media. Meaning we'll never

225

get justice because what's in the file can never be used if they indict someone.

And we had always believed this guy Ottis Toole had killed Adam, and there was never enough evidence. But when those files were opened, I was heartbroken to find out all the mistakes, all the cover-up, for example, there wasn't DNA testing in 1981, but they had taken a bloody piece of carpet out of Toole's car. Over the years they had lost the carpet. They had lost the car, they had lost the carpet. The FBI said to me, John, because I've caught twelve of their ten most wanted, they said, we'd put you at the head of the list, we'd test that carpet in one day and tell you if Ottis Toole killed Adam. So, I felt like if I couldn't get justice in this country, who could? And I should write about that.

PHILBIN: The man that you suspected finally admitted that he did it, on his deathbed.

WALSH: On his deathbed he finally confessed that he had killed Adam, and he was a serial killer, et cetera, and they never indicted him.

A day later Walsh elaborated on Toole's deathbed confession—which I'd never heard of before *Regis & Kathie Lee*—when he appeared on *Geraldo Live*. Walsh said the medical examiner at the Florida State Prison at Starke said Toole had told it to a nurse and psychiatrist: he'd killed Adam, and it was the only murder he was sorry about.

The next day I called Jack Hoffman to ask what he knew of Toole's deathbed confession. He said he'd never heard of it either, and there was "no reason why the prison would have withheld that information from the police." By saying it's Toole, Walsh is "just trying to get this off his conscience."

"I stand on my professional career that Ottis Toole didn't do it."

Also, Hoffman held to his theory that the head wasn't disposed of the day Adam disappeared. "Nobody believes that head was in the water for two weeks. I've handled lots of decomposed bodies. It's unbelievable what water, heat, and animals do to a body." Land crabs too.

The Broward medical examiner at the time, Dr. Ronald Wright, was now working in the pathology department at the University of Miami School of Medicine. On the issue of how long the head might have been in the canal, he was much less definitive than Hoffman.

On the whole, he thought it *had* been in the water for two weeks, "but it might not have been. It's so variable, with what's in the neighborhood." Still another unknown was how soon the head had been amputated after death.

Then he offered me a biology lesson—the reader is forewarned. The bacteria that speeds decomposition is in the intestines, he said: "You really spoil from the inside out." Newborn babies, which don't have much bacteria, don't decompose much at death, and Wright assumed the same effect happened here. "Assuming that, then this amount of decomposition is perfect for 14 days." Unless, he said, the head was severed more than 12-24 hours after death. Then bacteria would start to migrate.

By now I'd seen the police photos of the head. I was surprised how identifiable it was; everything looked fairly normal, save for some bleaching spots. I'd steeled myself for much worse.

He said crabs, fish and turtles "go after the eyes and mouth. But if the head's face down, then they can't get to it. "Heads alone have a very short float life. They leak. Whole bodies don't. You've got that whole bottom to let air out. They don't stay up as long. I always was surprised it was found. It was one of those really weird things, happenstance. My guess is that it wouldn't float more than a half day, maybe a day at the most. Obviously I don't have a lot of experience with that, just a few stories here and there."

Wright surmised, gas in the head caused it to rise to the surface, but once it leaked out, the head would have sunk back down, forever.

I asked, did the head look consistent with being under water all that time?

Yes, he said. "That's what bodies look like when they've been under the water all that time." The darker part is remaining skin, the bleached part is subcutaneous tissue.

Then could the head have been under water two weeks or so, and taken that long to surface? Was there any data on that?

"Not a lot. We tried some tests—I think we used pig heads—and it just varied all over the place. It was one of the various things we tried."

So Wright couldn't be sure how long the head was down, but "up I can tell you. It would have been very unusual that it would be up for more than a day. When it's up, flies lay their eggs—maggots—on them. No maggots. Therefore, not up very long."

I asked how long it took flies to do that to a body. "It depends a lot on the availability of pregnant females." The shortest he'd ever seen was a half hour post-death—that was near a manure spreader. In other areas with open dumping, he'd seen it within an hour. "Once they lay 'em, they'll go ahead and hatch. They'll even hatch underwater—they're anaerobic.

"It depends on the general availability of flies, and the general rule should be, yeah, there should be quite a few (it was summer in the swamp.) So therefore, it wasn't up very long."

In a canal, he thought a severed head would drop to the bottom immediately, and that's what happened with the pig heads. As he recalled, they surfaced 7-14 days later. But on the whole, the pig head experiment failed—a lot of stuff you try doesn't work, he said. "There's so much variability. I couldn't believe how variable these canals were." Factors that couldn't be measured included how much rain had recently fallen on the spot, and how much manure had been dumped in the waterways. Back then the canal was pastureland.

"It was always hard to believe that we got that head."

Wright said he'd heard of Afro-Cuban Santeria religious rituals where heads are severed. However, he never thought that had anything to do with this murder. "I always thought it was a sexual thing."

I asked him the sperm in the head question. He said flatly there was no evidence of it. "If it had been there, it wouldn't be"—meaning the submergence of the head would have washed it out.

I asked, had Toole left the body by the turnpike where he said he did, might an animal have eaten it and left no trace?

"We're a little short on the animals that would do that. Raccoons will eat dead bodies, but not very much—and not bones. Bears will, but we don't have them anymore. Panthers won't. Alligators, they won't eat it on land. Wild dogs, not really.

"If I were to guess, the rest of the body is probably in those canals," he said. Canal water there didn't have much movement, only from wind, and since the head hadn't floated long enough to get maggots, it likely didn't float more than a few feet before it was found.

How do you search a canal? I asked.

"That's the problem." Canals are so silty, he said, that only on clear days can you even see your fingers in front of your dive mask. And on the bottom is "gooey stuff." Every time he passes the site, on the turnpike, he thinks about it.

On the positive side, he said, bones stay intact a long time. Bones are still occasionally found from the 1928 Palm Beach hurricane that overflowed Lake Okeechobee. On the negative side, no machine can detect them.

(According to a document released into public record in 2008, in February 1997 Phil Mundy had 14 detectives from the

Broward Sheriff's Office dive team search a large area of the canal around where the head was found. Although the water had no visibility, the team searched in a grid with hand tools and rakes and found bones. However, the Broward Medical Examiner as well as a second opinion said they weren't human.)

I wondered out loud, could Toole, a noted blockhead, have had enough sophistication, even accidentally, to dispose of a body without it ever being found?

"That was always what bothered me about Toole. Toole was a quart low. He was never high on my hit parade." Yet, he thought, even if the body was ever found, it wouldn't be of much investigative use. "This is one case to be solved, if at all, by confession."

Two weeks later, Phil Mundy said Ralph Ray finally decided to let him discuss with me some of his investigative details.

First I asked him about the deathbed confession, as reported by Walsh. He said, after Toole died, Mark Smith went to the prison and wrote a report. "I don't think Toole, in my estimation, made what I would call a dying declaration.

"If John Walsh wants to believe he made a deathbed declaration, fine. And I can't blame the guy for wanting to think that."

Mundy didn't like William Mistler because in his interview he kept changing his story. "I wouldn't take this guy to the bank," he said. The case's star witness, he thought, was Mary H. As she was depicting the man she saw, "I thought, my God, she's describing Ottis. Not so much his physical stature but his mannerisms. Having sat and chatted with Ottis Toole myself, trust me, the man made an impression on me."

When she said that Toole had turned and smiled at her weirdly, Mundy thought he recognized something similar Ottis had done to him. Phil dramatized it: opening his mouth and tilting his head high to the right, almost 45 degrees, he gave a knowing wink. For him, Toole then brightened into a full smile and said, "Nothin' says you can't fuck 'em when they're dead."

"If you hadn't met Ottis, you wouldn't pick up on shit like that. You can't make that up, you can't."

She also described Adam wearing flip-flop sandals. "When I heard that, I went, *Excuse me?*" For emphasis, Phil flipped his coffee mug in the air by its handle. For an instant I thought it was full. "When I heard that, thinking Toole was still alive, I thought, your ass is mine. He's going to be indicted. You're going to be a witness at a grand jury." Later, Mundy created a photo lineup, for which he had to go through 2,000 pictures to find six men who looked anything like Ottis Toole. She picked him out.

"Bastard! I wish he would have lived longer! I think we were getting very close to a grand jury presentation." Then he added, "If Mary H. is a fraud or a liar, it would be one of the major disappointments of my career."

Two days later, I found myself arguing with Mundy. Mary H. had already seen Toole's picture before his lineup, and probably some video of him, at which time she learned his mannerisms. She'd also told Phil that Adam was wearing a red baseball cap. Phil admitted she likely remembered that from his missing photo. In her next interview, for John Walsh's book, she'd revised her description to a different kind of cap. And as Ralph Ray had said, because she'd waited 15 years to come forward she'd be vulnerable to a tough cross-examination. Although Mary H. told Mundy she'd gone to the police station weeks after the incident, she left before speaking to an officer. In sum, she wasn't bankable either.

Reluctantly Mundy conceded the issue. And without a bulletproof Mary H., Toole was no slam-dunk at trial. He tried to extract a weak compromise. "I don't think you can completely slam the door on this guy. You've got to leave a crack."

15
Tracking Down a Fledgling Serial Killer

AFTER LATE 1997, I SHELVED MY FILE since there wasn't much left to do. In the summer of 2002, in the true crime section of a used bookstore, I found a 1997 book by former FBI serial-killer profiler Robert Ressler titled *I Have Lived in the Monster* that included a transcript of an interview he'd conducted with Jeffrey Dahmer in January 1992. In it, Dahmer was talking about finding his last Milwaukee murder victim and had made light of a coincidence, that Konerak Sinthasomphone was the younger brother of Somsack Sinthasomphone, who he'd been arrested for sexually assaulting three years earlier:

"He was the brother of the one that [I'd photographed]. I was just walking in the mall, ran into him, didn't know him from Adam—how many are the chances of that happening? Astronomical."

When I read this, I stared at it. Was this a slip of the tongue by a serial killer who severed heads, who'd admitted being in Miami when the Walsh child was reported lost?

In 1991, Hollywood police seemed to have decided that Dahmer's movements here would be too difficult to trace, 10 years after the fact. Despite the handicap of another 11 years since then, I decided on the spot in the bookstore to do the legwork Hollywood hadn't done and learn everything I could about Jeffrey Dahmer in the literature—and especially his time in Miami.

My clues were the same as they were in 1991: Sunshine Subs, the Bimini Bay motel, and Ken Houleb. None were in the Miami phone book.

I did have one advantage by this point in time—the Internet. In Florida, county governments and the state had built websites allowing online searches of official records. With the advice of my friend Jean Mignolet, a Fort Lauderdale private investigator, I began.

Online, for criminal records, Dade County (now Miami-Dade County) posts docket sheets. For civil records it posts book and page numbers. To see more takes a trip downtown.

First, I searched Dahmer's name and anyone named Houleb—and found nothing. However, there were hits on Sunshine Subs and the Bimini Bay motel. I concentrated on the sub shop, the managers of which I thought would be more likely to remember Dahmer than anyone at a motel. Besides, in Hollywood's cursory investigation in 1991, someone had told them the motel manager had since died. They apparently hadn't located anyone from the sub shop.

Sunshine Subs had three references, from 1979 to 1983. In a small claims action, as a defendant, appeared the name Darlene Traux. Searching for her, I found no further hits. I tried Broward County records online and also found nothing. I checked the current Miami phone book—nada.

A trip downtown was beckoning. But first, since Dahmer said he'd collected state unemployment in Miami, and those records are not online, I called Tallahassee and eventually spoke to a supervisor in Unemployment Compensation's archives. Dahmer's records would be public, except they'd since purged all paper records dating back that far.

Possibly it was on their computer; a customer service operator offered to check under Dahmer's name and Social Security number (which I had from the Walsh file), but nothing came up. Still hoping, I mailed the agency a public records request. That produced no results either.

Downtown in Miami, I stopped first at the county main library's Florida room. They had the 1981 Miami phone book on microfiche. It listed "Sunshine Sub—pizza," at 17040 Collins Avenue.

I hadn't lived far away, so I knew the area. Everyone called it North Miami Beach, although the real city by that name is on the mainland. Now it is part of the city of Sunny Isles Beach. There was also a listing for the Bimini Bay motel, at 17480 Collins. Dahmer had said it was close to work. Also, an American Savings branch was located at 17066 Collins. Dahmer had told Hoffman he'd banked "right next to the sub shop."

So now I was convinced that Dahmer truly had been here.

From the library, the Dade County recorder's office was around the corner. To my dismay, I learned that in order to save on warehousing costs, in 1993 the county destroyed most all its court files older than five years. All that was left was whatever had been microfilmed.

Searching those microfilm reels of books and pages, I found that Traux was a misspelling—Sunshine Sub's principals were Darlene and Cecil L. Truax. On the computer, I searched those names—and found nothing more.

With a clerk's assistance, I tried to find land ownership records of 17040 Collins, Sunshine Sub's address. We uncovered nothing, but she showed me another database, then inaccessible online, for Miami-Dade County marriage licenses. On a lark I entered Cecil Truax and got a hit: a book and page for his 1980 marriage to Darlene C. Sortini. Since it was nearly closing time, I raced to another county building, where on a high floor newlyweds-to-be patiently sat for their bakery ticket number to be called, to buy a marriage license. Conspicuously out of place as well as out of breath, I ordered a photocopy from microfilm of the Truax's license. One dollar later, the license gave me dates of birth, both in 1945. Both had been divorced. Cecil Truax was born in New Jersey, Darlene in Massachusetts, and her maiden name was Famolare.

Back to the library's Florida room, which had a multi-diskette copy of the U.S. Social Security Death Index, 1999 edition. Bad news: Cecil Truax had died in November 1983, his death benefit sent to a Miami zip code. There was no listing for Darlene Truax.

Famolare sounded like a unique name, so still checking the death index, I found a number of elderly Famolares, all born and deceased in Massachusetts—Darlene's home state. I guessed, maybe everyone with that name was kin.

In 1992, at local public libraries, I could electronically search *Miami Herald* back only to 1988. They'd since added the years back to mid-1982, so I asked its database for "Cecil Truax." I got a one-line death listing on November 28, 1983. Realizing that the *Herald*'s database didn't include paid death listings, I manually searched the library's *Herald* microfilm and found one, published the next day. Survivors listed were Darlene, his five children and two sisters. It listed his employer, plus the fact that he'd died in Dallas on November 27. His nickname was Tex.

That left Darlene as my last tenuous link. But 19 years had passed, and certainly she might have remarried and changed her surname.

I had her date of birth, though. How many Darlenes could have been born on that specific date? I asked my friend Jean, could she run a check?

Eight, she soon replied, but none were apparently living in Florida. One was Darlene C. Hill, in Johnstown, Ohio—and my Darlene had been Darlene C. Sortini.

Checking online phone books, I found no listing in Ohio

for that name. A dead end.

I was down to one last shot. Asking for "Famolare" in Massachusetts, I found about two dozen listings. There were none in New York, New Jersey, and Connecticut, nearby states with large Italian communities.

I tried the listing in Boston for Charles Famolare, Jr., because there was a listing of the same name in Pompano Beach, Florida. That line was temporarily disconnected, which suggested he was a snowbird—it was summer. When I reached him, I introduced myself. "I'm looking for a woman I'm hoping is a relation of yours. She was born in Massachusetts and her maiden name was Darlene Famolare."

Charles Famolare couldn't have been nicer. "That's my cousin Darlene," he said. "She was just here a few weeks ago." The Florida house belonged to Sonny, his retired dad. He got him on the phone, too.

I explained why I was looking for her—twenty years earlier, ten years before anyone knew who he was, at her sub shop in Florida she might have hired Jeffrey Dahmer.

"Dah-mah!" exclaimed Sonny, in an unmistakable Yankee accent. I thought maybe this was a family joke, that in 1991 Darlene would have recognized Dahmer as a former employee. But the Famolare cousins had never heard this.

Without hesitation they gave me Darlene's phone number—she *was* Darlene Hill—but in Indiana. I called immediately—at that moment I envisioned her cousins thinking, what did we just do? then calling her themselves. I got her voice mail but didn't leave a message.

I reached her that afternoon. By then her cousins had called, and she was dying of curiosity. She was warm and helpful and wanted to know how I found her. Had I called several weeks earlier, she said, she was at the funeral for her cousin Ricky Famolare, a sergeant of detectives for Boston P.D. Their last conversation was about the Boston Strangler, one of Ricky's pet interests. In the old neighborhood, growing up, their friend's Uncle Albert was Albert DiSalvo.

Darlene said she didn't remember hiring Dahmer, but she had an excellent memory for names and faces, and wanted to see his photo before saying for sure she'd never known him. On MSN's search engine, I found a black and white mug shot from his August 1982 misdemeanor arrest at the Wisconsin State Fair—the same one the *Miami Herald* ran that Willis Morgan saw. His hair was similar in length to what it was in the 1991 photo.

Darlene still didn't recognize him, though. She said Sunshine was a small operation, and its employees basically consisted of her, Tex, and her teenage daughter Denise Sortini. But she remembered the Walsh case very well, and as we talked further, Darlene would become my gateway into the past. As it turned out the Dahmer story hinged less on Sunshine Sub and more on its sister store in a strip mall ten blocks north on Collins.

At the beginning, the tie-in was complicated. In June 1979, living on the beach, Darlene was diagnosed with a rare, fast-growing, life-threatening cancer. It came as a complete surprise. Her doctor wanted her to enter the hospital that afternoon, saying she had maybe two weeks to live. She refused; first she had to order her affairs.

Foremost were her two teenage daughters. Darlene was divorced, and their father was mostly uninvolved with them, so legal guardianship would have gone to her mother. That did not suit her, she preferred her sister.

From this extraordinary circumstance came an extraordinary solution. A tenant at Salem House, the apartment building she managed, offered a suggestion: he knew a gay Canadian who needed U.S. citizenship to stay in the country. On the shortest of notice he would marry her, and upon her death, he would assign guardianship of the girls as she wished.

(For this story I'm calling him Larry and his establishment Beach Pizza. Neither are their real names, although the business was a pizza restaurant. I've changed both names in all references to come, including in quotations. Everything else about them is accurate as I found and heard it.)

He was two years younger than Darlene, and she agreed to meet him. Months earlier he'd arrived from Montreal to manage Beach Pizza.

As Darlene would gather, there was a lurid reason for Larry's presence in Miami at Beach Pizza. On November 16, 1978, the original owner of Beach Pizza had been killed in his town house by three semi-automatic gunshots fired into his back and neck at near point-blank range. In his hand he'd been holding a pen. Two witnesses, the victim's wife and his school friend of 20 years, told North Miami Police they'd found him dead. Two days earlier, the victim and his wife had reported a home burglary in which they said a gun and $3,000 of cash and jewelry was stolen. Marks on the front doorframe around the deadbolt looked like they'd been left by burglary tools.

The friend, Jean-Guy St. Amand, told police he was an officer in the Montreal police department. At the victim's encouragement, he'd bought a share of Beach Pizza. He'd arrived from Quebec only a week earlier.

But in a late-night interview, conducted by Metro-Dade Police, the victim's wife said her husband had made impossible sexual demands on her. He'd even wanted her to have sex with her eight-year-old daughter, from a previous marriage. She was glad he was dead—and said St. Amand had killed him, to protect her.

At dawn, police awoke St. Amand at his beach apartment and brought him in for more questioning. He said the victim's wife had told him her husband had threatened to kill her and the child if they didn't have sex together while the husband watched. She said her husband had taken nude photos; at the murder scene, police had found a nude photo of the girl, plus a leather suitcase full of sex toys. St. Amand said the victim had threatened to kill him as well, and yes, he had killed him and arranged the scene to look like a break-and-enter. In May 1979, St. Amand accepted a plea bargain to manslaughter and was sentenced to eight years in Florida state prison. While awaiting sentencing, St. Amand offered Larry a partnership in Beach Pizza if he'd come to Miami and run it. At the time of the killing, Larry had been St. Amand's supervisor at Montreal Police.

Darlene married Larry on a Saturday, ten days after her introduction to him. On Sunday she entered the hospital. "I never, never expected to walk out of that hospital. Never, never, never. I'd said goodbye to my children." But she proved her doctors wrong. Three weeks and two major surgeries later, she did leave, although they told her she had only another month. They were wrong about that, too.

Given a proverbial second chance at life, Darlene and Larry struck up a friendship. Larry was kind and generous to her as well as to her daughters, Denise and Robin. He helped pay for her hospitalization and set her up in a restaurant she called Sunshine, a lunch place serving salad and homemade soup, a sort of ladies' tearoom, she said. Although Darlene married Tex late in 1980, she stayed friends with Larry. By March 1981, she and Tex decided to sell Sunshine to Larry, and he remade the shop into Sunshine Sub. But when she and Tex would return home to Miami after driving a semi-trailer they bought, they kept tabs on Beach Pizza.

When their mother went on the road, Denise and Robin went separate places to live. Since Denise had worked at Sunshine, in April 1981 she went to work for Larry at Beach Pizza. Larry even had her stay at his condo, two blocks behind the store. "If Dahmer was on that beach, my girls would know it," Darlene volunteered. They knew every teenage boy within a radius, she said. She emailed them both the mug shot, but neither recognized it.

I expected somebody to recognize the name Houleb, but

none of them did. Denise did remember a Ken, a mature man who worked at Beach Pizza. As she recalled, he made deliveries.

Pizza delivery. That required a vehicle. To Jack Hoffman, Dahmer's lack of one was his main alibi why he couldn't have come from North Miami Beach to Hollywood Mall for a kidnapping. But Beach Pizza made deliveries. And Sunshine Sub sold pizza too, I knew from the old phone book. Might they have delivered as well? Might Dahmer have made deliveries in a vehicle perhaps owned by Sunshine Sub or Beach Pizza, both owned by Larry?

In his interview, Dahmer hadn't mentioned pizza. Had Hoffman dug in the Miami library's phone books, might he have made the connection?

I asked Darlene to ask Denise, Could she remember whether Beach Pizza or Sunshine Sub had delivery vehicles? The answer returned, three. One was a Ford Escort, the other two were vans: a white one and a blue one.

A blue van, at the sister store where Jeffrey Dahmer worked, 15 minutes away from Hollywood Mall?

Darlene remembered it too. She'd used it when she moved, five times between summer of 1979, after she left the hospital, and the end of March 1981, when she began her trucking career and put her things in storage.

How easy was it, I asked, for drivers or just employees to take those vans?

"Easy," she said. "Anybody could grab a key to those vehicles. Larry ran such a mess."

I wanted to know more about Larry and his shops. Unlike Sunshine, Darlene said, Beach Pizza was a gold mine. For a time, it opened at six A.M. and closed at five A.M., and later it never closed at all. At different times of the day and night, it was a hangout for teenagers, college students, tourists, and after-hours people. A big part of the business was delivering to the nearby tourist hotels on Collins Avenue. They'd deliver well into the middle of the night.

Employees were forever coming and going. "He would hire racier people than I would have—people a little off-color. Gay people," she said. "But if someone worked for Larry and didn't have a place, he slept on the couch in his condo." That came "out of the goodness of his heart."

By his own admission, Dahmer had been homeless, sleeping on the beach before he got work at Sunshine Sub. Was this a match? Did Larry, a gay man who brought drifters into his home, meet Dahmer, a gay young drifter?

Might Dahmer have even made a reference to Larry? He'd described to Hoffman, "I remember sitting after work one night right on Collins Avenue, and there was this guy from Canada, and he tried to pick me up—which is a switch..." Dahmer had denied going off with this man. And Canadians did tend to congregate around Collins Avenue in North Miami Beach. Still, the possibility begged further research.

Larry had a side he didn't want Darlene to see. "Larry went places very late at night—I have no idea where he was. He never slept—or for two hours. I don't know what he did, or where he did it, but he did it in good taste." Or so she had thought.

"Everything Larry did wasn't done openly," Denise told me about the drifters. "I realize now who they were—at 16, I didn't realize then."

Like her mother, Denise hadn't seen Larry's actions as nefarious, but questions were gathering in her mind. "Larry was a generous person. He was helping down-and-out people—that's what I'd like to think."

At the time, Denise also didn't realize Larry was gay. She'd never seen him show any affectations, nor even physical contact toward anyone, male or female. She'd always felt safe with him.

The strays were always male and between 18-25 years old, she recalled. (In 1981, Dahmer was 21, Larry was 36.) The area was a magnet for runaways from all over the U.S. and Canada—like the more famous strip on Fort Lauderdale beach and the southern tip of Miami Beach. Everywhere was open all night, she said, and drifters were part of that life. When they needed work, Beach Pizza was a natural place to come. Considering his constant employee turnover, Larry always needed help, and "at the end of the night, if they didn't have a place to go, he'd bring them home."

That summer, Denise worked until four A.M. on weekdays, five A.M. on weekends, many weeks without a day off. She'd come home to Larry's condo, where she slept in the second bedroom, then wake up and discover someone she'd never seen before asleep in the living room or alone in Larry's bed. She knew the drifter—employee—must have come in with Larry, but she never saw him touch any of them. "And I lived in the apartment."

Although some drifters were alcoholics or drug addicts, Denise said she'd never seen any of them cause trouble, drink or do drugs—and Larry didn't drink or do drugs, either. "There were lots of drifters, and they stayed various amounts of time—a week, a couple days, a month, longer. It depended on the amount of trouble they were in, if they were on the run."

Generally, she said, she didn't pay attention to them, or for that matter, most of the employees. "The amount of people through both stores—unbelievable. Most were addicted to drugs, drank, or were just here to party. They got money, then left."

I asked about deliveries. If Dahmer worked at Sunshine, even though he said he only worked inside the store, did that mean he didn't make deliveries? "Employees weren't limited to a single job. You did whatever you had to do," she said. That included deliveries—for either store. On holidays, or when the hotels were full and a flood of orders came in, whoever could drive, did.

"I knew some people didn't have licenses, or had suspended

licenses, or Canadian licenses. It wasn't a concern to Larry."

Regarding the blue van, she said the white and the blue were the same model, although the blue came first. They were spartan inside, just the two front bucket seats, and the rears were empty. The white was for fetching supplies for both stores. The blue was "Larry's vehicle, for whoever needed it. Or if somebody wanted it for the night, whoever wanted it took it."

Did that include the drifters? "Yes, they had it too. A lot of times the drifters would just take a van and disappear for a day. I remember that van being taken and Larry not doing anything."

She couldn't remember the make and model of the vans, but they looked new, or maybe they were leased. The blue was a medium blue. It had automatic transmission, AM-FM radio, AC, windows on the rear doors but not on the sides, and blue seats. "They were never kept clean, there was no maintenance. They ran until they became a problem."

Darlene argued slightly with Denise's description. The color was grayish-blue, or a darker blue, depending on the light. "And you're talking to a former art student," she said. One of the vans had only a driver's seat, the other had only one seat additional. (Denise later agreed on one seat.) They were both extended vans, oversize. She doubted they were leased because then Larry would have needed to take care of them; otherwise, the leasing agency would have billed him penalties. "You have never in your life seen vehicles like these," she said. "You'd need a tetanus shot to look at them. I told him, do you realize you're delivering food? Do you know how unsanitary this is? This was a pigsty."

Next I wanted to find Larry. Over the years since leaving South Florida, Darlene and her kids had lost touch with him. I checked the Miami phone book, and he wasn't listed. Neither was his pizza restaurant (that is, its real name I am not using here). When I journeyed downtown again to read microfilmed county records for hints of where I could find him, I saw he'd recently sold his condo. A Fort Lauderdale attorney had handled the contract.

I obviously wasn't afraid of making cold calls, but since I'd have to leave a message with the attorney, I sensed this one might not be returned. I had enough trust in Darlene to ask to her to make the call, guessing that she'd definitely get a callback. She agreed. Three months before I'd first called her, Darlene's husband Glenn Hill had died of illness. When she called Larry's attorney she left a message there'd been a death in the family. Twenty minutes later, Larry called back, terrified.

They talked for a while, catching up. Larry had lost the restaurant and his condo, and was working in a church administration in Miami. To Darlene he sounded down-and-out.

Then Darlene explained why she was calling: a journalist was pursuing the idea that Jeffrey Dahmer killed Adam Walsh, and Dahmer at the time was working for Larry at Sunshine.

Darlene described Dahmer as an alcoholic living on the beach. Did Larry remember him? No, he said, but that was a long time ago. He'd had a lot of employees who fit that description.

Then he asked a question that struck her as odd: "Is he dead?" At that moment, Darlene said later, she got nausea.

When she raised the name Dahmer, she told me, Larry's voice quavered and his demeanor changed. Although he didn't seem scared, "Larry clearly remembered Dahmer." She hadn't posed the inquiry as a question. "I told him, not asked him, that Dahmer was at Sunshine, looking for a confirmation. That's when he asked me if he was dead."

He remembered the blue van—"that old van, with the carpet falling out, one seat in front." He couldn't remember the make and model, he said, but it had been stolen from him, and he'd personally reported the theft to county police—referring to Metro-Dade Police. It was returned with its ignition torn out. Unable to use it, he sold it.

I'd given Darlene a list of questions to cover. Larry solved the Ken Houleb problem—his name was Ken Haupert, and two of them, father and son, both had worked for him. The father, about 20 years older than Larry, had worked at Beach Pizza then Larry had him run Sunshine Sub. He'd divorced his wife and married an English girl who worked there—Maria, then later he said Susie. Then the two left town together.

Ken might have hired Dahmer, he said.

Darlene remembered: Ken Haupert had been a vice president for franchising at Nathan's, the Coney Island hot dog chain, but he'd quit or lost his job and went to work for Larry—a big step down.

After she left Sunshine, Larry installed a gas line and oven for hot subs and pizza. Larry had said the store had made deliveries.

Houleb instead of Haupert—was that Dahmer forgetting? Or inventing a deniably close name that Hoffman wouldn't be able to track, given no other clues?

After the phone call ended, Darlene was dissatisfied. "I've talked to Larry a million times. He remembers. He's never not remembered—until now. All of the sudden, names changing, memory diminishing."

Larry offered to look at the mug shot, but he emailed her back, saying he didn't recognize it. On a second call, he was more reticent, she said. As she pushed for answers, he complained, "You've changed. You never used to ask a lot of questions." That was true, she told me. Many things about Larry and his business she either hadn't wanted to know, or at least hadn't tried to find out.

"Whatever he's hiding from, I don't think he'll stick his neck out," she told me. Yet after that, Larry stopped taking her calls entirely. Denise and Robin tried him too, with no success.

I tried myself. I called his cell, but after telling him who I was, he quickly said he was busy and would call back. He never did. My later calls went unanswered.

16
The Blue Van

COULD I FIND ANYONE WHO RECALLED DAHMER and would admit it? And could I find, or at least document, the blue van? Could it still exist? If it did, might it still contain evidence from 20 years before?

A friend, Bob Foley, is a retired head of the crime-scene unit at the Broward Sheriff's Office. He had since become the head of the criminal investigation bureau of the Barnstable County Sheriff, on Cape Cod, Massachusetts. I called to ask him.

I knew about luminol. When it's sprayed onto surfaces, infrared light can detect a bloodstain, even if the blood is old or attempts were made to clean it. Spatter or pooling patterns indicate violence.

To find that in the van would be interesting, but DNA from the blood could be definitive. I asked Foley, can DNA be lifted from luminol-discovered blood? Yes, he said, and luminol can find 20-year-old blood on surfaces. He'd seen it detect 40-year-old blood.

Luminol works especially well in vehicles, he said, because

conventional cleaning can't completely remove blood. On fabric, like a seat cover or carpet, blood seeps even into stitched seams. Imagine spilling ink, he said. "You can't ever get it all cleaned." On an exposed steel floor or wall, as in a van, blood would fill scratches and slight cracks. Swabs could remove samples even that small, and DNA could be detected.

I told Foley my progress, and he was intrigued. On reflection, he thought the cops and the FBI were "stupid" to not pursue Dahmer further. He made an offer: if I could find the van, and Hollywood Police didn't care to check it, he would do it himself.

To obtain the blue van's vehicle identification number (VIN), I called a county vehicle registration office, which looked up vehicles registered to Larry. With the VIN, my plan was to enter it at Carfax.com to find later owners. There is no registry for junked cars.

The answer that came back was doubly discouraging. First, Florida state vehicle records on computer went back only 12 years; before that, the information is spotty. Second, a block on his file had been placed, stopping public disclosure of his records. The clerk, who suddenly turned accusing, thought maybe it was because Larry was a law enforcement officer. Which through the Seventies he had been in Canada.

Dade and Broward phone books had no listings for Ken Haupert. In online county official records, in Broward I found two separate divorces under the name Ken Haupert, in 1984 and 1985. At the Broward supervisor of elections, I checked the voter registration public database and found an address and date of birth for a Ken Haupert that suggested he was the son. In the online phone books I found a matching phone number.

After several attempts, I reached Ken Haupert on the first ring. Cautious, I told him I wasn't sure I had the right person, I was looking for the Ken Haupert who'd worked at a sub shop in North Miami Beach 20 years ago. At first he tried to sound like he didn't know what I was talking about.

"You sound too young," I said. "The man I'm looking for is older."

"I think you're talking about my dad," he said.

When I mentioned Dahmer, Haupert seemed genuinely surprised. He said he'd only worked at Sunshine and Beach Pizza to help out his father, and because he was between jobs. He didn't remember much because he hadn't stayed long. Susie was the name of the English girl his dad was involved with, although he couldn't recall her surname. "When I found out the relationship, what was going on, I got pissed off and left." He hadn't spoken with his father since.

But he did agree to help me find Ken Sr. Last he knew he'd opened a sub shop in Dewey, Oklahoma. He also gave me his father's full name and date of birth.

Ken Jr. wanted to see Dahmer's mug shot, which I emailed him.

I turned back to the Internet. Dewey was part of greater Bartlesville, Oklahoma, home of Phillips Petroleum, later ConocoPhillips. In the online phone books, Haupert wasn't listed. Its chamber of commerce had no exclusively sub shops. It was time to call my Delphic friend Jean again. Searching through a database of non-published phone numbers, she found Kenneth G. Haupert with a Dewey address. Yet the number seemed wrong. At first the phone just rang, then later, an electronic tone answered.

In the meantime, Ken Jr. called me back. As soon as he saw Dahmer's mug shot he recognized him from the shop. So did his younger brother, coincidentally named Jeff. "When I told him, he was floored, oh my God!"

They'd known him as Jeff, but may never have known his surname. "He wasn't anybody you'd remember. He just worked there. He cleaned tables, helped with food preparation. There was nothing that stood out about him. He was like the average person who came into work to make his money."

They had never had any meaningful conversation with him. Jeff Haupert thought Dahmer might have been in the army.

Nor had they made the association in 1991 when Dahmer made the news. Checking other pictures on the Internet, they reported, "He looked different as he got older. It didn't click in '91, hey, I know that guy."

In the shop, Dahmer had looked presentable, clean, clean-shaven, not seedy-looking. Compared to the mug shot, he said, his hair, which was dirty blonde, was flatter on top, combed more to the side, and he had no mustache, unlike in the later-1981 mug shot. "But the face, definitely," he said. He wore thick, out-of-fashion eyeglasses. "He looked like one of your friends, a guy you'd hang out with." He remembered him wearing a T-shirt that read "Sunshine Sub." He didn't know who'd hired him. "Funny you'd work next to somebody like that. I guess that's a claim to infamy."

He also thought that the store had an Adam Walsh missing poster.

After leaving Sunshine, Ken Jr. worked at Beach Pizza as an evening pizza chef. He remembered Larry's kindness and generosity. "If you needed money, he'd help you and never ask for anything in return." Sometimes Larry loaned him more than $100. Once when he tried to repay it, Larry wouldn't take it. He also knew Larry helped support Denise and Robin. "We wondered, what kind of person would do that?"

He also thought Larry had helped his father, who needed a break at the time, by setting him up at Sunshine and giving him money. "I don't think it was totally my dad's store. I think he was managing it."

He didn't know Larry was homosexual, though, or that he'd picked up drifters. He knew he didn't have girlfriends, but he never saw him make advances toward men, or look at them in a homosexual way. Larry never made him feel uncomfortable. "You'd think of him as your brother."

In about 1985, his father and Susan had had a child

together, Ian. About ten years later his father reached out to him, hoping he'd want to meet his stepbrother, but Ken Jr. refused.

To track down Ken Sr., I called county records in Washington County, Oklahoma, which encompassed Dewey and Bartlesville. They told me the Hauperts might have moved from the address I had for them. They suggested I call the electric company, which told me the same thing.

Next I tried the Dewey municipal water department. Getting the same answer, I asked the clerk if she knew of another city database, or property book, to scour for better information. While I kept her on the line, her boss, the city manager, peered over her shoulder and noticed Haupert's name.

Wait, said the clerk, my boss knows him. He moved to Bartlesville with his business—Ian's Sub Shop.

Could I speak to the city manager? She took the call. His new shop was in the lobby of a Bartlesville Best Western hotel. She politely offered to look up the phone number.

When I called it, the desk clerk said the Hauperts were away, it was their break time between lunch and dinner. Call back in an hour.

I did. A woman who answered had an English accent. I asked for her husband and she quickly put him on the line. Ken Haupert Sr. was friendly and of course surprised. He said he only had a moment, they were preparing for their dinner business. After asking how I found him—I told him—he said Dahmer in fact had worked for him, for a few months.

It was a Friday afternoon, and he asked if I could call back Monday. When I did, he was ready to talk about Jeffrey Dahmer.

He met Dahmer, he said, when he saw him rummaging through the dumpster behind Sunshine Sub. He was picking out pizza slices, to eat. "I said, why are you doing that? He said, I'm hungry and I have no job. I said, Come in, I'll give you something to eat.

"I gave him food, then a couple days later he was back at the trash cans. I asked, I needed a busboy.

"Who knows who you meet in life?"

Haupert said he assigned Dahmer to general cleanup, including bussing tables and mopping floors. He worked Monday to Friday, part-time, mornings to afternoons starting between 10-11 and ending between 4-5. He paid him minimum wage, plus meals.

Dahmer's first two or three weeks on the job were okay, but then he became erratic. "All of the sudden he came in filthy dirty—like he was drinking all night, drunk and dirty, unable to work. I'd send him home, and the next day he'd be okay."

But it became a frustrating pattern, starting again a week or so later. Once, he recalled, Dahmer came to work stinking, his eyeglasses broken. "He explained, I was running and fell down and broke my glasses." Losing patience, Haupert told him, "Get out of here."

Finally, after three months, "I got fed up and fired him." That was their last contact.

"He was a bum," he said. "He turned into a bum."

Could one of those weekday mornings when Dahmer came in drunk and Haupert sent him home been Monday, July 27, 1981? Haupert said he'd kept employee records, but hadn't saved them over twenty years.

I said, Dahmer had told the police he'd gotten unemployment compensation while he was working at Sunshine. Haupert said he didn't know that and asked how. I said, Dahmer admitted lying to the authorities. "He was quite good at lying," he commented.

Dahmer was also extremely quiet. "I'd ask, did you clean the bathroom good? He'd answer, but he was not one for conversation." Nor did Dahmer seem to relate to employees.

Haupert took his staff to a corner bar for occasions like birthdays, and "once in a while he'd join us." And then, "he listened but never talked."

He hadn't wanted Haupert to know much about him. He knew he'd just been discharged from the Army, but didn't know, until I told him, that the discharge was for alcohol abuse. He'd never seen Dahmer wear army clothing.

Dahmer had seemed "hateful" toward his parents, whom he said were divorced. "I said why don't you speak to your parents?" So one day at the store, Haupert called Lionel Dahmer, spoke to him then handed Jeffrey the phone. That may have been when Lionel first learned his son was in Miami—and how he knew he'd worked for Sunshine Sub.

When I asked about store vehicles, Haupert recalled a blue van. It was a Dodge, he said, and it was brand-new. Larry had bought it for both Sunshine and Beach Pizza. They used it for getting supplies and making deliveries.

Did Dahmer drive it? Given Dahmer's obvious alcohol problems, "I wouldn't let him drive anything. We had regular delivery people."

Unlike Darlene and Denise's description of the lax situation at Beach Pizza, Sunshine's copy of the keys was not easily accessible. Haupert said he kept them in his pocket. But, as Haupert described, Dahmer would have been familiar with the blue van—and undoubtedly knew it was shared with Beach Pizza.

Haupert said Dahmer had no car of his own. "He had no money for a car."

Did Dahmer know Larry? No, he didn't think so. Nor did he see any indication that Dahmer was homosexual. I also asked if Susan—Haupert's wife—was the English illegal alien who Dahmer said he'd been friendly with. No, he said, and she was legal. There were two other girls, one from England, another from Ireland, but they both had work permits. Or maybe one of them.

I emailed him the August 1982 mug shot, and he emailed back, "Yes, that's Jeffrey, but he had no mustache."

Next I looked for the two witnesses who in 1991 had told Hollywood police they'd seen Dahmer at the mall. Willis Morgan was in the phone book at the same number he'd given police in 1991. He still lived in Hallandale, sandwiched between Hollywood and the Dade County line.

Although 11 years had passed since his statement, 21 after the event, it was like he'd been waiting all that time for someone like me to call. No one ever had.

"I know the person I saw was the person who took Adam Walsh," he said right off the bat.

Was he still certain that the person he saw was Dahmer? Yes, 100 percent. But then he hedged, because the man he'd seen had long hair, to his collar, and Hoffman had told him Dahmer didn't have long hair because he'd recently been released from the military.

But he still thought that's whom he saw.

I asked him to describe what happened. He was in Hollywood Mall at Radio Shack, browsing the Red Tag sale table in the front of the store in the center aisle. The mall was dead, he remembered. Radio Shack was the second store inside the mall's north entrance, and in his peripheral vision, he saw a man come in through the mall's glass door and stop at the store entrance, about 12 feet from him. After they made eye contact, the man smiled and said, "Hi there, nice day, isn't it?"

"He was a nutcase. He wanted to talk to somebody. I didn't want to look at him. He stood and stared me down hard, for an eternity. If you asked me how long, I'd say probably 20 seconds, but it felt like 10 minutes."

When the man became angry, Morgan looked away, thinking he might leave. Instead, the man entered the store and approached him to within arm's length, hovering over him. As if he was starting over again, the man smiled and repeated—at the same volume and cadence as before, when he was further away—"Hi there, nice day, isn't it?"

Again Morgan didn't respond. "I was thinking, why is he talking so loud? He's standing right next to me. He must want someone to talk to really badly." Morgan pretended to be interested in the store item he'd already picked up, but he was keeping a peripheral eye on the man's hands. The man looked as if he was ready to fight or assault him. "A sense came over me—I thought he wanted to pull my arm and pull me out of the store. I thought, did he have a knife?" Just in case, Morgan used his left arm to cover his rib cage.

Because he had an artificial leg, the result of a motorcycle accident, Morgan couldn't quickly dart away from the man, nor did he want the man to notice his limp. Reluctantly he looked over his shoulder to look for a witness or someone to help. The only other person in the store was the clerk, in the back, stocking shelves. Then, abruptly, the man about-faced and stormed out, apparently feeling angry and rebuffed.

Morgan described the man as similar to his own size—5'10 or 5'11, 180 pounds. He wore blue jeans, but "everything about him was disheveled. He'd been drinking. He was totally unkempt."

What he remembered most about him was his eyes: "He had a look on him, like the devil was in him." When he'd stared at him, "I felt like he was trying to look at the back of my skull."

When the man left, Morgan decided he needed to follow him because he thought he'd approach someone else, and they might need help. He also decided he needed to commit his face to memory. "That's how scary this was."

From a safe distance, Morgan kept an eye on him as he walked the mall. He followed directly behind him, figuring the man would less likely turn 180 degrees than, say, 135 degrees, to the side. The man didn't realize Morgan was there. He continued following as the man entered Sears, then its toy department. As the rest of the mall was mostly empty of customers, so was Sears, he said. To hide, Morgan walked between clothes racks in the men's department, but because the toy department didn't lead anywhere further in the store, and the man would have to reverse his path, Morgan decided then to leave.

He thought about asking two young women at the perfume counter he'd passed to call security, but preferred to hurry on out of the store. He saw no kids in the toy department. He didn't feel safe until he got into his car and locked the door.

Morgan didn't think to note the exact time when he'd been in the mall, but thought it was sometime midday. In 1981, as in 1991, he was working four overnights a week, ending before dawn Sunday morning. He said after his work nights he usually slept until noon, but on the days he didn't work, such as Monday, he tended to awaken in the late morning after falling asleep shortly after midnight.

He did recall he went to the mall first thing that Monday, planning to eat lunch at the German deli. First he browsed at Waldenbooks for about 20 minutes. He remembered that because "it was a week or two before I went to Mexico. I was reading travel books at the bookstore." Then he passed Radio Shack and went in. After the incident, he ended up eating lunch elsewhere, at Denny's.

He said he first saw the Adam story on local TV news that night that a family was looking for their child lost in Sears's toy department. He was floored; he was sure it must have been a result of the man he'd followed. He told a neighbor the next morning, Tuesday, and when he returned to work Wednesday evening, his buddies urged him to report it to Hollywood police.

He stayed up after work and got to the police station around nine A.M., Thursday. In the lobby was an officer specially assigned to receive tips. To recall his name he thought out loud and said Officer Elvis—then said Officer Presley. He wrote down Morgan's name, address and information but wasn't much interested. He asked if he'd seen the man leave in a vehicle. He hadn't, he said; his encounter had been only inside the mall.

Did you get his license plate? the officer asked.

No, he said, I didn't see him outside.

Unsurprisingly, Morgan said police never called back.

I hadn't found any reference to Morgan in the file before 1991, but Hoffman had said a lot of early tips were lost.

Since his job was to prepare the presses, Morgan said part of his work was to read the newspaper's pages, cover to cover. Besides, the job had a lot of down time and he had nothing else to do. In 1983, he remembered, a *Herald* printing clerk named Monica showed him a front-page photo of Ottis Toole, destined for the press. She asked, "Willis, is this the guy?"

No, he said. But on a night in 1991, checking the inside pages before the presses would begin rolling, he saw a photo he did recognize.

"I was freaking out. This is the guy! This was the guy I followed in the mall! My supervisor had to calm me down."

The photo was Jeffrey Dahmer's.

When Morgan first sat down with Jack Hoffman in the detective bureau, Hoffman wasn't excited. Feeling ignored, Morgan decided to take his story to other ears. He wrote to John Walsh, went to Miami Beach police, who he said were rude to him (it wasn't their case), and spoke to an agent in the Miami office of the FBI. His sister Sondra even called Milwaukee police and talked to them at length, but despite a promise, they never called Willis back. He also tried, unsuccessfully, to get a *Herald* reporter and other local news people interested.

Three months after Morgan first called, Hoffman asked him to return and give a sworn taped statement. But later Hoffman told him, "It couldn't be Dahmer. Dahmer's been dismissed as a suspect."

"He so totally, completely discounted Dahmer. He kept convincing me it wasn't Dahmer."

His pressroom friends at the *Herald* began to tease him. When other serial killer stories hit the newspaper, they'd ask, "Willis, did you see this guy too?"

Much later, he said, he was watching John Walsh do an *America's Most Wanted* segment about a child kidnapped from a Kansas shopping center. "He said, I can sympathize, that happened to me, and no witnesses came forward. I called the show to say, I came forward. But they hung up on me. I called three, four times, and each time they got rid of me, like I was some kind of nutcase.

"I've always been so certain it was Dahmer because of the face, but they convinced me of the hair. Who knows? Maybe he didn't have long hair. I remember the eyes, the facial features. Maybe I got confused on the hair.

"I'm positive about what happened, how he approached me, what he said, and that I followed him to the toy department. Plus his eyes. Unusual eyes. The look.

"I stared at him about 15 seconds. I could be wrong about the hair."

Curious about this point of doubt, I called back Ken Haupert Sr. to ask about Dahmer's hair.

"He always needed a haircut," he said. "It was long in the back. I kept telling him to comb it."

That matched Billy Joe Capshaw's observation about the Army's lax hair enforcement in that era. I also asked Haupert if he'd ever seen Dahmer angry. He answered, he didn't have time to get into it, but yes. "I saw hell in his eyes, once," he said.

That sounded like Morgan's description, too.

Carrying library books with still photographs of Dahmer plus an A&E documentary about him, I visited Morgan at his small ground-floor apartment in the tri-plex he owned. He was

55 with thinning blond hair and large eyeglasses, from Long Island, N.Y.—on the phone I thought I'd heard New England. I saw how his gait was affected by his leg prosthesis. In 1977 he'd had a motorcycle accident.

In the mall that day, he explained, "If I'd had two good legs, I wouldn't have been so nervous."

My first impression of Willis was disappointing. He was kinda frumpy, and I wondered why Dahmer would have been interested in him. I think Willis picked up on this, and he showed me a photograph of himself, circa 1985.

The difference was striking. In the photo he looked like a male model. He wore a skin-tight polo shirt over a well-developed chest. His hand over his shoulder held a windbreaker, and he wore dark sunglasses. Willis said he was heterosexual (I apologized for having to ask) but in the photo he clearly matched a type that Dahmer had often repeated he sought out.

"I think I was his first choice. He went into the toy department, looking for somebody else."

I showed him a color news photo of Dahmer walking to his first appearance in Milwaukee County Court.

"That's the guy," he said.

Later, watching the A&E show, in which Dahmer wore a red prison jumpsuit, he added, "There's no doubt in my mind."

One of the books had another Dahmer mug shot, also from 1982, not wearing glasses. "That's him—with longer hair. I swear to you, when I look at the guy, that's the guy.

"I'm looking at his eyes, his face. We made eye contact—we locked. It was frightening."

On the videotape was the trial. Dahmer hadn't testified in his defense, but at sentencing he spoke to the judge in an attempt to humble himself. I'd hoped Willis could similarly identify his voice, but his reaction wasn't nearly as certain.

"That could definitely be the voice. But he's sober." At the mall, he said, Dahmer had been drunk, and was in a completely different mental state than in court. "I'm trying to give the most honest answer—it's not the same situation. He was loud and aggressive. Reading that speech, he was docile."

In 1992, he'd had a similar thought about listening to Dahmer, in person. When Hoffman told him he was going to interview Dahmer in Milwaukee, Willis asked if he could go too, so he could hear Dahmer say, "Hi there, nice day, isn't it?" Willis even proposed to pay his own fare and expenses. Hoffman told him, "That's not going to happen."

After Hoffman's Milwaukee interview, he called Morgan back. Hoffman said Dahmer had looked him in the eye and "was very, very frank with me. He even told me, I've got nothing to lose. If I did Adam I would have told you. And I believe him." Again insisting he'd seen Dahmer, Morgan asked for a polygraph test, but Hoffman refused him. "Listen, Willis, Jeffrey said he was working 10 hours a day, seven days a week and never took days off. Every once in a while they would just give him a day off. He was sleeping on the beach, didn't have a vehicle, and was drinking heavily." He added, "That little kid doesn't fit his M.O."

When Morgan heard that Dahmer had been killed in prison, "my heart sank because I knew nobody would ever believe me."

Online, I researched the *Miami Herald*'s initial coverage of the Dahmer story. It began with inside-page stories on Wednesday, July 24, 1991, and Thursday the 25th. On the front page of Friday the 26th they ran a photo, but the story was again tucked inside.

On Saturday the 27th, his story finally made the front page. On the jump page inside was the sidebar *Milwaukee mutilation suspect lived briefly in Dade.* On Sunday the 28th, the *Herald* ran its 10-years-after story of Adam's kidnapping, technically a day late.

I wanted to know, which photo caused Willis to react so strongly? Was it before the Saturday story that Dahmer had lived in Miami?

Back at the Miami-Dade main library, I copied pages from the *Herald*'s microfilm. Both Wednesday and Thursday's papers used the same thumbnail-sized Milwaukee County Sheriff's mug shot of Dahmer from 1982.

I'd already shown Willis the photo of Dahmer entering the Milwaukee courtroom, which the *Herald* ran Friday prominently in the middle of the front page, two columns. Saturday, on the front page as part of a three-column layout, the *Herald* ran his profile and a different shot from the court appearance. I mailed Willis copies of all the photos.

The photo he remembered seeing first was the thumbnail mug shot—run both the first and second day. In it Dahmer looks straight ahead—the way Willis encountered him, he said. Plus, it was the photo of him nearest to 1981.

"That thumbnail is the spitting image. That is him. That's the face."

The only difference, he said, was that in the shot Dahmer had a mustache and glasses. At Sears he wasn't wearing glasses, and Morgan hadn't committed to memory whether he had a mustache, and "his hair was longer and scraggly-looking, unkempt and dirty," like he hadn't showered or was living out of a car.

So Morgan was saying he'd recognized a photo of Dahmer before any media had reported he'd lived in Florida. Prompted by seeing the 1991 pages, Morgan said he remembered when his supervisor, several days later, showed him the Dahmer-in-Miami story. "That's when I got goose bumps."

Although Morgan had left the *Herald* more than five years earlier, he suggested I speak to printers there who'd remember him. He gave me the name Richard Herland, and I reached him at work, by phone. Herland said he hadn't spoken to Willis since he'd left, but vouched for his credibility and sincerity. He was able to recall the story Willis had told—he'd told everyone at the plant:

"He was at Sears mall, at Radio Shack, and a guy called to

him, Hey! He saw the guy, a lunatic, staring at him, Oh no he's talking to me. He got nervous, he only has one leg"—one real leg, that is.

He recalled Morgan's description of the man: "crazy-looking, something definitely wrong with him. His eyes bulged out of his head. He had messy-looking hair.

"He started walking toward the back, then Dahmer left Radio Shack, and Willis followed him to Sears, the toy department." Herland thought there was a commotion in the toy department, and that Willis had followed Dahmer to the parking lot, where he'd seen a van.

Save for the end, Herland echoed what Willis had told me.

Herland also remembered when Dahmer's photo made the *Herald* in 1991. Willis's story from ten years earlier stayed consistent, he said. "He's definitely sane, and definitely telling the truth of what he saw," Herland said. "Every time I heard the story, it was the same thing."

William Bowen, the other witness who in 1991 identified Dahmer at the mall, was also easy to find. In an online phone book, he was listed in a suburb of Birmingham, Alabama. Like Morgan, Bowen also seemed to be waiting for my phone call. He told me he'd emailed *America's Most Wanted* a year earlier, and although as a cameraman and director of production he'd once shot a segment for them, "nobody was very interested."

"I was there at Sears. To see how violent he was, it wasn't normal. I saw him take the kid up by one arm, like he was a sack of potatoes. He violently threw him into that car."

Car? I asked. In 1991 he'd told Hoffman he'd seen a man throw a child into a blue van.

There had been a blue van nearby, he said, which screeched away. He described the car as big, white or off-white, with a Florida license plate lettered BAC or VAC. "I was distracted by the blue van—which may have had nothing to do with the white car."

In his 1991 statement, Bowen hadn't mentioned any car—much less one that sounded like Ottis Toole's Cadillac. And BAC or VAC were the same letters he'd said were on the blue van's plate.

Rather than say more, I let him continue.

After finishing college, he said, in 1981 he'd come to Hollywood from Alabama and taken a job at Calder Race Track, in north Dade County. He stayed only eight months before returning home. On the day in question, he went to Hollywood Mall to pay his Sears bill—which he did in the moments after the incident. He remembered getting his statement time-stamped—but in 1991, ten years later, he couldn't find that month's statement.

[In 1991 Bowen had in actuality shown Hoffman a Sears bill, date-stamped for payment July 22, 1981. He said he'd returned to the mall five days later, to browse.]

In 1981, he didn't immediately tell police what he'd seen because it took a few days before he realized the possible significance. "I saw a missing poster at a Kentucky Fried Chicken drive-in, near the mall, and that's when I thought, maybe I saw what happened."

At that time, his apartment had been burglarized and his high school class ring stolen. When Hollywood officers responded, he told them what he'd seen at Sears, and they promised to pass it on to the case detectives, but when he got no callback he suspected they didn't.

Upset at South Florida's violence—in 1981, homicides hit an all-time peak—for Bowen his apartment break-in was the last straw. He impulsively resolved to go back home. "I literally loaded up my car one night and left." He thought he was back in Birmingham when Adam's head was found, but didn't know about it at the time because he didn't see the story in the local papers there. He finally read it several months after.

Two years later he read that Hollywood had solved the case. "Then [in 1991] I found out that they hadn't."

Talking to me, Bowen said he felt tremendous pain because he hadn't done more to tell police what he'd seen. "I feel to this day, if they [the officers responding to the burglary] would have taken this seriously, something would have happened."

In 1991, after giving his taped statement, he said Hoffman told him, "Thanks for helping, but we have our man." He was referring to Toole.

I had Bowen start again from the beginning. He said the incident had occurred near Sears's customer pick-up entrance, which had a carport. That was on the Hollywood Boulevard side, facing the police station. It was around lunchtime, he thought, because he had to be at work at the racetrack between 12:30 to 1 o'clock. The mall was about a 25 minutes' drive to Calder.

[In 1991 he told Hoffman he was off work that day.]

He saw a small boy, maybe five years old, wearing a funny hat—he couldn't describe it any better, since he saw him from the back. He was wearing dark-colored shorts—blue, he thought, and a polo-type shirt the color he couldn't recall.

[In 1991, he told Hoffman the child was about five or six, had a Chinese bowl haircut, and wore a striped shirt, perhaps red and blue. He didn't mention pants or a hat.]

The man he saw had a balding spot on the back of his head and his pants were paint-splattered. "He was nuts. He turned toward me. He reminded me of David Letterman—the way he had a gap between his teeth."

I said he seemed to be describing Toole. He agreed. "It looked like Ottis Toole—from what I've seen of him."

I then read Bowen his words to the police, as transcribed:

He said he'd seen a blue van leaving, with a screech. And the man who he'd seen throw the child into the van resembled Jeffrey Dahmer, whose photograph he'd just seen in the *Birmingham News*.

Bowen didn't believe me. He insisted the newspaper story had been about Toole.

But I had the clipping, from the police file. I read him the headline: *Dahmer denies killings outside Wisconsin, Ohio*. And its subhead: *Florida police investigate possible links to Adam Walsh*. It had a profile photo of Dahmer. And handwritten on the photocopy page was a phone number for Hollywood police.

He still didn't believe me. Look it up on microfilm in the Birmingham library, I said. I gave him the date—Sunday July 28, 1991. Page 4A.

A stunned silence followed. Bowen didn't sound like a flake. He was 44, a media professional like myself, and university-educated. "Maybe I was confused," he conceded, trying to save face. "It shocks me to think... the only name I remember was Ottis Toole."

Turning off any trial attorney bluster I incidentally might have shown him, I began probing why he might have replaced references of Dahmer with Toole.

He thought he knew: he'd recently read *Tears of Rage*. For years he'd resisted, believing it would alter his memory. Oddly, he'd looked for his name, as someone Walsh would have criticized as a witness who hadn't done enough to help at the time.

Bowen's name wasn't in the book. For that matter, Walsh mentioned Dahmer only briefly, while concluding that Toole had killed his son. Toole was in the photos, severely gap-toothed and badly dressed.

"It all happened in ten seconds," he explained.

I needed advice, so I visited Brian Cavanagh, the Fort Lauderdale homicide prosecutor. Did Bowen's reversal ruin his credibility?

No, he thought, he could be rehabilitated. He suggested I mail Bowen a full copy of his transcribed words, plus the *Birmingham News* clip. It was crucial to the case, Cavanagh said. "He is the hub of the wheel in which all of the

265

circumstantial evidence comes together." Without Bowen's blue van, Dahmer's access to a similar vehicle at Sunshine Sub or Beach Pizza didn't matter.

Back to the online phone books, I obtained Bowen's address. Apologizing in a letter for the intrusion, I mailed him the papers. A week later I called and left a message, then reached him the next night. The night of the first call he'd reluctantly read what I'd sent. "It was eye-opening," he said.

The handwriting on the newspaper clipping was his, as I'd guessed. Yes, now he remembered, it *was* about Dahmer.

As he'd said in 1991, he'd only seen a blue van. He explained: "After I read the [Walsh] book, it tainted my memory and I saw a white car."

He still thought the man was gap-toothed. But talking more, he agreed, the book might have affected that impression too.

What he remained certain of was that he'd seen a man who'd "lifted a kid by one arm, kicking and screaming, and slung him into the vehicle." Later he described the throw as "like a pendulum," with a windup. The throw itself, when the child hit the inside wall of the van, must have injured or even killed him.

"That's something you will never, ever forget. My memory of all this is very vague. Certain points I do remember; other points, I don't know."

On the abduction, I noted, he was consistent from Hoffman's 1991 interview to mine.

"The guy was nuts, out of his mind, he was raging. He turned around for just a brief moment. I was scared to death. How could a father treat his child like this? Others around me were in shock, too.

"At the time I remember a blue van—it was nondescript. I read the book, thought maybe I'm wrong, it was a white car."

Again, I thought, Willis Morgan had said when Hoffman told him Toole was the prime suspect, Morgan had questioned himself whether he'd really seen Toole.

A van is higher above the ground than a car, I reminded Bowen. You just told me the man lifted up the kid.

He agreed. "He had to lift the kid up into the van. Big blue van. Held him up. Threw him in, peeled off." Again, later, he added the van sped off almost before its door was closed. In its dust was the sight and smell of burning rubber.

I asked if he could say for sure he'd absolutely seen Dahmer. He wouldn't commit—but he hadn't said that in 1991 either. I offered to email him Dahmer's August 1982 mug shot.

Days later, Bowen called me. "It doesn't ring a bell. But I saw the guy from the back. He turned around [for just a moment]. At first I thought it was an angry parent. Looking back, I've never seen a parent like that. Maybe this wasn't an angry parent."

Within the last year, he said, he'd watched an MSNBC documentary about John Walsh, which I'd seen too. After that he emailed *America's Most Wanted* asking, is this solved or not? He then re-volunteered his information.

He got a callback from someone who said he represented the Walsh family. He'd said he'd follow up, but no one ever did.

"I don't know how to make this right. I have a lot of guilt that maybe I could have helped more." At that moment, he added later, "I didn't think evil. Why would somebody abduct a kid in broad daylight? It just didn't cross my mind. It's been a thorn in my side all this time. What could I have done differently?"

17
Calling The Cops

I WEIGHED THE PROS AND CONS of sharing my information with Hollywood police. At some point they'd have to become involved, since it was their case. Especially if the blue van could be found, they'd have to do crime scene tests. Also, I needed help finding the van's vehicle identification number. As well, it didn't look like Larry would talk to me, but maybe he'd talk to them.

On the other hand, I expected they'd see me as intruding. Police don't like reporters to compete with their investigations, certainly not to propose dismissed solutions in their department's highest-profile case ever.

In November 2002, I re-contacted Mark Smith. It had been five years since we'd last spoken. As I expected, Smith was interested but skeptical. To give him the full context of my theory I offered a draft of my Dahmer chapters. He accepted, and I emailed them.

Smith was then chief of detectives, but was about to take a promotion to road patrol lieutenant, initially on the graveyard shift. For the time being he would keep the Walsh case but eventually his successor would inherit it. Because he wouldn't know details like Smith, it sounded to me like pretty much the end of the line. Smith insisted no, every new lead would continue to be investigated.

Smith promised to track the blue van and interview Larry and Darlene Hill after he finished reading what I'd sent. To keep after him, I'd call after midnight. During late-night lulls he'd read a few pages then put it down. Weeks of good-natured nudging turned into months.

In March 2003 he told me he'd heard Jimmy Campbell had died, of illness. The newspapers hadn't reported it. If so it would leave another permanent hole in the story. In 1995 Smith wanted to interview him, but Campbell's parents wouldn't say where he was. Smith said he didn't press because he didn't think Campbell was guilty.

Online I searched the *Miami Herald* and *Sun-Sentinel* and found death listings for James Campbell, 47, died on February 28, 2003. From the microfilm I had Campbell's date of birth, and I called the funeral home, in Hollywood, to confirm whether it was the same. It was.

Meanwhile, Smith said, he'd asked the head of the auto theft unit to check Larry's vehicle registration records. What came back, he emailed me, was an '81 Olds station wagon and a '76 Buick. Which was odd, because when I'd checked, months before, they'd reported a '76 Dodge, no Buick, and a Lincoln Town Car.

Months passed and Smith still hadn't finished my Dahmer pages. Finally, in July, he said the new chief of detectives would assume the case.

His name was Scott Pardon. When I reached him, he promised to read my material and interview Larry. Since it would be an official police action, he wouldn't let me be present, but he promised to share its results with me when it was written up in a police report.

In August Pardon gave me an appointment, with Smith

present. They were looking for Larry—he'd since left the church. His driver's license gave the address of the condo he'd sold a year earlier.

Meantime a detective had spoken to Ken Haupert Jr., who couldn't remember a blue van, and was adamant that Sunshine Sub didn't have delivery vehicles before 1982. In '82 Haupert entered the insurance business and wrote policies on either vans or pickups Larry purchased that year. They were registered to Beach Pizza.

Reviewing my notes, Haupert Jr. wasn't my source on the blue van. His father was, as well as Darlene and Denise. I suggested Pardon contact them.

Scott Pardon found Larry—within the Hollywood city limits, at that. He was living in a motel, apparently fallen on hard times. He'd explained why he hadn't spoken to me—he doesn't talk to reporters.

The news was Larry said Beach Pizza never had vans, contradicting what Haupert Jr. had told them. He had white pickup trucks but never a blue van.

When he saw Dahmer's photograph in the news in 1991, he didn't recognize it. The sub shop might have had a guy named Jeffrey, but he never remembered him using delivery vehicles, and besides, Sunshine didn't even do deliveries. And he couldn't have taken a vehicle without Larry's knowing.

Also, Larry said he'd kept no records of his vehicles.

Between Larry, Haupert Jr., and a records search, police had failed to confirm the existence of a blue van. Pardon said he'd have his detective call Darlene and Haupert Sr. in the next week, but he expected to close out the investigation as inconclusive.

I'd been patient for most of a year, but as I'd originally anticipated, they weren't interested. They never called Darlene or Haupert Sr., and as a result I didn't call Hollywood police again, either.

I was going to have to document the blue van myself.

If it was no longer in state DMV files, where could an errant mention of it be hiding? A speeding ticket?

I asked Denise. Larry drove like a cop, aggressively, and he could have gotten tickets. Besides him, two kids who did deliveries, Gino Cocco and Joey Trapasso, would take the van. They liked to party in Broward, and neither had his own car. Joey would often take Larry's keys, say he'd be back in an hour, and not return for two days.

Darlene had told me Gino and Joey's names before, along with Joey's sister Connie, who'd also worked for Larry. The Trapassos were a family who'd lived in Salem House, and she'd introduced Joey and Connie to Larry for jobs. Connie became Denise's best friend.

At his core, Joey was a sweet kid, Darlene said, but wild. He was heavily into drugs and drinking, and likely would have gotten tickets or DUIs.

She thought about him some more. Joey was gay, and Larry had been very good to him.

"Do you see why my stomach got a knot when I talked to Larry?" she said. "Now I see a different rationale" for him helping Joey. "Joey's a handsome boy. But to get money for drugs, he did tricks. And Larry was taking care of this dumb-assed kid."

I searched for Gino and Joey. Gino was easy, because he had phone numbers in Hallandale. Joey wasn't. Darlene remembered his full name, same as his father, and Denise remembered he was born in 1963 and the month.

I called my Metro-Dade detective friend for a favor. Would he look up Joey to get a current address? He did and found he was dead. He gave me his Social Security number, which I looked up online in the Social Security Death Index. He'd died in 1996, in New Jersey.

Darlene was shocked to hear the news. I was deflated

myself—another consequence of arriving too late. The next best thing was to look for his sister Connie.

A year before, Denise had told me about a 1983 car accident she'd been in. Connie had been driving in a car Larry leased for her. They were hit someplace around N.E. 163rd St. and W. Dixie Hwy.—inside the incorporated city of North Miami Beach. Hoping to get a VIN that could connect me to Larry's other vehicles, I'd gotten a copy of the report, but the car, a white Chevy Chevette, was registered to a rental car agency.

Now I was glad to have it. It gave me Connie's date of birth and Florida driver's license number. I called back the detective and he offered to run an "Auto-track" report, a database used by police and private investigators. I went to visit him, and he ran the Auto-track on both Larry and Connie, amounting to 18 and 28 pages respectively. Most of the information was garbage—names of completely unrelated persons who over the years had lived at addresses used by, or near, the subjects. The more you knew what you were looking for, the more valuable the report.

Connie's married name was Daramola, and her most recent addresses and phone numbers were in Pennsylvania. Connie's phone numbers didn't connect, or weren't right. I tried the online phone books for any Daramola in Pennsylvania or New Jersey, and still found nothing useful.

Neither Dade nor Broward post traffic citations online. But they were available at courthouses. In Broward, the database goes back to 1980. For Joey I found a 1985 DUI and marijuana arrest by the Broward Sheriff's Office. It didn't list what he was driving. Because of later probation violations, the case remained open and active. That was good, because the file would still exist.

Larry had nothing—a 1999 citation for an expired license tag, driving a '94 Ford. Gino also had nothing old.

In Dade, online, I found a March 1984 Metro-Dade Police

arrest of Joey for cocaine possession. I asked the department records office to search their microfilm and they sent the report: an officer saw him sitting at a bus bench at 4:40 A.M., asked him for ID and saw a baggie with traces of white powder in his wallet. Charges were later dropped.

At the same time, I asked for the 1982 lost/stolen tag report Larry had made on his '76 Dodge. Could I have overlooked that the Dodge might be a van? The report gave a license tag and VIN number, but when I called Chrysler customer service, the VIN corresponded with a Dodge Coronet sedan.

For Dade traffic records, at the criminal courthouse I had to take a number behind people waiting to pay their traffic fines. An hour later, given my unusual request, I was shown a supervisor who offered to look up all three names in purged computer records and microfilm for 1980-87.

A day later I got answers. Two more tickets for Joey: one in 1984, and an arrest by Florida Highway Patrol in 1985. I submitted Joey's three citation numbers to the state DMV records department. I also requested Larry and Joey's driving records and Larry's vehicle registrations (again), but everything that old was gone.

Darlene had thought she remembered Larry telling her in 1981 that the blue van had been stolen. Now she began to doubt that memory, but she didn't doubt that he had a van. "If Larry didn't have a blue van, then my furniture walked itself to storage."

"The van was there about a year," Denise said. She thought it was new—possibly a Dodge, as Haupert Sr. said, but no more than a few years old. She didn't remember if it was stolen, or when, but she thought they had used it in 1981.

Gino Cocco called back. He didn't know Joey had died, but did recall a blue van—and its single seat. He agreed with Denise it was relatively new then, somewhere between a '79-'81 model year, and agreed with Haupert Sr. it might have been a Dodge. It was dark-blue, regular-sized as opposed to extended, as Darlene recalled, and had automatic transmission and AM-FM. He didn't remember any dents or signage, but added that all Larry's vehicles "had a lot of shit in them—papers, cups, whatever."

"I remember driving it," he said.

He remembered Larry driving it in January 1981 when he picked him up at Fort Lauderdale airport after flying in from Montreal, as well as after other flights he took from Montreal. "Larry used that van. Early in the morning, he went to the farmer's market" to buy supplies, he said. Gino knew because he worked the breakfast shift, starting at six.

But in April '81 Gino returned to Montreal, and when he came back a year and a half later, "the van wasn't there anymore." He didn't know what had happened to it.

He remembered cleaning up the Sunshine store after Darlene left, before it reopened as a sub shop. But because he left just after that, he didn't recognize Dahmer as an employee. "Larry was gay," he blurted with a laugh, in case I hadn't already heard. Most of the delivery drivers "were his boys," including Joey (who was 18 in 1981) and Larry let them take the delivery vehicles for their own use. Without me asking, Gino said he himself wasn't gay.

"Larry was weird. His life was sexually oriented. He was fat, bald, and had crooked teeth—not the most attractive guy on the planet."

He was uninterested in making money. The "boys" would take from his cash register but "he didn't care." Once, Joey broke into Larry's safe to steal money to buy drugs. In fact, Gino said he was with Joey at the time, and they both did drugs together. Gino added that he's been clean since April 1985, after his second overdose. Had he then been alone then, he thinks he would have died.

One of Larry's friends who was a waiter elsewhere would recruit drifters in Haulover Beach, a park two miles south of

Beach Pizza. Larry would hire them for the shop and have sex with them. Coincidentally, that waiter was the same person who'd introduced Darlene to Larry after she'd been diagnosed with terminal cancer. He had lived in Salem House. She'd known he was gay, but didn't know the rest of Gino's story until I told her.

When I asked Gino where the waiter was, he didn't know.

Gino also described gay prostitution on Collins Avenue around Beach Pizza. Once, while he waited at a bus stop, a man tried to grab his genitals—a pickup ploy.

That again reminded me of Dahmer talking about being solicited on Collins. Maybe he wasn't referring to Larry. I asked, even if Larry hadn't hired him, and he was working in his other shop, would Larry have had, in effect, radar for someone like Dahmer, a drifter?

"Absolutely," he said.

On Gino's list of other Beach Pizza insiders, the first I found was Chuck Marcus, who'd managed Souvenir World, next door. Gino said Larry would let Chuck eat for free, and Darlene said, "Chuck was in Beach Pizza more than Larry. He knows everything."

Marcus agreed he'd hung around Beach Pizza. As for Larry's delivery vehicles, he remembered Chevy S-10s—small pickup trucks, and either Chevettes or Escorts. I asked if there were any others. He thought about it.

"Larry's blue van!" He described it as royal blue—"not regular blue-blue." It was a basic van, two seats.

How easy was it to take any of the keys? "Real easy," he said. "I used to take them myself." He remembered the vehicles always had "that pizza smell."

Marcus knew Larry was gay and also that he had guys stay at his place. He didn't recall Dahmer, from his mug shot, but thought he looked like one of Larry's boys. "He had the profile. He could have stayed at Larry's," he said.

Could he have had access to the vans? "Yes, definitely."

Marcus forwarded the mug shot to a friend, Robert Gaines, who also knew Larry and Beach Pizza. Gaines did recognize Dahmer, he said. He and Gaines were working together in Gaines's shop that made yacht blinds, and he gave me his phone number.

Back then, Gaines told me, his father had a clothing store in Sunshine's strip mall, and Robert managed the shop after five. "He'd bring food," he said, referring to Dahmer. "He bought something—a shirt."

You remember Dahmer bought a shirt from you?

"I have a good memory." When he saw the mug shot, he said, "That's him."

Dahmer was quiet, an introvert, he said. He wore raggedy clothes. I asked, do you remember him with Larry?

"I can't say yes, can't say no. Larry always had young guys with him." Robert's words for Larry were uncomplimentary, the most printable being, he had a "very weird personality."

He remembered the blue van—he thought it was a Chevy, a dull, dark, cobalt blue. "I was in the van. It was an empty cargo van." Echoing Darlene, he called it a "pigsty. It was always a mess."

The keys were easy to take. "Larry was around, then he wasn't. Drivers would take the vans for personal use."

Gaines thought Larry had bought the van, used, from a nearby dealer, Bill Kelley Chevrolet, in Hallandale. I called the dealership to see if they'd kept old records.

Bill Kelley Jr., the owner, told me he was the only employee still around from 1981. Just last summer, in 2002, he'd trashed all his oldest records.

I asked him, if I found the VIN, what were the chances of a circa-1980 standard van still being on the road?

"Very slim," he said. "Highly unlikely."

After leaving a voice mail for Linda Trapasso at a New Jersey number, she called back. She was shocked that I knew her son Joey was dead. I insisted I only knew from the Social Security Death Index, I didn't know the cause. Her reaction made me suspect it was AIDS.

But she said she'd pass on my number to Connie.

Days later Connie called. Joey did die of AIDS, she said. He spent his last two weeks in a hospice situation at his mother's apartment. Seven years later, Linda was still traumatized by it.

He'd been diagnosed as HIV-positive twelve years earlier—which meant 1984. Later, he'd also been diagnosed as paranoid-schizophrenic, a result of his drug use. After a while he got tired of taking his meds, both for the mental illness and AIDS. The only good that came from it was it inspired Connie to get a degree that enabled her to work in a behavioral hospital setting. Currently she was studying for a master's, at night.

But back when both she and Joey were working for Larry, Joey had confided in her. To Connie, "Larry was like my grandfather." He was also nurturing with young men, but for them there was an exchange that included sex.

"Larry gave my brother money, a job. There was a hierarchy for Larry; if he liked you, you got to do whatever you wanted."

But Larry played favorites. "When Larry found a new boy, he would toss out the old boy—which was Joey. Then when he'd toss out the new boy, he'd come back looking for Joey."

I asked Connie to recall the delivery vehicles. She remembered Escorts (Chevettes, actually), and a white van and a van she at first thought was green. When I asked, if it could have been blue, she said yes, it was dark-colored. It was old and cruddy, and missing a seat.

"Only my brother drove the vans," she thought, he and Larry. And they were both reckless drivers, and likely got tickets in them.

Using the number I'd found, Darlene had called Linda to offer condolences. For three and a half hours, Linda had poured out her heart. "My blood was boiling," Darlene agonized.

"Joey wasn't gay—Joey was gay for money, so he could take girls out, or get money for drugs." Because she'd helped both Joey and Connie get jobs with Larry, "now the guilt is on me—I fixed it so [Larry] could stay there. I wasn't unobservant, but never in a million years I thought he would do something [like this]. I knew my girls were fine with him. I never thought their friends would be at risk."

Another name supplied by Gino, as well as Darlene, was Walter DiGrazia, one of Larry's pizza chefs. Gino thought he was in Fort Lauderdale, and there I found his ex-wife Ella.

"Larry had a white van," she recalled. I asked if there were others.

"Blue van. The picture just popped into my mind."

She described it as not new, with old-style round headlights, its color between light blue and a darker sky-blue. It had just one seat, and its two back doors opened.

She remembered that Joey Trapasso did a lot of drugs. "I never had a problem with Joey. He was always sweet to me." But she knew that he took Larry's vehicles. "He even took the keys to our car one night. The car reappeared at eight A.M. Walter was very angry." But with Larry's vehicles, "that happened all the time."

Larry, she said, was "always, always bailing out kids." Walter would know more, she said, and gave me his cell phone number. But when I reached him, Walter didn't want to talk. He didn't recall Dahmer at one of Larry's stores, or from his mug shot. He said he never worked at Sunshine Sub, although Darlene said Larry had told her he had, and Denise told me the same. He said he only vaguely recalled Sunshine Sub. He also said he didn't recall the blue van, or any van Larry might have owned.

Although Connie didn't remember Dahmer from his mug shot, I still counted four who did. For the blue van, I had eight witnesses, even if their descriptions varied. But I still lacked someone who saw Dahmer and Larry together. I called back Ken Haupert Jr. and asked how often Larry had visited Sunshine while he worked there.

"Anytime at all, day or evening," he said. "He'd bring supplies, or sometimes I'd take supplies to Beach Pizza—cups, a box of pizza cheese."

Sunshine didn't have many employees, he said, two at night when he was mostly there, maybe three during the day. Unlike Beach Pizza, it wasn't a moneymaker. "I remember no great rushes when you were so busy you couldn't handle it."

The third employee, unneeded at night, would have been the busboy—Dahmer's job.

Then likely, Larry would have known Dahmer, then? "I would imagine so, at least seen him."

18
25th Anniversary

HOLLYWOOD POLICE STILL AIM TO CLOSE
ADAM WALSH MURDER CASE OF 1981
—*Hollywood Gazette*

IN JULY 2006, AS THE 25TH ANNIVERSARY of the case approached, I learned that Mark Smith, now a Hollywood police captain, had once again taken charge of the case. To a monthly community paper called the *Hollywood Gazette* he said, "The best thing about cold cases is that the older they get, it actually works in our favor." He added, "We do get some tips—none that have panned out. To this day, we're still actively pursuing tips."

In July, Congress passed then President Bush signed at the White House on July 27, in front of John and Reve Walsh and all their children born since Adam, the Adam Walsh Child Safety and Protection Act. Among other provisions it mandated the creation of a national sex offender registry.

In a White House press conference, Walsh spoke about the murder investigation:

I never give up hope. I always talk about how my wife and I have never gotten justice. A lot of people think that Ottis Toole, who died in a Florida prison for some horrible crimes, he died of cirrhosis and AIDS in prison, was never charged. The sad thing is that they found a piece of bloody carpet in his car years ago when he was a suspect, and there was no DNA, and unfortunately the Hollywood police over the years misplaced that carpet, which is a real tragedy, because the FBI lab said to me, 'Mr. Walsh, if you could give us that carpet, even now, in one day we would tell you whether Adam was in that car or not and whether that man, who is the main suspect, murdered Adam.'

I made another attempt to bring my evidence to Mark Smith, and as well tried to enlist the Broward State Attorney's office.

At a proposed meeting, I offered to bring in Willis Morgan, Gino Cocco, and Darlene Hill. On the phone I would present Ken Haupert Sr., Bill Bowen, Billy Capshaw, and Linda Swisher.

Although Morgan was willing to go to a meeting, he didn't think Mark Smith would listen to him. In 1994, when Smith first took on the file as a cold case, Willis had called him. When he said he'd seen Dahmer in the mall, Smith replied, "Yeah, right."

I spoke directly to Chuck Morton, the Chief Assistant State Attorney, whom I knew, but couldn't convince him to commit one of his office's investigators. Smith told me he was ready to take the meeting if the State Attorney became involved. In the end it didn't happen, especially after I told Smith I wanted to bring in Willis.

Reviewing the case file, I found a reference to Neil Purtell, an FBI agent assigned to its Madison, Wisconsin, office, who in

1992 had called and asked Jack Hoffman to come to Milwaukee to interview Dahmer. When Hoffman did come, Purtell was supposed to have sat in on it but he was sick that day and Dan Craft had substituted. I found him easily on the Internet, now retired from the FBI and working as a private detective in Madison.

On the phone, Purtell was a friendly, folksy guy who still thought the Dahmer-Adam theory was viable. He was on the case starting the morning after Dahmer was captured. As police quickly learned from Dahmer where he'd lived over the years, Purtell said he made eye contact with a Milwaukee detective, both thinking the same thing: Could he have been connected to Adam Walsh?

The FBI's behavioral sciences unit had trained Purtell as a profiler. After Dahmer's murder convictions, he was able to meet with him a number of times in prison where he revisited the possibility he'd killed Adam.

"I asked, do you want to tell me anything about that?"

Dahmer paused. "Honest to God, Neil, I didn't do that."

"Let's leave God out of it," Purtell responded. "It's my experience, when people overemphasize their denials, it's usually an admission. When someone says, Honest to God, I know they're lying.

"Did he do Adam? I think he did," he said. "My impression was, he admitted it."

As he'd said to Hoffman, Dahmer told Purtell he "didn't do children."

"Bullshit, you do," Purtell berated him, reminding Dahmer of his conviction for sexual assault on a minor. Dahmer then said that whoever killed Adam would not be able to live in any prison.

When Purtell asked if he'd take a polygraph, Dahmer responded that Florida had the death penalty.

I knew that Dahmer had kept photographs of people in his Milwaukee apartment, some of whom were his victims. I'd been trying to find if any children had been discovered among them. Purtell didn't know. I'd called Milwaukee Police, first speaking with a detective lieutenant who as soon as I said Dahmer referred me to the public information officer. That was Anne E. Schwartz, a former *Milwaukee Journal* reporter who'd written a book about Dahmer. After unanswered messages left on her voice mail, I obtained her email address from the police chief's office and sent her the question.

This was my response, in full:

> Police thoroughly followed the lead regarding Dahmer and Adam Walsh, and it was proven to be false. There was no evidence to indicate that Dahmer had anything to do with Adam Walsh's murder. If I can help you in the future, please let me know.

I told that to Purtell. He wasn't surprised. He'd run into the same attitude in 1992, trying to get Hollywood Police to investigate even only as far as they did. They didn't want to spend the money, he said. He wished me good luck in changing their minds.

Serial killers usually fixate on specific kinds of victims, but Dahmer was an atypical serial killer, he said. In fact, "Dahmer broke our profile. He was morally indiscriminate. He'd do anything when he was in the mood." Although he had his victim preferences, he was willing to take whoever was available. Purtell called him "opportunistic."

"The whole motivation is power. If it was a woman, fine." Or a child, because he or she was easy to control. He paraphrased a line from prosecutor E. Michael McCann's closing argument at his Milwaukee murder trial, that Dahmer's ejaculations were more important to him than someone else's life.

Purtell was also shocked to hear that Billy Capshaw had said Dahmer had come looking for him in Arkansas in late 1981, driving what he thought was his father's old car. Neither Jeff nor Lionel Dahmer had mentioned that to any police, who therefore had discounted reports of killings or missing person from anywhere but Milwaukee, Chicago, and Akron. "We always thought, what if he had a car?" Purtell said. "That would break open everything."

Purtell suggested I speak to Dan Craft, also since retired from the FBI, who'd also interviewed Dahmer several times in prison. He too had been trained as a profiler. I found him on Internet, teaching criminal justice classes at Metropolitan State University, in Minneapolis.

Craft had believed Dahmer's denials. I let him read my full argument then he called me back with a mixed response. It remained his personal and professional opinion that Dahmer told him the truth. Yet he thought all the new information leading to Dahmer seemed real. "Dahmer was very, very believable. I looked him in the eyes and pressed him. His answers looked truthful, and sounded truthful," he said.

But, he said, as a polygraph examiner for the FBI, he was used to people lying to him, and he'd even complimented Dahmer on how good he was at it. "I know that people can lie, and very convincingly. I'm very good at detecting lies. But with that said, I'm not naïve enough to think I can't be fooled."

He spoke what sounded like Rule One to his classes: "In law enforcement there are no coincidences. There may be coincidences in real life, but not in law enforcement. They don't pay us to believe in coincidences, they pay us to get off our ass and talk to people and to investigate every lead thoroughly."

Craft agreed when I said that nothing Dahmer said should have been believed on its face and that Dahmer didn't give up anything he didn't have to. He had no choice but to detail his murders of those whose skulls, other body parts, identifications and photographs were in his apartment. He gave up Steven

Hicks, in his hometown of Bath, but sooner or later police would have approached him on that, too. Since his father knew he'd been in Miami and worked for Sunshine Sub the summer of 1981, he had to talk about that, too.

"If I had the case, even feeling how I feel, if somebody came to me with what you did, I'd take a look at it. Put him in or put him out. Don't let it sit there, like a matzo ball."

Craft said he'd seen everything taken from Dahmer's apartment, and although Dahmer had a large amount of porn, there were no photos of children as young as Adam. And because he'd handled a number of sexually motivated crimes, he'd learned that the offender's "motivating turn-on" was usually consistent, especially in pedophiles.

"Homosexuals usually don't like sex with the opposite sex. Bisexuals will swing both ways. But occasionally you will find a 'try-sexual,' meaning they will try anything, with anybody, at any time. Sometimes it just boils down to convenience—any port in a storm, or as the song goes, 'If you can't be with the one you love, love the one you're with.'"

19
Was Willis Morgan Right?

HERE WOULD HAVE BEEN MY ARGUMENT to Mark Smith and Chuck Morton:

That summer of 1981, Dahmer was clearly in South Florida. By then he'd already killed at least once and maybe more times, severing the head of at least Steven Hicks. He was interested enough in children to masturbate in front of them, in Germany, as he did later in Wisconsin. Where he worked that summer of 1981 there was a blue van at the sister shop close by, and access to its keys sounded easy. In addition, some days when he went to work in the late morning he was drunk and immediately told to go home. Two identifications placed him that midday at Hollywood Mall, and later in Dahmer's career he picked up at least three victims in shopping malls—the last of whom he "didn't know from Adam." Plus, an FBI agent who'd interviewed him thought he'd admitted the murder.

In the other corner were witnesses William Mistler and Mary H., who said they'd seen Toole at the mall that day. The credibility of all the mall witnesses suffered because none were in the police records before 1991. However, Willis Morgan and

Bill Bowen said they'd told police what they'd seen just after the murder.

No one but John Walsh thought Mistler was a reliable witness. Only Phil Mundy and Walsh thought Mary H. was useful. Neither of their stories was well corroborated. Jack Hoffman's dismissal of the Dahmer witnesses had stopped anyone else from seriously considering them, but in fact, Morgan and Bowen's stories were well corroborated.

As to identifying Dahmer, Morgan was more valuable than Bowen. Bowen had been an observer, Morgan had been approached as a pickup. But Bowen connected Dahmer with a blue van.

Both said they'd never forget the essence of what they'd experienced. About that I believed them entirely. Potentially suspect—certainly at any trial, which would never happen because Dahmer was dead—were their memories of details.

The problem with all four witnesses was time—and continued publicity so long after the case, much of it generated by John Walsh. His belief in Toole's guilt muddied Bowen's recollections, and possibly also Mistler's and Mary H.'s. Morgan seemed the least affected, since his 1991 statement was so consistent with what he'd told me later.

Since I'd gone as far as I could to put Dahmer in a blue van that might match Bowen's statement, I decided to work a second track. I organized similar fact evidence from descriptions of Dahmer that might match Morgan's statement.

Was Jeffrey Dahmer the man Willis Morgan saw in Hollywood Mall?

Morgan said the man he saw in 1981 was 20-25, 180 pounds. That matched Dahmer, 21, 180 pounds.

1. Drunk and disheveled.

One of the most striking remarks Morgan said to me was:

"Everything about him was *disheveled. He'd been drinking*. He was totally *unkempt*."

a. To me, Ken Haupert Sr. said that after he hired Dahmer, he was sober for the first few weeks. "Then all of a sudden, he came *in filthy dirty—like he was drinking all night. Drunk and dirty,* unable to work. *I'd send him home,* next day he'd be okay. Two months later [as his problems persisted] I fired him."

b. The Army had discharged Dahmer early for alcoholism. David D. Goss, his platoon squad leader, said Dahmer's heavy drinking began late in 1980 when he'd go on three- to five-day binges: "It started to *affect his job and appearance.* He started missing work. He would come to work at battalion aid station under the influence. You could smell it on his breath. *He'd be staggering.* Or he wouldn't show up for work."

According to an August 16, 1991, FBI document, Dahmer's military records show that he'd been counseled on seven dates between August 8, 1980, and March 9, 1981, "regarding his behavior and actions that were a result of his alcohol abuse." On February 5, 1981, he was enrolled in an alcoholic rehabilitative program but refused treatment, indicating "he was not willing to control his alcoholic intake."

c. In his book *A Father's Story*, Lionel Dahmer wrote that at the end of the summer 1981, Jeff had phoned from Miami Beach asking for money because he was broke and had no prospects. Taking the call, Lionel's second wife Shari instead offered to buy him an air ticket home to Ohio. "I picked him up at the Cleveland airport a few days later... Once he came closer to me I saw that Jeff was *filthy and disheveled.* He'd grown a mustache which he hadn't cleaned or tended and was now *scraggly and unkempt.* His clothes were unwashed and covered with stains. *He stank of whiskey...*"

d. Later, Lionel Dahmer wrote, his son's alcoholism revealed a vicious edge: "Only two weeks after returning home [from Miami], Jeff was *arrested* at the local Ramada Inn. He'd been asked to leave the lounge because he'd been drinking straight out of a vodka bottle... The police had finally been called, and at their arrival, *Jeff had suddenly turned violent.* It had taken three officers to restrain him."

e. Speaking in his interview to Robert Ressler, Dahmer spoke of how he'd found hitchhiker Steven Hicks, his first admitted victim, near his parents' home in 1978. "I had the car, about five o'clock at night, and I was driving back home, *after drinking...*"

Ressler pursued the connection between Dahmer's alcoholism and his desire (or need) to find sexual partners.

Q: *Were you always drinking when victims were picked up?*
A. *Mmm-hmm.*

f. Although Dahmer didn't drink all the time, he drank a great deal, said Billy Capshaw. "*The drunk Jeff w[ould] kill you,*" he said.

2. The Devil in Dahmer's eyes.

Also interesting was how Morgan described to me the man's eyes, which had briefly locked with his: "He had a look on him, *like the Devil was in him.* It was so scary, I was afraid to look at him... *Eyes. Unusual eyes.* The look."

a. In summer 1978, just before Jeffrey left home for his only semester of college, Lionel Dahmer recalled in his book when Shari discovered two rings missing, one garnet-and-diamond:

Jeff denied that he had any knowledge of the robberies. He appeared insulted by the accusation, and actually rose to leave the room.

At that moment, Shari, a woman who is over six feet tall in heels and who has a commanding voice, told Jeff in no uncertain terms, that he was to sit back down. For a single, chilling instant, Shari, as she later told me, *glimpsed a flash of terrible rage as it passed into Jeff's eyes.* In an instant the rage was gone, but in that moment, Shari had seen the other Jeff, the one who looked out from behind the dull, unmoving mask.

Shari told the *Milwaukee Journal* something similar in 1991. After Jeff was released from jail for molesting Somsack Sinthasomphone, she said "He had no light in his eyes."

b. On July 22, 1991, after Tracy Edwards escaped Dahmer's apartment, he ran to a nearby police car and gushed: "He threatened me, and made advances. Suddenly he had this big knife in his hand and pressed the blade on my breastbone, right here, by my heart. He said, 'You die if you don't do what I say.' *His face was completely changed.* I wouldn't have recognized him. *It was like he was the devil himself.*"

c. Talking to me, Ken Haupert Sr. said that during an argument with Dahmer, "*I saw hell in his eyes* once."

d. Another Dahmer victim, Ronald D. Flowers, Jr., 25 at the time of his sexual assault by Dahmer, testified at Dahmer's murder trial that the day before Easter in April 1988, Dahmer met him at a gay bar. Flowers's car wouldn't start, and Dahmer offered to help. They took a cab to Dahmer's grandmother's house, then, unknown to him, Dahmer drugged his coffee:

> The next thing I recall happening was thinking to myself, '*Why is he looking at me like that?*' For the first time his eye contact was solid. He didn't divert it at all. It was almost as though he was waiting for something. So, naturally, I started drinking the coffee quicker because I was getting uneasy to get out of there. The next thing I remember was becoming extremely dizzy and my head started to go down and that's it.

Flowers awoke in a Wauwatosa hospital with contusions to his head and hip, his underwear inside out. Dahmer told police he wanted to kill Flowers but didn't because he thought his grandmother had seen him.

e. In another recollection of Dahmer making concentrated eye contact, wrote Richard W. Jaeger and M. William Balousek in *Massacre in Milwaukee*, "Jeffrey once pulled out a can of beer in a McDonald's restaurant and drank it in front of a police officer sitting a few tables away. *The officer stared at Jeffrey but the young man just stared back, finally backing the officer down.*"

f. During his interview, Robert Ressler asked Dahmer about the yellow contact lenses he liked to wear:

DAHMER: The two central characters in both of those films [*Return of the Jedi* and *The Exorcist III*, two of his favorites] had glass tints to their *eyes that exuded power.* And that was part of the fantasy.

Q: You actually wore these [contact lenses], did you not, sometimes?

DAHMER: Only in bars.

Q: Did people comment on it?

DAHMER: They noticed it. *I didn't get a sense of power from wearing them, but it fit in with my fantasy.*

g. In trial testimony, Dennis Murphy, the Milwaukee detective who took Dahmer's confession, said Dahmer *likened himself to a character in The Exorcist III.*

Murphy: "He states that he felt the main character was driven by evil and *he felt he could relate to him because he was driven by evil.*"

h. In closing argument at trial, Dahmer's defense attorney Gerald Boyle quoted his client: *"Now I'm totally evil, totally depraved, totally out of control."*... He says, *"I'm Satan. I'm Satan."* Milwaukee police, in his confession, quoted him, "I have to question whether or not there is an evil force in the world and whether or not I have been influenced by it.

Although I am not sure if there is a God, or if there is a devil, I know that as of lately I've been doing a lot of thinking about both, and I have to wonder what has influenced me in my life."

i. Capshaw had described Dahmer's eyes, when he was about to turn violent, as "kind of like he was cross-eyed. An expression like he just wasn't there. I've never seen it on anyone else's face. *In a millimeter of a second, he turned from good to bad—and then he'd attack. If you've ever seen that—I promise you, you will never forget that eye contact.*"

j. Linda Swisher's snapshot of Dahmer was of him smiling, but "*his eyes were like ice.*"

"It was so clear to me at that minute of time. The violent evil I was looking at in his eyes. I've been haunted by this one tiny piece of information."

3. To gain control of victims, Dahmer grabbed arms and used knives.

In my interview, Morgan said of the man, "*I felt he was going to pull my arm and pull me out of the store... I thought, did he have a knife?*"

Bill Bowen said he saw something similar. "As I looked up toward the Sears to start walking I heard the racket of *a man dragging a boy out by his arms*, really manhandling him..."

a. Inside his Milwaukee apartment, Dahmer was showing Tracy Edwards his aquarium, blandly talking about how the catfish cleaned the bottom of the tank.

Edwards: "A split second later *he throws a handcuff on one arm and (presses) a big-ass military knife right below my rib cage, right below my heart.*"

b. In his interview, Jack Hoffman asked Dahmer about the types of tools he used to dismember his victims:

Large hunting knife with a rubber grip, very large. Bought it at the knife store in the Grand (Avenue) Mall (in downtown Milwaukee)... Just slit from the sternum to the, you know, pubic area, removed the internal organs and then cut the flesh starting from the calves, legs, and then up, removed the head and put that in the freezer, and, uh, the bone, the skeleton that was defleshed I would put in that large 80-gallon cooking pot that I had, pour in a box of that wall-cleaning solution, I'd strip the remaining flesh off, turn up to a boil, and did the same with the heads so I had a clean skeleton...

Occasionally, Dahmer said, the drugs he used to subdue his victims weren't sufficient. "I had to *stab him in the throat with a knife* 'cause he wasn't completely out..."

c. When Capshaw opened Dahmer's Army locker, *he found an ice pick and six-inch buck knives,* which Capshaw would dispose of each time he found them but Dahmer would always replace. Once he saw blood and mucus on one. Capshaw said they were easily purchased at the camp Post Exchange. He added that Dahmer always carried a six-inch lock blade knife with him, concealed in the pocket of his all-weather green army jacket. He also said that Dahmer would attack him, unpredictably, *by lunging.*

Did Willis Morgan fit the profile of Dahmer's victims?

In 1981, Morgan was 34 and only slightly smaller than the man who approached him. Back then *Morgan had a well-developed body and the look of a male model.* But he also had a subtle handicap; an above-the-knee leg prosthesis, from a motorcycle accident. He said when the man came closer he hovered over him.

a. From his book, Robert Ressler:

I moved on to victim selection. The *people Dahmer picked up from malls* or on the street *were not always gay.* He said that hadn't mattered, because *he had been looking for physique*, and in any case, the sexual activities that he performed were not consensual and took place while the victim was unconscious or dead. He said that *one of every three he approached in a mall would agree to come back to his place* and be photographed, while in the gay bars the proportion was two out of three.

I asked him again about his sexual preferences—if all things had been equal, what sort of person he would have wanted as a sexual partner.

DAHMER: I would have liked to have, like on the (gay pornographic) videotape, a *well-developed white guy*, compliant to my wishes...And if I had met, like, *one of the guys that did a striptease act*, but it's awfully hard to find somebody like that.

b. Dahmer told Jack Hoffman, "As I said, I was interested in finding the type, *the Chippendale-type, good-looking swimmers-type build.*"

c. A man who *Newsweek* described as a *muscular black model* said Dahmer had picked him up at the end of the night at a Milwaukee gay bar. Dahmer's line was, "*Hi. I'm Jeff.* I like the way you dance." The man had gone back to Dahmer's apartment, saw that his mattress was bloodstained, and managed to escape.

d. *Dahmer looked for victims he could control, and that usually meant smaller or younger.* As well as being smaller, at 17 Capshaw was two years younger than Dahmer and before joining the Army had never left his Arkansas hometown. Told of *Morgan's leg prosthesis*, he said, "*Jeff preyed on people who had that kind of problem.*"

e. When Morgan refused his blatant pickup offer, the man in Hollywood Mall became extremely upset and left Radio Shack for Sears. Rather than Adam Walsh, Morgan said, "I think I was his first choice."

*When Jeffrey Dahmer lived in North Miami Beach,
did he prowl for partners (or victims)?*

Dahmer had a history of being beaten up and mugged. Either he had a black cloud over his head, or, a more logical explanation, the assaults were responses to his failed homosexual overtures.

a. Ken Haupert, Sr.: "He came in once, *eyeglasses broken*, stinking... he explained, I was running and fell down and broke my glasses." Haupert later said that Dahmer came to work on three occasions with broken glasses—each time, Haupert bought him a new pair, and the money was repaid from Dahmer's earnings.

b. Dahmer told Jack Hoffman, "I would hate going back to the beach to sleep on the beach and so I'd stay up drinking til maybe three in the morning and this one time *I got mugged. The guy took a hundred from me.*"

Q: Did you report it to the police?
DAHMER: No. Another time I remember going back to the beach... where I had my sleeping area set up and there were some other guys there and *I almost got knifed* 'cause they didn't know who I was.

c. Lionel Dahmer wrote, while Jeffrey lived with his grandmother in West Allis:

He roamed around bars and repeatedly stayed until closing time, then he'd demand more drinks, they'd usher him out, *sometimes there'd be fights, he'd get hurt badly,* several times he got hurt resisting arrest.

He was *attacked several times and had stitches over his eye and broken ribs. He had $300 stolen from him* outside a bank downtown.

d. Reporting trial testimony reflecting Dahmer's police confession, the *Milwaukee Journal* wrote that in Milwaukee, "a man he had hoped to get into his apartment *struck him from behind in a stairwell and took $350 from his pocket.*" In a Chicago bathhouse, a man "realizing he had been drugged, *slugged him in the face.*"

Also, while he was in the Army, "he was *beaten bloody once by two angry privates.*"

e. Capshaw said soldiers sometimes violently answered Dahmer's advances. Once, he was *slugged in the face so hard he needed dental surgery.*

Was Jeffrey Dahmer a thief?

Although Ken Haupert Sr. said he never let Dahmer drive the blue van, Larry owned all the delivery vehicles and, according to Darlene Hill and Denise Sortini, left keys to them at Beach Pizza, available to anyone who needed to make deliveries. Larry, they and others said, kept exceedingly poor tabs on those vehicles, and delivery drivers and others occasionally took them for personal use. That is, they disappeared from time to time.

Knowing that, could Dahmer have taken the keys to the blue van from Beach Pizza—blocks from Sunshine Sub—and used it, perhaps after Haupert Sr. had sent him home on a weekday morning for coming in drunk? Might this have been the blue van Bill Bowen saw at Hollywood Mall, where he said a boy fitting Adam's description was tossed into it by a man fitting Dahmer's description—similar as well to Timothy Pottenburgh's statement to police?

In fact, there are many instances of Dahmer's thefts:

a. After Dahmer drugged his coffee at his grandmother's house in April 1988, Ronald Flowers filed a *theft report* with the West Allis Police Department. *About $250 in his wallet was missing, as well as a gold bracelet.* When Milwaukee police in

1991asked about it, Dahmer said he gave Flowers a dollar and walked him to a bus stop. Flowers awoke at a hospital.

b. Lionel Dahmer: "My mother told Shari that she had found a full-size department store *mannequin* in Jeff's closet. It was a male figure, dressed in sports shirt and shorts... I called him up... Jeff's reaction was completely calm and unemotional. *He said that he'd taken it from a store* only to demonstrate that he could do it..."

c. When Dahmer briefly attended Ohio State in 1978, wrote Keith McKnight for Knight Ridder newspapers, "campus police questioned him as the only *suspect in the theft of a watch, a radio and $120 that were taken from another room* in the Morrill Tower dormitory."

d. Capshaw called Dahmer "a good thief." *He stole anatomy posters* from the hospital, *hid a small stereo in a box with a larger stereo he purchased,* and apparently *diverted Capshaw's direct-deposited Army pay* to his own account. He also said Dahmer *pilfered drugs* from the base hospital to administer to Capshaw.

Could Jeffrey Dahmer be trusted to tell the truth?

Dahmer consistently denied murdering Adam Walsh. However, even before Jack Hoffman interviewed him, Hollywood Police told the *Miami Herald* they'd dropped Dahmer as a suspect. After the interview, Hoffman wrote for the file that he believed Dahmer, citing that he'd confessed to more murders than the evidence would have proved against him. Also, his likely lack of a personal vehicle—as well as his denial of knowing where Hollywood Mall was—to Hoffman suggested his innocence. He also told Morgan that he'd looked Dahmer in the eye when he denied the killing, and he believed him.

However, Dahmer had a long history of lying to law enforcement, as well as to his father.

a. Lionel Dahmer:

Jeff would lie, and we'd catch him in lies. At other times, he would be absolutely frank, and I'd check up and find him to be frank. You can't tell with a person like that whether you're getting the truth or not.

He had become that most *artful of all deceivers*, one who *mixes falsehood with just a pinch of truth.*

However, he also wrote: "I allowed myself to believe Jeff, to accept all his answers regardless of how implausible they might seem."

b. To Hoffman, Dahmer explained his work at Sunshine Sub:

DAHMER: I had all types of positions, *cashier, cook, cleaner.* And the guy was paying me under the table so he wouldn't have to, you know. And at *the same time I was collecting unemployment.*

I was working every day, about every day, once in a while I'd get one day off on the weekend, I was working *ten, twelve (hour) shifts,* um, days from morning to night, uh, didn't leave any time for recreation at all.

Q: Do you remember your supervisor's name?

DAHMER: Yeah, he was, uh, let's see, Ken Houleb I think his name was.

Q: What was his last name?

DAHMER: Houleb, I think. H-O-U-L-E-B.

c. Ken Haupert, Sr. described his employee's responsibilities differently:

"I paid him minimum wage and meals." He said Dahmer's hours were *part-time,* weekdays, roughly midmorning to late afternoon. *He worked "bussing tables, mopping floors, cleanup.*" In Haupert's entire career, managing restaurants, he said he never overworked employees the way Dahmer described.

Asked whether he knew Dahmer was collecting unemployment at the same time, Haupert said no, but he'd recognized that *Dahmer "was quite good at lying."*

d. Arrested in 1988 for sexual assault on 13-year-old Somsack Sinthasomphone, Dahmer denied intent to molest a minor. Lionel Dahmer:

> 'I'll never do anything like that again, Dad,' he reassured me. But with this assurance came another lie.
> *'I didn't know he was a kid,'* Jeff said.

e. Somsack Sinthasomphone told Milwaukee Det. Scott Schaefer *that he'd told Dahmer he was a high school freshman,* and that Dahmer had intentionally drugged him, touched his penis, placed his head on his stomach to listen to it, and then kissed it.

The night of the arrest, *Dahmer denied all of that.* If the victim was drugged, he said, it was from leftover sleep medication that Dahmer hadn't washed out of his cup before serving coffee to his guest. Police located the coffee cup, and found traces of Halcion and Irish Cream liqueur.

f. In court on the sexual assault offense, Milwaukee County Assistant District Attorney Gale Shelton told the judge that *Somsack Sinthasomphone didn't look like an adult, and that Dahmer preyed on him because he looked like someone who could be easily victimized.* The boy told her that Dahmer had asked him what grade he was in. He answered, "a freshman." "So, Dahmer knew full well he was not dealing with a consenting adult. He instead was tricking a person who he knew was a child."

Further, Shelton said, the boy remembered Dahmer pouring white powder into his mug, and Dahmer had repeatedly suggested he keep drinking.

g. After his guilty plea to the sexual assault, at his sentencing Dahmer blamed his actions on alcoholism. Appealing to the judge for leniency, he asked for treatment, which, he suggested, he'd more likely get outside of jail.

Don't buy it, said Shelton, who asked the judge to impose a five-year prison term. She called Dahmer "*very manipulative*":

> Mr. Dahmer's version is simply not the truth... His perception that what he did wrong here was choosing too young a victim—and that's all he did wrong—is a part of the problem. He appeared to be cooperative and receptive, but anything that goes below the surface indicates the deep-seated psychological problems that he is unwilling or incapable of dealing with.

After listening to the prosecutor, Dahmer personally addressed the court:

> What I have done is very serious. I've never been in this position before. Nothing this awful. This is a nightmare come true for me. If anything would shock me out of my past behavior patterns, it's this.
>
> *Please give me a chance to show that I can, that I can tread the straight and narrow* and not get involved in any situation like this ever again. This enticing a child was the climax of my idiocy. I don't know what in the world I was thinking when I did it. I offer no defense. I do want help. I do want to turn my life around.

h. Lionel Dahmer:

> On the day before Jeff was scheduled to be sentenced for child molestation, I drove to my mother's house in West Allis in order to accompany Jeff to his

court appearance.

... as I went through his room, I found a small wooden box with a metal rim. It was about one foot square, and its lid was tightly sealed and locked.

I asked "What's in here?"

"Nothing."

"Open it up, Jeff."

"But why, Dad?" Jeff asked. 'There's nothing in it."

"Open it."

Jeff suddenly grew very alarmed. "Can't I have just one foot of space to myself? Do you have to look through everything?"

"What's in the box, Jeff?"

... I turned and started for the basement to get a tool with which I could open the box myself.

Jeff leaped in front of me... "You're right, Dad," he said quietly. "It's magazines, that kind of thing."

Jeff promised to open it the next morning, out of the presence of his grandmother. The next day he did—revealing pornographic magazines.

Watching him as he faced the judge that day, it was hard to believe that this same son would never be more than he seemed to be—*a liar, an alcoholic, a thief, an exhibitionist, a molester of children...*

i. Billy Capshaw said Dahmer made a cat-and-mouse game out of outsmarting others. He was *"sneaky, conniving, and cunning. He c[ould] make you believe things that weren't true.* That's why he kept me in that room so long."

j. In a memo written on FBI stationery dated August 16, 1991, entitled *Jeffrey L. Dahmer: Foreign Police Cooperation - Murder*, found in the Hollywood Police file, an investigator wrote that Dahmer *"denied any homosexual activities while in Germany.* He further denies ever having traveled to any location to meet with homosexuals and *has not had any correspondence with anyone residing in Germany after his return to the United States."* Dahmer did say he'd traveled on short trips around Baumholder but never stayed overnight.

k. From Dahmer's interview with Hoffman:

Q: There was another incident... where the police came, which was after the arrest of (Somsack) Sinthasomphone and they searched your apartment and you had the skull.
DAHMER: That was, uh, even before that there was a time, well, I'm not going to say that on tape. That was the time I had that mummified head... *They searched my apartment,* I had an apartment on 24th Street (in Milwaukee) and they looked, *they just didn't pull a towel up, that's why they didn't see the skull...*

And another time *I had that mummified head in the, uh, small metal chest I had in the closet* and I took that to work, that's where I kept it, at work, for about a year. And then the time that the police came around asking questions about the guy that was shot upstairs or strangled upstairs, he came into my apartment and looked around and didn't see anything...

Then the time that 15-year-old guy I met working at the gay bar, he ran and told the police that I had assaulted him and they didn't believe him...

l. Dahmer continued to insist that Somsack Sinthasomphone was older than he looked:

DAHMER: ... I never intended to hurt him.
RESSLER: This was a young guy, wasn't he? How old was he?
DAHMER: Thirteen, fourteen. I thought he was older. *You know, an Asian guy can be 21 and still look like he's a young kid.*

m. Two 18-year-old girls, out after midnight in Milwaukee in May 1991, *saw 14-year-old Konerak Sinthasomphone butt naked, bruised, bleeding, and dazed.* They called police, who responded, but by then Dahmer had showed, beer under his arm. He tried to regain control of the situation.

"Look, we've been drinking Jack Daniel's, and I'm afraid he's had too much." *When an officer asked how old the child was, Dahmer answered nineteen.* "We live together, right here at 924 (25th Street, his address). We're boyfriends, if you know what I mean."

One of the girls argued that the dazed boy was obviously much less than 19, but trusting Dahmer, the officers told the girls to leave and escorted Dahmer as he took Konerak home.

Inside his apartment, Dahmer kept the officers in the living room. *Had they entered the bedroom, they would have found a body.* When the police left, Dahmer admitted, he killed Konerak then dismembered him.

n. To Hoffman, Dahmer spoke of yet another close call with police, in 1978 after he'd killed Steven Hicks and was taking bags of his dismembered bones to the dump:

In the middle of the night, 3 o'clock on a deserted road where I was pulled over by two policemen in Bath, Ohio, and *had the body parts in the back seat* and they gave me a ticket for driving left of center. Had to take the drunk test and everything and *they asked me what's this stuff? And I said, it's just garbage* that I hadn't gotten around to drop off at the city dump earlier today.

o. In 1986, *Dahmer was arrested for masturbating* in a Milwaukee riverfront park, pants around his thighs, *in front of two 12-year-old boys.* He told an officer he'd done it about five times before in the last month, but *to his probation officer he said he was merely urinating* after drinking too much beer:

After a few cans of beer, I needed to go, so I did, behind some trees. I was sure there was no one else around, but I was wrong. Two boys saw me and called the police.

However, to Jack Hoffman, Dahmer admitted that the event was not unique, besides his getting caught:

In West Allis there was some *lewd and lascivious behavior in a park that I was involved in for about a year...* There was no assault on any children or anything, it was just masturbation.

Capshaw said *military policemen caught Dahmer at least twice in Baumholder masturbating in a local park where children swam,* and brought him back to his room, although they never charged him.." They told Capshaw that Dahmer was doing it in front of "kids."

p. At trial, psychiatrist George Palermo, a prosecution witness, testified that *Dahmer "has lied for years and still lies today."*

He lied to the judge in 1989 [in the sexual assault case]. He lied to his lawyer. He lied to many doctors to get the [sleeping] pills [he used to drug his victims]. It is my feeling he has embellished a great deal in the things he has said he did.

In a 2007 interview, Palermo said he never believed that Dahmer didn't kill between 1978-87, and thought the German murders likely were his. Dahmer told him, he awoke once in Frankfurt with no memory of how he got there. Frankfurt is about 25 miles from Bad Kreuznach, where five mutilated women had been found in the vicinity while Dahmer was stationed at Baumholder, another 50 miles south. The cases were never solved.

He also thought Dahmer might have lied about not killing Adam in order to avoid Florida's death penalty.

q. In his closing argument, Milwaukee County District Attorney E. Michael McCann suggested that Dahmer might have killed elsewhere in addition to the instances he'd admitted:

> Don't be fooled by him. He fooled the police in Bath, Ohio. He fooled the West Allis police. He fooled the Milwaukee police. He's fooled a lot of people, including the court who gave him probation for sexual assault.
>
> Ladies and gentlemen, *he's fooled a lot of people. Please, please don't let this murderous killer fool you.*

r. To Dahmer, Hoffman summarized Morgan and Bowen's statements identifying him at Hollywood Mall on the day Adam disappeared:

> DAHMER: Coincident.
> Q: Excuse me?
> DAHMER: *What a coincidence, huh?...* And people said they seen me in Arizona and in California... never been there. And uh, but the, I can't prove I didn't do anything to them but the biggest, the biggest I can, I can say is Why would I have admitted to half of them (the 17 murders) that they would have known nothing about and then leave him out?

s. To Milwaukee police detective Patrick Kennedy, who asked if Dahmer had killed more than 17, Dahmer was quoted in his confession:

> Pat, what good would it do for me to admit to just half of my victims, or to a few of my victims, or not to tell

you of a couple, when I know that in the long run, it will be me that has to stand before God and admit to my wrongdoings and He'll know if I was truthful and honest when I finally was caught.

(Elsewhere in the confession, Dahmer said he considered himself an atheist.) At the end of the session he concluded, saying *"I'm telling you the truth now and I've not left anything out."*

Not entirely so, pointed out reporter Bob Springer of the *Akron Beacon Journal*, who wrote:

"Yet he had left something out—about cannibalism." In his statement on August 8, 1991, Dahmer asserted he'd only cannibalized one of his victims. But on August 22 he told Kennedy and Det. Dennis Murphy, who wrote, "there were other times in which he had eaten part of the victim." When the detectives asked him about this revision, Dahmer said he'd held it back "because it was not very appealing and he did not want us to think less of him."

t. Donna Chester, a Wisconsin state probation and parole officer, supervised Dahmer after his release from jail on the sexual assault charges. She called Dahmer "one of the most cooperative clients [she] ever worked with." She referred him to a psychiatrist, who found no serious mental disorder or any threat he might pose to others. Chester asked her supervisor for and got approval to waive any home visits at his apartment. Unknown to Chester at the time, during the more than year he was under her supervision, Dahmer killed 12 times.

Did Dahmer decapitate Adam as he decapitated so many others?

Adam Walsh's head was found, seemingly discarded, although no other part of his body was ever discovered. Eleven skulls, some still with flesh, were found in Dahmer's Milwaukee apartment. He also admitted to mutilations of additional bodies.

a. Regarding the body of Steven Hicks, his first admitted victim, in 1978, Dahmer told Ressler:

And then I cut the arm off. Cut each piece. Bagged each piece... put them back, under the (house) crawl space. *Took the head, washed it off, put it on the bathroom floor...*

b. Regarding Steven Tuomi, who Dahmer said was his second victim, in 1987, when he was living in the basement of his grandmother's house in West Allis:

DAHMER: When my Gramma goes to church for a couple hours, I go down and get it; take a knife, slit the belly open, masturbate, then de-flesh the body and put the flesh into bags; triple bag the flesh, wrap the skeleton up in an old bed sheet, smash it up with a sledgehammer; wrap it up and throw it all out in the trash on Monday morning. *Except the skull. Kept the skull."*
RESSLER: *How long did you keep that?*
DAHMER: *About a week.* Because I put it in undiluted bleach. That cleaned it, but it made it too brittle, so I threw it out.

Did Dahmer victimize other young children he didn't acknowledge?

The man who rented the Milwaukee apartment directly beneath Dahmer's, Aaron Whitehead, told the *Milwaukee Sentinel* he'd often been awakened and scared by loud pounding and "tussling noises" above him. "*One night, I heard what sounded like a kid up there. He was crying like his mother had just walloped him.* Then I heard a big falling sound. Sounded like he was being hurt."

In the days after Adam's head was discovered, both the police and press had turned to criminal profilers. Hollywood police spoke to a Los Angeles Police psychologist, Dr. Mark Reisner, the *Miami Herald* asked Dr. Sanford Jacobson, director of forensic psychiatry at Miami's Jackson Memorial Hospital.

I thought I'd compare their opinions at the time to the case's later main suspects, Campbell, Toole, and Dahmer.

Reisner had thought the killer was male, white or Latin, 19-35, but probably early to late 20s.

All three were white males. In 1981 Campbell was 25, Toole 34, Dahmer 21.

Reisner thought the killer had borderline psychopathic/psychotic personality with a tremendous homosexual conflict expressed in violence and rage. He was probably a loner and not liked by many people. He was unlikely to brag or talk about the murder, nor was it likely he'd show remorse, guilt, or confess to it.

Jacobson had agreed that the killer was a loner and as well as about remorse; he expected none, at least that was sincere.

As Reisner used the word rage, Jacobson used the word hate. He thought the killer's choice of a weak victim reflected both self-hate as well as envy. It may have referred to how he himself had been a victim of child abuse, possibly sexual.

"There is a hatred of what they were and what they still feel about themselves. By doing this to the victim, they identify with the person who aggressed against them in childhood and kind of master their own trauma."

Campbell had had some childhood conflicts, but otherwise didn't seem to fit these extreme descriptions. The Jacksonville psychologist who examined Toole in July 1983—before he volunteered he killed Adam—told a judge Toole should be committed for psychosexual problems, among others. Toole was a loner and admitted his homosexuality, he wrote. However, "he has no homicid(al) thoughts and he is not given to violence."

Some people who knew Toole saw his occasional fury, but the profilers' descriptions seem closest to matching Dahmer.

Dahmer was a loner and clearly had a homosexual conflict expressed in violence and rage. At four, he'd had a double-hernia operation, after which he asked his mother if the doctors had removed his penis. The same year he first became fascinated with dead animals. By six his first-grade teacher noted he was profoundly unhappy. At eight, his father said, an older boy in the neighborhood sexually abused him. Even if Dahmer wasn't repeatedly physically or sexually abused, he was noticeably embraced less by his parents than other children around him— his younger brother and their middle-class neighbors and friends.

Dahmer confessed to murders, but only when police found skulls in his apartment. And only at sentencing, in the glare of high-publicity television, did he show even the least bit of remorse. If he killed Adam he never admitted it, except possibly to Neil Purtell.

Reisner thought the killer had little formal education and came from a lower socio-economic background.

Campbell was one semester from getting a B.A. and came from a military family. Dahmer also came from the middle class, but spoiled his chance to get a good education. Toole fits this one best—he dropped out of seventh grade and lived in a flophouse neighborhood.

Reisner thought the killer probably had held a number of unskilled or minimally skilled jobs. Jacobson agreed that he was able to function and go about his business, seeming merely unusual to other people, but not outrightly strange.

Campbell was Adam's baby-sitter, but later he opened a business, renting beach watercraft. Later he was a self-employed landscaper. Toole worked for a roofing company, picking up trash. Dahmer was an army private, a busboy at Sunshine Sub, then later mixed chocolate in a Milwaukee factory.

Reisner said the killer identified with and was attracted to children. He had poor relationships with both females and males.

Campbell liked Adam very much, but his affair with Reve showed he could have good relationships with women. Toole told his analyst that although he was homosexual he didn't have sex with children. Milwaukee police arrested Dahmer for masturbating in front of 12-year-old boys in a park in 1986, exposing himself in front of 25 people including women and children at the state fair in 1982, and according to Billy Capshaw, in 1980-81 military police removed Dahmer two or three times from a German park where he'd masturbated in front of children.

Reisner thought Adam's decapitation indicated there had been sexual contact. The killer "almost certainly" had abducted or tried to abduct a child in the past, "almost certainly" had sexually assaulted a child in the past, and "very likely" had been arrested and imprisoned for such acts.

Campbell fit none of those criteria. Although Toole confessed to abducting and sexually assaulting children, those confessions were dubious, vague, often recanted, and hadn't stuck. Dahmer had a sexual assault conviction on a 13-year-old, although it came later.

I'd already presented my case to a Broward prosecutor who I cannot name. He'd given me his opinions freely, but in July 2006 his boss Chuck Morton implied that my using his name would risk his career. I assured that prosecutor I would not place him at such risk. Morton's reasoning was it would compromise the case if one of his prosecutors was on record saying that Dahmer killed Adam Walsh and the office ever brought charges against anyone else.

Meanwhile, the prosecutor still agreed with me.

I'd asked him, if official investigators found that my evidence checked out—plus the hypothetical that Dahmer was still alive—would you accept this case for prosecution?

Yes, he said.

Looking for weaknesses in the evidence, which the defense would likely exploit, we discussed the problem of memory, 20-plus years later, of Morgan and Bowen. Morgan seemed strong, but Bowen was on thinner ice because of his initial statements to me contradicting his 1991 interview with Hoffman.

But that could be explained and was mostly rectified after I re-familiarized Bowen with his police statement, the prosecutor thought. Back in 1991, it was compelling that both Bowen and Morgan so quickly contacted police, and that Bowen—who happened to be in town from Alabama days later—came in to give a statement.

We agreed that Bowen seemed to be describing the same incident outside Sears, of a man dragging a child into a blue van, that 10-year-old Timothy Pottenburgh told in 1981. But their descriptions of the blue van differed. Was that a problem?

No, he thought. Witnesses commonly vary in their recollections of specifics. In fact, it would be *more* suspicious if they matched perfectly. That might suggest a later witness was influenced by what an earlier one said, perhaps by reading about it in a newspaper.

"Assuming the IDs are good, absent an alibi that [Dahmer] was elsewhere, you're in the realm of probable cause" for arrest, the prosecutor said. It was clear that Dahmer was in South Florida that day; he'd already admitted it to Hoffman. So yes, even without physical evidence, there was "certainly enough" to take the case to a grand jury and ask for a first-degree murder indictment.

"Whether it would be proof beyond a reasonable doubt" at trial, that at present was a question mark, he said. But what I'd presented him, he said, met the American Bar Association ethical standard for a prosecutor to bring a case to a jury: he or she must believe it has a reasonable prospect of conviction.

Then he discussed similar fact evidence—that Dahmer severed his victims' heads, possibly in the same manner as

311

Adam's head was severed. He complained that in his Florida state judicial circuit, the court of appeals has made it difficult for trial judges to admit such evidence, and that in this case, the defense would argue that the murder of Adam wasn't a similar fact because of the age difference between him and Dahmer's acknowledged victims.

But he would still argue for its inclusion. Applying the legal test, he asked, "Does the relevance outweigh the prejudice? I think it does. If evidence of Dahmer's other crimes came in, conviction is certain. The jury would never let him walk out the door. It's overwhelmingly damning—which is why the other side would fight so hard to keep it out."

That part of the trial would be a contest of behavioral experts, he said. The prosecution would need to establish that Dahmer could have been interested in a boy of Adam's age. Dahmer was a pedophile, at least of older boys. As for whether Dahmer admitted the murder, as Purtell thought, the prosecutor said he often reviews defendants' statements with psychiatrists, who testify whether or not innocuous statements are actually admissions.

I explained a theory, proposed by my friend Christina Spudeas, by now working for the state defending its death row inmates: Although a 15-year age difference existed between Adam, 6, and Dahmer, 21 in 1981, Dahmer later chose victims with similar and even greater age differentials. At 31 he killed a 14-year-old, and another 14-year-old at 28. His youngest acknowledged attempted murder victim was age 13 (when Dahmer was 28), and he'd been arrested (at 26) for masturbating in front of 12-year-olds.

Dahmer, white and raised middle-class, chose white middle-class young men as his first two admitted victims, in 1978 and 1987. In an abrupt switch, the next 14 he admitted killing were persons of color, mostly black, of the urban underclass, including runaways and homosexual patrons of gay establishments. Most themselves had criminal records, from male prostitution to rape to use of a weapon. In general, Dahmer's choice of these victims was suspiciously notable for the lack of priority and attention police and media gave them once they were missing.

Was that because he'd learned a lesson after killing Adam Walsh?

Until forced to face the families of his victims in a Milwaukee court, Dahmer seemed to hide behind a conceit that the people he'd confessed to killing were nobodies. But the parents of white, middle-class Adam had relentlessly gone to the police and press, turning Adam into a media figure, later even launching his little league photo into a crusade, a permanent national awareness of missing children. Every high-energy TV appearance John Walsh has since made—and that Dahmer would have had trouble avoiding—continues to remind the public of the torment of his son's brutal murder.

If Dahmer killed Adam, might he have been sufficiently shocked not to repeat the mistake of killing such a young child—perhaps, a young white child?

Then I asked the prosecutor a slightly different question: Aside from whether it's a prosecutable or winnable case, do you think I'm right?

He told me: "I think you're right."

I recalled a comment Dan Craft had made:

"I'm old school," he said. "We work for God. It doesn't matter the subject's dead. Who speaks for the victim? Adam needs to be spoken for." If he were still at the FBI, he'd sit down with John Walsh and ask, What do you want to do?

On the day Adam was found dead, John Walsh was quoted making a remark that now seemed prophetic:

Whoever did this had to have a vehicle, it had to be registered somewhere. He was functioning in society. And now he'll probably just move to another state and get another dishwasher's job.

20
The Dahmer Story Breaks

IN DECEMBER 2006, I BROKE THE STORY in the *Miami Daily Business Review*, then in February 2007, local news stations WSVN in Miami and WISN in Milwaukee did their own versions. Within days CNN picked up the story, followed by the Associated Press, and other television networks, newspapers, and Internet blogs.

In advance of the *Daily Business Review* story, I called *America's Most Wanted* for comment. They offered none, but the night before publication I did receive a call from Joe Matthews—who'd polygraphed Walsh for Hollywood Police in 1981, helped the Broward State Attorney during their cold case investigation, and was now representing either the show or Walsh personally—and shared with him case facts as I had discovered them.

After two hours, I asked Matthews what he thought. Although he remained convinced that Toole killed Adam, he called my work "an impressive piece of investigation."

For the story, the paper quoted a Broward State Attorney's Office statement calling the theory "hunches and suspicions."

On WISN, reporter Colleen Henry quoted Mark Smith: "If we found no more on Jeffrey Dahmer, and I don't believe we will find any more than this circumstantial evidence we have now, we would never get to a conviction. I don't believe we'd ever get to an indictment."

Dahmer's trial attorney Gerald Boyle told Henry he didn't believe Dahmer killed Adam because doctors had spent hundreds of hours interviewing him, and not one suggested Dahmer was withholding information. "He was very honest. By that, I mean, he seemed to unload everything. I don't see any reason he wouldn't have said that he killed the boy. But of course, that was not his profile. Young boys was not his profile."

John Walsh wouldn't let himself be interviewed, but did respond on camera to questions from WSVN's Patrick Fraser, the tape of which WSVN shared with WISN. Walsh said he wanted investigators to talk to the witnesses who said they saw Dahmer at Hollywood Mall. "I think the ball is back in Michael Satz's court, the Broward prosecutor's court, to thoroughly look at this case, even though it's a cold case. People have come forward who are claiming one thing, who are saying we were not taken seriously back 25 or 26 years ago, so I think they have to look at this case."

Added Colleen Henry, Walsh said "more than 25 years later, he can't believe he's still fighting for a competent investigation into Adam's slaying."

Walsh: "That's a bitter pill for me to swallow. As someone who's a big supporter of law enforcement, that the law enforcement agency investigating my son's murder would lose—blatantly lose—key pieces of evidence and not interview people who thought they had important information about the case, it's really a tough thing."

Henry reported that the Broward State Attorney's Office told her they would investigate. But five days later, *America's Most Wanted* posted a release on their website:

Despite news stories prompted by the publication of a recent article in a Florida newspaper, *America's Most Wanted* is aware of no credible information connecting Jeffrey Dahmer to the murder of Adam Walsh...

According to the police in Hollywood, Florida, where the abduction of Adam Walsh took place, a potential Dahmer connection was first investigated in 1991, and nothing was found to validate the story. Then, two years ago, when writer Arthur Harris approached the Hollywood Police Department with his theories, a detective was assigned full-time to reinvestigate the Dahmer leads and any new information provided by Harris. According to investigators, they found Harris's claims to be totally unsubstantiated.

The remainder of the release restated that Walsh had long believed Toole killed Adam, but Walsh did repeat that the Broward State Attorney's Office should thoroughly investigate any potential new information.

To a *Daily Business Review* staff reporter, Hollywood Police spokesman Capt. Tony Rode said police had re-interviewed Morgan and Bowen after I went to the police with my information. Morgan responded in a letter to the newspaper, calling that "blatantly untrue." His last call from Hollywood Police was in 1992, and his last contact was in 1994, when he'd called Mark Smith to say that Dahmer had approached him in Hollywood Mall, and Smith dismissed him, "Yeah, right." On Fox News Channel, Bowen said he hadn't been re-contacted either.

Within weeks, Morgan and Bowen got calls from Chuck Morton personally. On March 10 Morton took Morgan's sworn statement. He also told Bowen he would fly him in for a similar interview. However, on March 21 after a producer for ABC's *Primetime* had tried to reach Morton, office spokesman Ron Ishoy called him back to deny that Morton was investigating the case because Morton "doesn't investigate anything. We rely on the police for that." He added that "we and Hollywood Police and John Walsh all believe it was Ottis" who killed Adam.

Mark Smith told the same producer, Geoff Martz, "to a high degree of certainty" Hollywood Police had ruled out that Dahmer used the blue van, and therefore they would not be investigating any further.

Morton never got back to Bowen, so that interview never happened. But in April State Attorney's Office investigator Terry Gardner interviewed Larry (the former owner of Beach Pizza) then Darlene Hill. According to transcripts of their taped statements (released two years later as public records), Larry changed his story slightly from what he'd told Hollywood police five years earlier. According to what Scott Pardon had told me, Larry said he had no vans, only pickup trucks. However he told Gardner he did have a used van, which he described as plain. It was for his personal use, but it was also used to move stock between his stores. He said he thought its color was beige, and he'd told that to Darlene when she'd called and asked him about a blue van. He added, "Listen, I might be wrong. I don't know. I really, I really don't, ah, to me it was always beige."

Gardner asked Darlene about it two days later. "He said he told you that he recalled a van, but his recollection was that it was beige, not blue," Gardner said.

"No. He recalled a blue van," she answered.

Unlike the other major witnesses I'd found, I'd never had the chance to spend unrushed time talking to Ken Haupert Sr. When I tried to call him in 2007, I found he'd since closed his Oklahoma sub shop and his home phone number wasn't working. To find him, I used the water records at Dewey city hall—again. When he answered the phone, he was just as surprised at how I'd found him as the first time. He was in the process of opening a new restaurant across the Kansas border in Caney, not far from his home.

He'd seen Morgan's quotes in the *Chicago Tribune*, how Dahmer had looked at him. "That could only have been Dahmer," he said. "The way Dahmer looked at people he disliked, you wouldn't know it unless you saw it. There's not another person in the world who had that look."

Haupert recalled again the moment Dahmer had given him a similar look. Haupert told him off: "You ever look at me like that again, you're in big trouble."

Haupert also remembered something he hadn't thought of before. A week or two after he hired Dahmer, Jeff told him there was a dead man behind the dumpster. For two or three days he'd been stepping over him.

"Why didn't you say something to me?" Haupert asked him, sounding exasperated to me. "Maybe he needed help, maybe he was still alive."

When Haupert saw the body it had already turned blue and had flies. He immediately called police. He thought the man was about 50, sickly, and didn't look like he'd been beaten. Haupert guessed he'd been eating out of the dumpster—as he'd seen Dahmer eating out of it before he hired him.

Haupert said there was a police report of the incident. He didn't know the date, but the address must have been the store's, 17040 Collins Avenue.

I called Miami-Dade Police Central Records. Although they had 1981 police reports on microfilm, without a victim's name I needed a case number.

I knew the Miami-Dade Medical Examiner kept good records. I asked a clerk there to search their deaths in June and July 1981 for a body found at that address. Days later, she had it. The M.E. had his name as Jaida Bohumil, age 55. He'd been identified by his fingerprints—he had a record in Dade County for vagrancy and drunkenness. The police report date was July 7, 1981—20 days before Adam disappeared.

The medical examiner had the police case number. I ordered it from Miami-Dade Police, as well as the autopsy report from the M.E. When I received the police report it listed as the reporter of the crime "Dahmer, Jeffrey." For his address and contact phone he gave the address and phone of Sunshine Sub.

Finally, here was official evidence, which Hollywood police had failed to find, that Dahmer had been in Miami. And Jeffrey Dahmer finding a dead body, how suspicious was that? No one in the larger Dahmer case seemed to know about it. Apparently, in those hundreds of hours of interviews when he admitted everything, he'd forgotten about it. Nor when Geoff Martz asked Lionel Dahmer did he know about it.

The report was three pages, its supplement written by a homicide detective:

> According to Mr. Jeffrey Dahmer the victim was an old derelict living at the rear of his business in the meter room. The victim was always seen walking around on Collins Ave. and had been complaining of ill health. The victim was discovered by Mr. Dahmer face down directly south of the meter room on the gravel. The victim was known [as] "Bobby" possibly Janosky (phonetic).

In fact, all the information taken at the scene was "according to Mr. Jeffrey Dahmer." But Dahmer clearly knew the dead man. On his rap sheet, two of his arrests were as Robert Janda. Another, that sounded closer to his given name, was as Bohumil Vaclau Janda.

It wasn't obvious to the detective this was a homicide. The body had no bleeding or obvious marks of violence other than indentations from gravel. He was found cold, and was wearing only one tennis shoe—the detective found his other shoe in the meter room, about 20 feet away. His last known address was from 1970, and police had found no kin to notify.

According to the report of his autopsy, done the next day, he was 5'4" and 78 pounds. His stomach had less than a half-ounce of fluid—he must have been hungry. Assistant Medical Examiner Charles Wetli wrote that his probable manner of death was natural, caused by chronic ethanolism. His findings were fatty metamorphosis of liver—suggesting alcoholism—dehydration, and cerebral edema with possible encephalomacia. But in a note for the file dated six days later, after viewing microscopic slides, Wetli handwrote, intriguingly, "no fatty metamorphosis."

Haupert remembered there had been a man living in the meter room, although Haupert said he never went in there. Too smelly. Around the time of the police report, he realized that Dahmer didn't seem to have anywhere to live—which would have been consistent with Dahmer giving his address as Sunshine Subs. Of course, Haupert had hired him after twice seeing him look for food in the store's dumpster. Within the next week or two after the deceased person incident, Haupert said, he arranged for Dahmer an inexpensive room at the Bimini Bay, which rented by the month or week. He advanced whatever money was needed to get Dahmer in, and Dahmer later paid him back in full out of salary.

When I told the story to Billy Capshaw, who believed Jeff had lied about killing only 17, he thought Jeff likely had murdered the man. He said Jeff knew how to suffocate someone without leaving a trace. It was simple—he'd sit on the person's chest or upper back until he stopped breathing. Jeff had done it to him, and Billy had learned to breathe shallowly and not complain, otherwise Jeff would clobber him with an iron bedpost. That the homeless man was so small made it that much easier for Jeff, who was very strong. Haupert had made the same point about Dahmer's strength, especially in his hands. He'd seen it when he scooped ice cream.

I also told the story to Willis Morgan, and it was he who

When I raised it, below was a gravel crawlspace, about four feet in depth. Martz lowered himself down to examine it, and said it was about 15 by 15 feet. Aside from two empty plastic grocery bags and some PVC piping, he saw nothing else.

I knew that Dahmer had admitted dismembering Steven Hicks in the crawlspace beneath his childhood home in Akron. That was in 1978, three years before Adam. Police had searched the space in 1991 and found blood and a few human bones. When Dahmer returned home in 1981, after his South Florida adventure, he said he'd exhumed Hicks's remains from the drainpipe he said he'd left them in, then sledgehammered and scattered them in the woods behind his backyard.

A news broadcast videotape Martz later found showed the crawlspace looking remarkably like the one we'd just uncovered. But we didn't have the time to excavate ours.

Jan marked interesting stains on the walls with stickers printed with arrows. But it wasn't until she pulled out colored goggles for us, and aimed a colored light on one of those corners, that a pattern emerged to our eyes.

On the southern wall, almost at the southwestern corner, strikingly obvious, was a rain of stains, maybe a hundred droplets, starting about a foot above the floor to above where we could reach. When Jan turned off the light and we removed our goggles, it was no less obvious.

The rain of stains was in two directions, she showed us. Assuming a chopping motion down, the cast-off droplet stains rose, climbing the wall. As the chopping instrument was pulled back, other droplets were cast off in a down direction, the reverse. There were less of those.

Looking at the scene clinically, I thought it was spectacular. Jan agreed. I asked if it looked to her like it might have been related to a homicide. She did.

Was this blood? Using a swab kit, first she showed us what a positive result would look like, using a control. She soaked the swab with distilled water, placed a drop from a vial she'd brought containing horse blood, then doused it with phenolphthalein. The swab turned magenta—to my eyes, the whole swab burst with blood color.

Next she tested a spot on the wall about ten feet from the spatter corner. She dabbed the water-soaked swab onto the concrete wall, hoping for transfer then added the chemicals. Concrete, she said, is one of the toughest surfaces to get transfer from. The swab failed to turn color at all.

Then she took a sample from a spot in the corner. The swab reacted just as it did in her control test.

I shivered. In an obscure room that connected to Jeffrey Dahmer, paces away from where he was employed that summer of 1981, was a large pattern of spatter, possibly indicative of a homicide, which tested positive for blood.

Was this Adam Walsh's blood?

Unfortunately, this was the peak moment. Nothing else would get us further. After taking two more phenolphthalein samples that indicated blood—then one that didn't—Jan tried a field test called Hexagon OBTI, a sort of litmus paper that can determine whether blood is human or animal. The emergence of one band on the paper would indicate negative but that the test is working, two bands positive, that the blood is human. The horse blood resulted in one band. And so did our sample, twice. We were left to wonder whether we'd just proved the blood was animal and not human, or merely gotten an inconclusive result, as Jan suggested. The field test shouldn't be relied upon, she said.

By now the business day had begun and our time was up, as the shopping center management told us in no uncertain terms. To earn time for Jan to gather a few more samples that she could submit to a private crime laboratory, outside I stalled the maintenance men, regaling them with the story of why we were there, what infamous person had trod these steps. If the lab could prove the blood human, we were hoping they could spin DNA from it—which potentially could be tested against hair samples of Adam kept by the Broward Medical Examiner. But when the results came back about two weeks later, the news was uninspiring: the samples, as biologic material, had degraded and told us nothing. Probably because they had been in that warm, humid room for years they simply weren't testable.

Jan wanted to return to the room and chisel off some of the stained concrete and submit those samples to the lab. She also wanted to take, with permission, the axe and sledgehammer to test for blood, and excavate the crawlspace to look for bones.

I'd never heard of a crawlspace anywhere in sea-level South Florida. What a stroke of luck for Dahmer to discover one in that room—if in fact the crawlspace existed in 1981. I checked the Miami-Dade Building Department for plans. The original architectural records, from the fifties, were on microfilm, but unreadable. We'd noted that the scalloped cut in the concrete floor looked modern, as of course was its Home Depot door. Had the cut in the floor been enlarged, or was this the first cut? We had no way of knowing.

Also to note was that the concrete cinderblock on the corner adjoining and above where we'd found the blood had been partly (and sloppily) repaved, who-knows-when. As well, higher above on the adjoining wall was post-original construction metal and PVC pipes. However, where the blood was the wall seemed to be original. After we got the cold case squad of the Miami-Dade Police interested in the room, a detective tried to get shopping center manager Danny Katz to sign a legal consent to search. Instead, Katz told the detective there had been a fire in the shopping center in October 1994, and that the electric room had been completely redone after that.

Katz hadn't told us that. When I checked online in the Miami Herald, there had been a large fire in the shopping center when Katz said. Chemicals in a print shop on the second floor had ignited, and flames collapsed its floor—the ceiling of a

Chinese restaurant. As to whether the electrical room had been upgraded and that wall repaved then, building permit plans might give the answer. I asked a researcher at the county Building Department to check their files. He found two demolition permits for the shopping center dated November and December 1994, but no records of rebuilding or electrical permits. From our look into the electrical room, most of the electrical boxes looked upgraded from 50 years ago. But one box seemed original. Inside it, I had noted, handwriting referring to the fuses was in fountain pen ink. Later, Darlene Hill told me, when she had run Sunshine in that space, there was no second floor. It was logical that the new electrical boxes were installed when the second floor was first built, sometime in the 1980s.

Speaking himself to Jan, a Miami-Dade police lieutenant had thought he understood her to say that her negative field test result for human blood meant we had proved the blood was animal, not human. By contrast, Jan told us the negative result was merely inconclusive. I checked on my own.

I emailed Bluestar, the company that marketed the Hexagon OBTI test, and received a reply from the president, Jean-Marc Lefebvre-Despeaux, in Monaco. He wrote back that a negative result could mean three things: that the sample wasn't blood; it wasn't human blood; or it was human blood but the hemoglobin was too degraded to get a positive reaction. Although he doubted the last explanation, he added that the Hexagon OBTI is "only a presumptive test," and that DNA testing could tell more. But we'd already tried that.

I then spoke to Mike Grimm Jr., vice president of Evident, located in Virginia, a distributor of forensic investigative products including the Hexagon OBTI test. "In general, the test is very inconclusive," he told me. Rather, it's meant "to point the investigator in the right direction." Before the Hexagon test existed, officers would make arrests for stains on a suspect's clothing that a crime lab would determine weeks later was red paint, or dog blood.

The result of a single bar on the test, as we'd gotten, doesn't even indicate blood, he said, it only indicates that the test is working. He suggested I speak to a criminology expert in blood and stain pattern analysis—Jan Johnson. When I told Grimm we'd already hired her, he said, "I would to defer to Jan."

In April 2008 I received public records from the FBI's Adam Walsh file. One document stood out. It was an interoffice teletype stamped-dated April 30, 1992, sent by the FBI's Miami bureau and read that "Miami received information from [blackout] that three separate witnesses have come forth and have placed Dahmer at the Hollywood shopping center the morning Adam Walsh was kidnapped from a Sears department store.

"[blackout] described his witnesses as being reliable ordinary citizens and not individuals seeking notoriety or publicity. One of the witnesses is a [blackout] in the Fort Lauderdale area, and like the other two, after seeing Dahmer on the news they independently contacted [blackout] at different time frames. There is no information to reflect that the witnesses know each other."

Three witnesses. There was nothing in Hollywood's file to reflect that. And no way in this document to identify who it was.

It continued about efforts to interview Dahmer about Adam. An FBI supervisor had spoken with Dahmer's attorney Gerry Boyle, who'd initially agreed to assist "if it meant not placing his client in jeopardy. As the Bureau and Milwaukee are aware Dahmer has refused to implicate himself in case in those states which carry the death penalty."

Boyle never did let Dahmer speak to the FBI about Adam. (When Dahmer spoke to Jack Hoffman, it was after Boyle had withdrawn from the case.) Boyle "indicated that Dahmer had information (possibly an alibi) that would eliminate him as a suspect in the Walsh case; however, this information was never shared with Miami."

The last interesting line in the document was that the Miami Bureau "would still like to interview Dahmer since he is currently the only suspect in the case."

I asked Neil Purtell if he knew about a third witness at the Hollywood Mall. He didn't, aside from what he'd told Geoff Martz and I in 2007 of a man in Pigeon Forge, Tennessee, who had called the FBI's Knoxville office to say that he had been in a mall in Hialeah and thought he had seen Dahmer there. That mall, I knew, was called Westland Mall, it also had a Sears, and was approximately as close to where Dahmer was living on the beach as was the Hollywood Mall. Hialeah is in west Miami-Dade County, Hollywood is in south Broward.

Martz and I had failed to find the man but there was a report in the FBI file about him too. He'd first called the FBI on July 29, 1991—the day after Bill Bowen first called Hollywood police—after he too had seen Dahmer's photo in the newspaper. He said that he'd seen "at the mall a man who looked just like Dahmer propositioning young males. He was carrying a camera and taking pictures. His behavior was strange and remembers him because of his actions. He also describes him as a cold-eyed, very disturbing-type person."

In a second conversation days later with the Knoxville office the man went into more detail. He said that in 1981 he'd had a business near the mall in Hialeah, and about a month before Adam had disappeared, he'd taken his son shopping to that mall.

He recalled "standing outside a shop window and noticed a guy there he now believes to be Jeffrey Dahmer taking photos and passing out cards. This person asked [blackout] if he knew of some young men who wanted to get into the modeling business. [blackout] recalls this person because of the scene created by him. A young man was approached by this individual. The young man cursed, backed off and said 'Hell no, you son-of-a-bitch.' The young man tells [blackout] 'He thinks I'm a queer and wants me to pose nude.'"

I mailed a letter with copies of these documents to the newly installed chief of Hollywood police, Chadwick E. Wagner. He forwarded the letter to Det. Lyle Bien, and he returned my call. He said he wasn't familiar with any third witness of Dahmer at Hollywood Mall and he'd asked the FBI to provide him an un-redacted copy of the documents, but frankly, it didn't make any difference to him. "It's of no value to us," he said. "I don't believe there's anything there."

He didn't believe the stories told by Morgan or Bowen. Willis had recently demanded that Bien re-interview him, and as Bien recalled (and Willis had told me), Willis "didn't leave here happy."

"I don't believe that Morgan came face-to-face with Jeffrey Dahmer," Bien said, although he did think that Willis had "convinced himself it happened." A normal person, he said, does not do what Willis had said he'd done, following a suspicious person through the mall. Willis had told me he'd done it because he'd expected the man would approach someone else, who'd need help.

Nor was Bowen credible. He'd had just a "brief side profile encounter. I just can't believe somebody saw that and remembers it so many years later." He said that wasn't how it went in police work.

Willis's complaint to Bien was that he, currently in charge of the case, had dismissed Dahmer without re-interviewing any of the important Dahmer witnesses—despite Capt. Tony Rode telling the press in 2007 that they had. I got Bien to admit that he hadn't spoken to Bowen, Ken Haupert Sr., Jan Johnson, or gone into the meter room. He said our inconclusive field test results were enough that they didn't have to do their own.

He thought a dead bird in the room was the source of the blood on the wall. The Miami-Dade police cold case detective had seen the bird when he'd gone inside.

In fact there had been a dead bird on the concrete floor of the meter room. It was a baby bird—a chick—the day I was in the room I'd only seen it because I'd put my pint container of orange juice on the floor right next to it. It had come to its final rest inches from the wall opposite the bloodstains, about 10 feet away. There was no blood on or around the bird, or any trail from it to the bloody wall. Frankly, the idea that that little birdy was the source of so much blood, rising so far up the wall— well, it was ridiculous.

Bien also tried to convince me that the meter room had been rebuilt since the fire. I told him about the meter box with the fountain pen writing. He dismissed that too. "That's in TV crime shows. That doesn't prove anything."

I wasn't getting anywhere. At least he didn't suggest to me that I had done the murder, as he had to Willis. (Since I mentioned it, I have an alibi. I was then living in Los Angeles.) I mentioned the eight witnesses who'd seen the blue van, none of whom they'd questioned. "We proved there was no blue van from the guys we talked to," he said.

In October at an award dinner for Broward County prosecutor of the year I ran into Mark Smith, who Wagner had promoted to Assistant Chief of Police. He said he was still working the case. In the next few weeks he was about to pursue a new lead, although it probably wasn't earth shattering, he admitted. All he would tell me about it was that it didn't connect to Dahmer or Toole.

21
Resolution

THE MORNING OF DECEMBER 16, 2008, Hollywood Police Chief Chadwick Wagner announced he would hold a press conference that afternoon to close the Adam Walsh case. His killer? Ottis Toole.

It seemed like a Christmas gift to John and Reve Walsh, who were present. At last they could have closure, the killer of their little boy, taken 27 years before from the shopping mall across the street from the police station, finally determined. The event was carried live on cable TV news networks. In the room the media had an edge of skepticism, but it seemed inappropriate to argue with the crying victims. Also on the dais was Mark Smith. Someone asked him what he thought of the decision; he said he agreed with it.

National media presented the news as a good day for the Walshes. Bloggers generally agreed. If it was a fiction or wishful thinking, it didn't much matter because Toole was dead (as was Dahmer), and the Walshes felt so relieved.

But it did matter. Closing a murder case on the wrong, if convenient suspect doesn't inspire confidence in the police.

Endorsing it didn't make for the media's most shining day either. Some in local Miami media dissented. That evening, WSVN aired *Questions Still Surround Adam Walsh Case After Its Official Closure*. Outside the police station I was quoted: "I came here because they said they had new evidence. There was no new evidence." In the following days, the Associated Press ran *Case Closed? Questions Linger in Adam Walsh Probe*, and the *Miami Herald* led a Sunday paper with *Doubts About Adam's Killer Loom Large*. The brashest headline was in a *Broward New Times* blog, *According To No New Evidence, Deceased Pathological Liar Killed Adam Walsh*.

But what everyone saw on television was only the surface story. For the last two years I'd repeatedly asked Hollywood to open the remainder of their case file as public records. Florida state law requires the police to make their files available on request unless the case is in active investigation. I kept arguing it wasn't. They kept responding that it was. Now, with the case officially closed, they had to open the file. In fact, the police had already prepared copies of it on CD-ROM to hand out to reporters that day. Because I was there I got a copy. On one CD was everything that had been released in 1996, on a second everything since then.

One of the most notable things about the case had been that police for years had not felt they had any credible witnesses, aside from Reve Walsh, who said they had seen Adam at Sears that day. Actually, they had Timothy Pottenburgh, but within a month they had dismissed him, Jack Hoffman thought his timeline was an hour too late. In 1991 came William Mistler, but none of Hoffman, Mark Smith, or Phil Mundy had considered him credible enough. Like Pottenburgh and Mistler, Bill Bowen had reported seeing Adam and an abductor, but he had been dismissed. Willis Morgan had only seen a possible abductor.

So in the end, what was this vaunted case against Ottis Toole? Besides his confessions. There was the 1996 statement

Mary H. gave to Mundy—from the new files we learned her full name was Mary Hagan, but she had died in 2006, at age 85. There was little more in the transcript of her interview to Mundy than he had told me in 1997. There was Bobby Lee Jones, who had worked with Toole in 1982 and was with him in the Duval County Jail in 1983. Mundy had re-interviewed him in 1996, but again, he'd already told me most everything in that statement. And then-security guard Kathryn Shaffer, now Kathryn Shaffer-Barrack, had changed her mind in 1996 to say she *had* thrown Adam out of the store. Whether her first or later impressions were correct—and it seemed that her first impression was best—we knew in 1997 what she had said.

There was one new name, Nellie Schreck, who in 1996 said she'd seen Toole hold open for her an entrance door to Sears. She remembered his ugly face and that he tilted his head to the side. But she said she'd been in the store between 2-5 that afternoon, which was when she always did her shopping. And could she have seen and been influenced by WSVN's oft-repeated 1984 jail interview with Toole, where he notably tilted his head to the side? Schreck had died in 2006 too, at age 86.

In 1996, when I'd first approached this story, I'd speculated that the police had the solution in their files, they just didn't know it.

Thirteen years later, in the first weeks of 2009, going through the new case file reports, I finally realized for certain I'd been right.

There were at least four additional witnesses who had all seen Adam at Sears that day. Two had seen him with his abductor, the others had seen a suspicious man nearby. Their statements were dated 1996 and 1997. As I found each of them in the file, I interviewed them.

Phil Mundy had interviewed three of them and showed them a six-picture photo lineup that included Toole. All three had failed to identify Toole as the man they had seen that day. On that, Mundy seemed to have dismissed each as a significant witness.

A fourth witness's statement was on a tip sheet page from *America's Most Wanted* that had been forwarded to Hollywood police. Neither Mundy nor Mark Smith had interviewed her. Why not? Because she'd mentioned seeing a blue van outside Sears? And Mundy was looking for an old white Cadillac?

When I interviewed them, I showed them a photo of Toole. All four had seen him before. The three who hadn't identified him for Mundy emphatically said to me the man they saw wasn't Toole. The fourth, who hadn't been interviewed, thought maybe that was who she had seen.

Then I showed pictures of Dahmer. All four knew who Dahmer was, although one didn't know his face.

What happened next, I have never experienced anything like.

Each of the four reacted emotionally. The woman who thought she'd seen Toole got goose bumps. It was Dahmer, she realized, not Toole who she'd seen. Another woman cried at the mention of Dahmer's name. Seeing his picture years ago she had concluded it was him, and she identified the first photo of him I showed her.

A man who was 9 years old in 1981 and said he had been playing videogames with Adam, and had seen him leave with a man, stared at a picture of Dahmer I showed him. His voice broke and tears came. Although he wouldn't say absolutely it was Dahmer he'd seen, he admitted having an emotional reaction. "You know what's bothering me?" he asked. "That it's bothering me."

Another man did a double take when I first showed him Dahmer's picture. He was skeptical that he was the same man he'd seen until a couple weeks later we looked at a number of photos of Dahmer on the Internet. Then he came to one and stopped. "Oh, my, god," he said. "You have a picture that is strikingly similar to the man I saw." He said if Mundy had shown him that picture in a lineup, he would have picked him out.

What's more, two of the four, entering Sears that day, saw a blue van parked in the store's fire lane just in front of the toy department entrance. Police had dismissed Timothy Pottenburgh's similar statement, and then Bill Bowen's, but now there were four witnesses total who had seen a blue van in the same spot all at about the same time.

In the order in which I found the witnesses:

Philip Lohr

A 1997 summary memo written by Phil Mundy attached to an interview he'd done with Philip Lohr was dismissive. Lohr had already sought out Mark Smith, who told him what he'd seen had no relation to Adam. Lohr had complained to Smith's sergeant then found Mundy. Mundy agreed with Smith. When Lohr got sarcastic, Mundy wrote, he decided his best course was to just take his statement.

Mundy wrote that Lohr couldn't say for sure he saw Adam, couldn't be certain it was the same day as the abduction, and his description of the man he saw didn't fit Toole "or any of our other 'suspects.'"

In the transcript of his statement, Lohr said he'd passed a man carrying a child out the west side lawn and garden entrance of Sears, and overheard the child say something unnerving: "You are not my daddy." The child was about six, too large to be carried. For comparison, in 1997 Lohr's own son was then six. The child had a freckled face, brown hair, was missing his front teeth, and looked flustered, like he'd been crying. Lohr couldn't be certain of the day it happened, but recalled it had been a day or so before he first heard the news about Adam missing and had seen search helicopters flying. The time of day could have been anywhere from noon to three P.M.

The man, he described, was about 25-30, 6-foot, medium

build, brown hair, wearing glasses, sideburns, and a "short chin beard" hair connected to a mustache, possibly like a goatee.

He said when he saw Adam's picture on the news he immediately thought it was him. Mundy asked why he didn't immediately contact police.

"Well, I was forced to make a determination as to whether did I see something significant or was it not significant... I hate to bring it up but it boils down to I was able to convince myself that it probably wasn't the same child, the police probably have other witnesses, that I couldn't have been the only person who saw anything. Every reason in the book just so that I don't have to say that I was the one who could have stopped the man."

Mundy asked why he was talking to police now. Before he went into the store, Lohr mentioned, outside the entrance he'd seen a van parked. It was blue. "Let me sum it up, I guess I have always felt that I made the wrong decision in not going to the police. Maybe I've felt a little guilty about not doing that."

The van had been parked in a traffic lane within twenty feet of the store entrance, and no one had been in it. To Lohr's annoyance it had interrupted the traffic flow. He didn't know if it was connected to what he'd seen moments later, but "to make a long story short with the van, every time we get behind a van I eventually start to get bothered by, should I have gone to the police, and every time that happens I just put it out of my mind... I do U-turns in the middle of the street because I quite frankly... I don't want to go through another one. I don't want to actually end up being somebody that sees this thing twice."

On that, Mundy ended the statement.

In 1996-97, Mundy was trying to prove the case against Toole. Toole had a white Cadillac; rightly or not, Pottenburgh's blue van had been discredited. So had Bowen's blue van. When Lohr brought up a blue van, Mundy seemed not to want to hear about it.

On the other hand, I was very interested in a sighting of a

blue van. Although Lohr recalled it as somewhat deluxe, as had Pottenburgh, he'd also placed it in nearly the same spot as Bowen and maybe Pottenburgh had said it was.

"I know absolutely it was Adam Walsh" I saw, Lohr gushed when I came to his Hollywood home to see him. He was also "absolutely positive there was a blue van."

He'd expected someone to contact him after the Hollywood press conference. He was equally positive Toole was the wrong man.

I took his story from the top. He was a regular shopper at Sears's tool department. That day in 1981, driving in the parking lot lane next to the west side of Sears, headed south, Lohr had spotted a good parking space. Next to him in the northbound lane was a blue van, inappropriately parked and stopping traffic. A county bus was behind the blue van and then a white car, possibly a Ford (not a Cadillac, he insisted). He was about to make a right turn into the parking lane when from behind the bus the white car darted into his lane, cut him off and turned towards the spot.

Lohr was incensed—enough to animatedly recall it for me so many years later, as if it had just happened. It was weird but I understood. I knew from living in South Florida back then, you sneaked into someone's intended parking space at the risk of violence.

The white car didn't take the spot but Lohr remained irate by the episode. On his way into the store he walked past the van, the root cause of the problem—it was right in front of the entrance, about 20 feet from the door.

As he passed through the door, a man exiting was carrying a child. Something was inappropriate; the child was about 6 years old, too big to be carried. And he was either crying or had just stopped. That child was Adam, he said after seeing his picture in the news.

"I heard Adam say, 'You're not my daddy.'" The man responded, "I'm taking you to your daddy."

"It startled me. I thought, everybody down here is divorced. There's a boyfriend. Okay, maybe he's taking him to his daddy." Stopped in his tracks, Lohr wondered, "Should I do something? Go out there and take a look?"

He didn't follow them but did decide to commit to memory what he'd seen. He focused on the child. He noted his three-color striped shirt, khaki shorts, his face covered with freckles, and that his front teeth were missing. Also, "I remember saying to myself, sailor's cap." Later he called it a captain's hat. "I thought, what kind of parents would give a kid a captain's hat?"

All that matched Reve Walsh's original description of Adam, except for the color of his shorts. Reve had said they were green.

He didn't concentrate as much on the man. All he could say was, "He was not really dirty. He had reasonably acceptable clothes, a neat appearance. I did not consider him to be unsavory." He recalled the man was wearing glasses, possibly sunglasses, and was maybe 6 feet tall, or in any event, a few inches taller than Lohr, who is 5'6". He had a very calm voice.

"Oh God, could I have done something? Could I have stopped it? I don't want to be known as the person who didn't stop it," he said. He's felt guilty all these years—although he realized that at the time he couldn't be sure there was any reason to do anything. "Ever since Adam, I've stopped people when their kids say, I don't want to go!"

In 1997, with the case back in the news, he saw another blue van driven by someone who made him think of the man who carried the child out of the store. Considering now his own son, he thought, what if "Oh my god, he's back!"

He called Mark Smith at Hollywood police and came in to give a statement. Smith gave him a photo of a small boy who looked like Adam but wasn't, then left the room. Lohr got the feeling he wasn't being taken seriously. At the State Attorney's office he found Mundy, who showed him a six-photo lineup that included Toole. Lohr insisted Toole wasn't the man.

I showed him a photo of Toole, from John Walsh's book. "He ain't got enough hair," he said. "That is definitely not the person."

I showed him Dahmer's 1981 black-and-white mug shot. He was dubious. Then I showed him a color shot of Dahmer at his first appearance in a Milwaukee courtroom in 1991. He did a double take. Pending showing him more pictures, I left that day with his conclusion: "I can definitely say that I cannot rule out Dahmer, but I cannot rule him in."

Lohr had an email address but warned me he wasn't good with the Internet. I sent him links including A&E Biography's Dahmer story, then realized he probably hadn't opened them. Two weeks later I arranged to put him in front of a computer.

After a few minutes, he said, "For every picture I see that says, that looks like him, I see another that says, that's not him."

Dahmer's 1981 mug shot came on the screen. I printed it, and Lohr borrowed a black felt pen and drew on it glasses, longer hair brushed to the side, and a mustache and goatee. "If I had a police officer set this down in front of me (in a photo lineup) and ask, can you I.D. any of these people, I would gravitate to that," he said. "He has the eyes."

A few pictures later, he added, "He's demonstrated he has facial hair, and combs his hair over," as Lohr had just drawn. He was looking for a shot of him wearing glasses, if possible photochromic lenses, which in sunlight darken to sunglasses. Lohr called them PhotoGray, a brand name.

And then we came across a family portrait, first published in Lionel Dahmer's book *A Father's Story*. Jeffrey was about 17, he wore his thickest mustache, and a hint of hair lined the bottom of his chin (although it might have been only a shadow on the photo). He also was wearing dark amber glasses. Lohr stopped.

"Oh… my… god. That's getting real close. And he's wearing sunglasses indoors."

He thought about it for the next few minutes. "I find it amazing how similar (that picture) is to the man I saw. You have a picture that is very, very similar." He wouldn't commit to certainty, but he repeated about the "striking similarities."

"I only saw the man for a split second while I was doing the left/right dance to get around him, when I heard Adam say, you're not my daddy."

"I'm amazed that Jeffrey Dahmer could be that similar to the person I saw. Seeing that picture there starts making it real creepy."

I later asked Billy Capshaw whether Dahmer had ever worn transition glasses. He had. "They were a smoky color when they changed," he said. "I had never seen glasses like these, I was pretty impressed with them." He remembered they weren't army-issue, and were in the 1970s style of pilot glasses, square-looking. That description matched the glasses in Dahmer's family picture.

Vernon Jones

In 1994, Vernon Jones wrote a letter addressed to John and Reve Walsh in care of John's show:

"I was playing Atari and Intellivision with your son Adam on that eventful day in July [1981]. The reason why I am informing you of this is to give you my sincere apologies for my being too young and naïve to realize that I possibly could have made a difference in the outcome of your family's life."

In 1981, Jones was nine. He offered further explanation to the Walshes or anyone who would get back to him. He wrote that he'd just spoken to 1500 people at a convention for a group called Youth Crime Watch and told them what had happened to Adam "could have been me" instead, or possibly it might have happened to both of them together.

America's Most Wanted forwarded the letter to Hollywood police, which never called him. Rummaging through the file in 1996, Phil Mundy found it and went to Jones's office to speak to him. Jones was then working for a youth crime prevention program funded by the U.S. Attorney's office for the Southern District of Florida.

On tape, Mundy spoke to him for fifteen minutes. Jones described a man who motioned toward both he and Adam while they were playing the videogame. Jones knew not to follow a stranger. But a short time later he saw Adam leave with the man. Towards the interview, Mundy showed him the photo lineup that included Toole. Jones couldn't pick out the man he'd seen.

Mundy thanked him, and in his summary wrote that Jones didn't match what Mary Hagan and Kathryn Shaffer-Barrack had told him. And despite that Jones had sullenly written to John Walsh he'd played a videogame with Adam, Mundy wrote that Jones did not identify Adam as the boy he'd played with, and likely was in the store at some other time than when Adam was there.

In fact, Jones had told Mundy on tape he'd identified Adam as that child when he'd first seen his picture in the news in 1981, and that he and his grandfather had tried to tell the police what he'd seen. Instead of asking whether they'd made such a report, Mundy ended the statement there.

Jones was anxious to talk to me and had a lot to say. It was definitely Adam who he'd played with. He'd been telling that to people for years, even in other speeches he'd made to Youth Crime Watch groups. He'd even mentioned it to Attorney General Janet Reno and Florida Senator Bob Graham when they were honored by the organization, and a number of local police chiefs. That the man he saw wasn't Toole, that was true.

Adam's murder changed Jones's life. He knew how close he'd come to Adam's fate. The man had motioned to either or both of them, and what probably saved Jones is that he was three years older than Adam, plus Jones is black and the man was white. He thought, "Oh, man, I'm not goin' with you" and turned away.

Just after that, Jones's parents enrolled him at a karate school for kids, to learn self-protection. Five years later, Jones opened his own karate school for kids, which he still has. He earned a black belt and taught his dad to be a black belt.

That summer he was staying with his 78-year-old grandfather Otis Williams at his home in Hallandale, next to Hollywood. They got up early each weekday to cut lawns. Often they would be in Sears because Williams would need to replace a broken blade or some other yard tool. While he shopped in the tools department, Vernon played videogames.

That day in 1981 he was playing Intellivision's baseball game with Adam. They were both standing, Vernon on the left, Adam on his right. It was the last inning, Adam trailing but he had the bases loaded.

It was at that moment that a man tried to get their attention. Or was it just Adam's attention? Vernon thought he remembered hearing a noise, like Hey, hey. "I looked over, you talking to me? I didn't know him," he said.

Distracted, Vernon returned to the game. "I pitched the ball. Crack! Grand slam home run! Oh, man!"

He remembered Adam's smile at having beaten the bigger boy. As the loser, Vernon put down his controls and moved around the side to another game in the store's display, probably Donkey Kong. A bit later he looked to his right and saw Adam leave with the man. There was contact between them, possibly the man's right hand holding Adam's left hand. They went out the closest door to where they were playing, the west door.

He couldn't remember if it was the same night or just after when an aunt called his grandfather to turn on the TV news about a little boy missing from Sears. At least two of Vernon's aunts worked either at Sears or elsewhere at Hollywood mall.

He remembered seeing Adam's picture. "Grandpa, grandpa, that's the boy I was playing with," he said. "Are you sure?" his grandfather asked. "Yes, sir."

Next morning, before starting work, his grandfather took him to the Hollywood police station. "I'll never forget it. Parked the truck, getting out, walk the walkway, holding his hand." An officer was "hanging out" and Vernon's grandfather "literally ran into him, bumped into him." Vernon explained that his grandfather always had a fast walk.

"I'm sorry, sir," his grandfather excused himself. Vernon never knew the officer's name, but remembered his gun belt and his belly. It was Vernon's first encounter with a police officer. "My boy here, my son here..." his grandfather tried to say.

The officer spit a black wad of what might have been tobacco at Vernon's grandfather's feet. It hit the ground but splattered back onto his shoe.

"Listen boy," said the officer, "I don't have time for this." "I'm sorry, sir," said Vernon's grandfather, who grabbed Vernon's hand again. They turned around, walked back to the truck, and went to their first job that morning, cutting a lawn in Bal Harbour.

Vernon said that was the first time he'd encountered racism. "Why was he calling my grandfather boy?" he wondered then. The result was, Hollywood police never got his tip.

I showed him a Toole picture. "*Uh uh*," he said. "I would have remembered a face like that." Then I showed him a 1991 courtroom shot of Dahmer.

"Wow," he said.

I put him in front of a computer screen and played MSNBC's 1994 prison interview with Dahmer. He stared, rapt. He knew who Dahmer was but hadn't associated his face.

I watched what was happening to him. He narrated for himself. "Looking at him, hearing his voice is bothering me. I feel my eye twitching, I feel my heart rate elevating. Looking at him right now, putting the headphone on and hearing his voice is literally bothering me."

As well, his voice was breaking, and the eyes of this black

belt karate teacher were tearing. "When I heard the case being closed, my family and others know I've been talking about this for years…" he trailed off.

"Looking at him, I wouldn't have been scared. The other guy [Toole], I would have gone *ecch*, get away from me. He was revolting."

Janice Santamassino

On September 21, 1996, the night *America's Most Wanted* ran what was supposed to be its last-ever segment, a full hour about Adam's case, a show operator taking tips wrote this down:

"Hollywood, Fl. Caller saw by toy entrance a dk color van was parked there (maybe blue) w/curtains in windows (old beat up van). It was around 11 A.M. (morning hours). Caller reported this information to Hollywood Police that night Adam disappeared. Caller had seen Adam playing near the arcade when she walked in, and 10-15 mins later she heard on the loudspeaker he was missing."

The caller left her name and phone number.

It was the same night Mary Hagan had called. The show had forwarded the tips to Hollywood police, along with others as they had gotten them. There was no evidence in the case file to show that Hollywood police had called her or Hagan back. Phil Mundy had found Hagan, but to me or in the file he hadn't mentioned this caller.

I found her easily. Her name was Janice Santamassino, and in fact my call was the first time anyone had ever gotten back to her about Adam Walsh. No one had called her back either in 1981 either.

She first wanted to talk about was the van. Before she'd entered the store, it had been inappropriately parked directly in front of the toy department entrance, and in trying to get around, she'd almost rammed it. She'd gotten her first driver's license only months before. "I wasn't too good at making turns then," she said.

She was so upset about the van that she'd tried to remember its license plate number, to tell police. That afternoon, when she'd called Hollywood police immediately after seeing Adam's photo on the 5 o'clock news to tell them that was the boy she'd seen, she'd mentioned the van to an officer, even volunteering that if they'd arrange a hypnotism session, she possibly could recall the whole plate number. 27 years later, the letters and number still in her head were K, L, and 6. The only other description of the van she could add, besides what the show operator had written down, was that it may have had heart-shaped windows in the rear, covered by a curtain.

She described Sears that day as "relatively like a morgue—empty. The only person I saw was Adam." She estimated it was between 10 A.M. to noon. She had brought her 11-year-old son Anthony and her 4-year-old daughter Lori to buy white little girls' sandals. That Monday was the first day of Janice's vacation and she'd planned to spend the rest of the day poolside with the kids.

Walking through Sears on their way to Kinney Shoes, they passed the videogame display. Lori wanted to play.

Adam was already playing, Janice remembered. "The kid was talking about the video. He was telling her how it worked. She had her hands on the game. We were there a good ten minutes—too long, I thought. She wanted to stay with him. I thought it was a little strange, the boy being there alone, so long."

She remembered Adam wearing a cap—she thought it was a baseball cap, maybe blue or red or white.

Lori, now 31 and married, had a memory of it too. "He was standing to my left. It was a game with a joystick, I remember where his hand was, on the joystick. I was watching him play. I just remember, it was me and him. He was slightly taller."

"I wanted to pull her away from that game," Janice said. Lori had responded, "Five more minutes!" "No!" said Janice.

Leaving the games they walked through the toy department, Janice holding Lori's hand. There was a man with his head down holding a toy, possibly reading it. He looked up at Janice and briefly their eyes locked.

"I remember thinking he was weird" and out of place, she said. "He was scuzzy and he had no kid with him. I had a creepy feeling."

She described him: disheveled, unshaven, no mustache, thin face, no glasses, about 6-feet tall and lanky, in his 30s. His hair was brownish or sandy-brown, and "was a wreck. He was scary-looking". I asked if she was scared of him. "Now that you mention it, yes, for a fleeting moment."

She'd seen Ottis Toole's picture—obviously, since she'd watched that episode of *America's Most Wanted*—and although she said she couldn't be 100% sure, she thought it was Toole.

They'd gotten to Kinney Shoes but when Janice found they didn't have the white sandals she was looking for, they went back to Sears and saw a pair in its shoe department. When I came to meet Janice at her home, she showed me the shoebox they'd come in, now stuffed with old bills. Sears's price tag was still on it: $4.99, children's size 8½.

While back in Sears, she recalled hearing the store's public address page for Adam, missing. On her way toward the garden center exit, passing the catalog desk, she saw a woman who she figured was the mother of the missing boy. "She looked distressed, crying, or about to cry," she said. She was leaning on the counter with one hand, the other hand holding what Janice remembered was a lampshade or a lamp. Her hair was disheveled, like she'd just gotten out of bed.

She was with someone, "I thought, a husband, a friend." His hair was similarly disheveled. She described him as late 20s to early 30s, dark hair. Janice left the store, expecting the child would show up. Maybe he was just hiding.

On television, Janice recognized John Walsh .She knew him because she'd worked at the Diplomat Hotel for a number of years. She remembered he worked for the hotel's convention services; she'd seen him in the catering department. He was good-looking, she added.

But the man she'd seen with Reve at the catalog desk wasn't John. When I showed her two newspaper photos of Jimmy Campbell she said it might have been him.

I was more interested in the man in the toy aisle. She had gotten two good looks at him; his profile and straight on. On her computer screen I found on the web MSNBC's Stone Phillips 1994 prison interview of Dahmer and played a few seconds.

"He's got the right nose," she said.

I skipped to A&E Biography's Dahmer show. They had him walking into a Milwaukee courtroom for his first appearance.

"That's his profile!" she got excited. "His hair. That's what I saw, when he was looking down. I can't believe it, this is like the profile."

I found Dahmer's 1991 color mug shot, with both a profile and a forward shot. "That's it! His hair was a little bit more messier. I'm getting goose bumps." She was; I saw them on her arms. "I never thought I would get that emotional. But that is him. That looks like him. I can't believe it! I was 99% sure it was Toole until I saw this."

We talked about the forward-looking mug shot. "That's what I saw, at me." I said others had told me that Dahmer could look right through you. "Right!" she said. That's what she thought he was doing in the mug shot, and when they'd locked eyes.

"Wow. It's so eerie looking at him. He's scary."

Jennie Warren

A report by Mark Smith briefly details a phone call he got from Jennie Warren on October 30, 1995. She told him she had never before spoken about Adam's case to Hollywood police. She said on the day of the abduction she was in Sears with her 8-year-old granddaughter, and had seen Reve and Adam enter the store from the catalog desk door. Reve then left Adam at the videogames.

Several children were already playing the games, so Adam had to wait his turn. Mrs. Warren left her granddaughter in the toy department then followed Reve as she walked toward the lamps department. Mrs. Warren continued on to the store's business office. When she returned to toys, she saw a suspicious man she described as 5'9", 30s, dirty blonde hair, wearing khaki-colored shirt and pants. He was talking with a catalog department employee she knew. Although she felt "uneasy" about the man in khakis, she didn't think much of it and left the area with her granddaughter. About 30-40 minutes later she heard an intercom page for a missing child.

Smith had tried to find the catalog desk employee who had been talking to the man. Sears referred him to two men, both of whom denied working on the day of the abduction. One suggested another employee who was homosexual and effeminate and during his tenure at Sears had been arrested for a fraudulent report about a stolen vehicle.

Smith found the police report, dated 1978. A criminal check showed the man also had arrests in the Sixties and Seventies for soliciting lewd acts in Hollywood, New York, and Phoenix, and in the summer of 1982 in California. Also in California he also had a 1979 forgery arrest. Sears couldn't confirm that the man had worked for them. Smith later found him in Oklahoma. Smith had grilled him, but he wouldn't back off on his story: he'd left Florida before 1981 and therefore wasn't working at the Hollywood Sears that day.

Almost a year after Mrs. Warren called Smith, Phil Mundy taped an interview with her. She was then 73. It turned out Smith in his earlier report had made some mistakes.

First, Mrs. Warren said she'd gone to Sears with her three granddaughters, ages 14, 8, and 3, the youngest in a stroller. It was "between mid-morning and mid-afternoon." They had entered the west side and first gone to toys, where the 8-year-old wanted to look at Barbie dolls.

Mrs. Warren saw a mother and child she later recognized as Reve and Adam. Reve "dropped off" Adam at the videogames. Elsewhere in toys, Mrs. Warren did the same with her 8-year-old.

Adam was standing behind and watching two boys about 12 already playing the games. Smith had written that Mrs. Warren saw the man in khakis when she returned to the area, but she told Mundy she saw him before she left. He was "right beside Adam." Although the man in khakis and the catalog department employee were talking while watching the boys play the game, she described the khakis man as "alone".

She thought he was wearing a cap but underneath it he had dirty blonde hair about two inches below his ears. The khakis were "like army fatigues clothes" and he had a T-shirt underneath. His hands were in his pockets. "He was just standing there watching," she said.

She followed Reve as far as the lamp department, then Mrs. Warren continued on to the business office to pay her Sears bill. She took a service ticket but because she had to wait she got an "uneasy feeling" about leaving the 8-year-old alone. She told her 14-year-old let's go, and when she didn't move fast enough, Mrs. Warren said she kicked her in the rear to get her going.

She hollered for the 8-year-old, who answered. She didn't notice whether the khakis man was still there or not. They left Sears and went into the mall, then later heard a store announcement about a missing child. Mrs. Warren took the moment to lecture her 14-year-old on why you shouldn't leave a child alone.

Mrs. Warren said she was a hairdresser, so she had taken note of Reve's hair. It was damaged, she said, probably bleached and permed. Since it was straight at the roots and frizzy at the ends, it looked to her like she was trying to grow it out. All she could remember about Adam was he wore dark clothes, and she wasn't sure about a cap or hat. "But I know he was engrossed in watching the Nintendo," as she called the videogames.

Mundy showed her his six-picture lineup that included Toole. She picked out Toole but not, as Mundy wrote, to identify him. She said Toole's picture gave her "a sick feeling in the pit of my stomach when I saw him but I can't really say that was his face."

At the doorstep of her Hollywood home, at the mention of the case, Jennie Warren, now 85, began to cry. Blubber. She knew that the man the Hollywood police had just decided killed Adam was the wrong man. It was the other guy.

Jeffrey Dahmer.

Warren couldn't say exactly when she'd made the Dahmer connection. But her grandson-in-law, married for the last ten years to the granddaughter who'd been 14 in 1981, told me she'd said it to the family a few times.

The story she told me of her day at Sears was consistent with what she'd told Mundy except for naming Dahmer. At the computer games, Dahmer was there when Adam arrived. The two boys already playing were white, and Dahmer was standing right behind them. Adam took a place on Dahmer's left, and they both watched the game.

"Adam could have cared less who he was next to," she said. "He was wanting to play the games." Did Reve see Dahmer too? She must have, Jennie answered. "I was right behind her." Reve also must have seen the catalog department employee, she said. Did she see you? Probably not, Jennie said. "Reve was all wrapped up in herself."

When Mark Smith had discovered that the former catalog department employee he thought was the right person had a record for homosexual solicitations, he'd pursued him hard because, it seemed, he thought maybe he was the abductor's inside guy. That would have been wrong, Jennie said, the catalog guy was only there because he wasn't busy. They were just talking. He was valuable to find because he was another witness, she thought.

Since the man she said was Dahmer was wearing army-type clothes, did she think he'd been in the army? Yes, she said. Bill Bowen had described the man he'd seen outside as wearing an army shirt, but he'd said it was green. Khaki meant beige, she said.

"He was kind of shy," she said. "His expression was, he was sad, or lonely. After I left I had the sense he was intent on watching the boys."

We looked at Milwaukee courtroom pictures of Dahmer. "See where his hair is? It came that far down, below his ears." To another one, she said, "The hair, the beard, an overgrowth. That's him."

To the picture on the cover of a Dahmer book, she said, "That's the man I saw. All these pictures, he has hair below his ears. I'm a beautician, and I notice all these things."

I showed her a picture of Toole. "That's not him. He's ugly. This Dahmer was not ugly."

At Sears's business office, when she decided she needed to retrieve her 8-year-old, she told the 14-year-old to hurry up. When she didn't, Jennie said, "No! I want to get back there, let's go!" When the girl still didn't react, she threatened, "I'm going to kick you in the buttinski if you don't move!"

Back in the toy department Jennie called the 8-year-old's name. "Yes, I'm here! What do you want?" she answered. "Come here!" "But I want to see the dolls!" "Come here right now!" "Okay, nanny."

•

Two of the four new witnesses had first contacted authorities in 1996 or 1997, but the others had tried to tell Hollywood police what they'd seen within the first days of the case. That made six witnesses at Sears that day who saw Adam's possible abductor and said they'd gone to Hollywood police in 1981 with their tips: Santamassino and Jones, plus Morgan, Bowen, Pottenburgh, and eventual-Toole witness Mary Hagan. All but Morgan saw Adam as well.

Here was the problem: of the six, detectives only knew of Pottenburgh. In fact, he was the only one of the six who hadn't on their own volunteered or tried to volunteer his or her information to the police. Acting on someone else's tip, detectives had found and interviewed him. Then they dismissed him—as police would eventually dismiss, ignore, or repulse each of the six individually, except in Phil Mundy's case Hagan in 1996.

Had the police had all six from the very beginning, they could have shown them lineups of Campbell in 1981; Toole in 1983; and Dahmer in 1991.

The case would have been over in 1991.

The Walshes would have been spared the last 18 years of grief. The citizens of Hollywood wouldn't have had to pay for all that police work, documented in this story. Toole and Campbell would have been eliminated early on. Dahmer would have gone to trial and faced Florida's death penalty. Wisconsin didn't have a death penalty, and he wouldn't have faced it in Ohio had they tried him there for Steven Hicks.

What seemed increasingly obvious through all my work was now certain. The Hollywood police blew this case beginning on the very first day, when Janice Santamassino called police with what she knew, and was never called back. The cops also blew it every day after, up to the very last day in December 2008 when the chief closed the case on Toole, he and his detectives choosing to ignore the most important witnesses who even gave them second chances to listen to them.

John Walsh said it himself, in 1982, to the Miami Herald: "There were thousands of leads that they never followed up. And I saw detectives write them down on matchbook covers, scraps of paper. I'm afraid that in their ineptitude they've let the real killer get away. That's the horror of this thing."

Walsh was wrong about Toole in 1996 and after. But give him credit, in 1991 and 1992 he was right about Jeffrey Dahmer. He let the cops talk him out of it.

3704850

Made in the USA